kraft foods

RECIPE COLLECTION

WEST
SIDE
PUBLISHING

Pictured on the front cover (clockwise from top): PHILADELPHIA Blueberry No-Bake Cheesecake *(page 310)*, Roasted Red Pepper-Basil Spread *(page 38)*, Dark Molten Chocolate Cakes *(page 224)*, Cheesy Chipotle Vegetable Bake *(page 122)*, Creamy Layered Peach Squares *(page 392)*, Cucumber Roulades *(page 26)*, Easy Cheesy Potatoes *(page 130)*, Cheesy Pizza Dip *(page 47)*, and Texas Sheet Cake *(page 230)*.

Pictured on the back cover (top row left to right): Eggnog Eclair Dessert *(page 194)*, Bruschetta Chicken Bake *(page 96)*, Caramel Apple Dessert *(page 268)*, PHILADELPHIA New York Cheesecake *(page 315)*, (middle row left to right): OREO Milk Shake *(page 369)*, PHILADELPHIA Chocolate-Vanilla Swirl Cheesecake *(page 313)*, Spinach-Garlic Pizza *(page 180)*, PHILADELPHIA New York-Style Strawberry Swirl Cheesecake *(page 316)*, (bottom row left to right): Triple-Layer Peanut Butter Brownies *(page 357)*, Chocolate Mousse Torte *(page 220)*, OREO No-Bake Cheesecake *(page 308)*, and Firecracker Bites *(page 196)*.

Nutritional Analysis: Every effort has been made to check the accuracy of the nutritional information that appears with each recipe. However, because numerous variables account for a wide range of values for certain foods, nutritive analysis in this book should be considered approximate. Different results may be obtained by using different nutrient databases and different brand-name products.

Microwave Cooking: Microwave ovens vary in wattage. Use the cooking times as guidelines and check for doneness before adding more time.

Preparation/Cooking Times: Preparation times are based on the approximate amount of time required to assemble the recipe before cooking, baking, chilling, or serving. These times include preparation steps such as measuring, chopping, and mixing. The fact that some preparations and cooking can be done simultaneously is taken into account. Preparation of optional ingredients and serving suggestions is not included.

contents

Welcome to the KRAFT Foods Recipe Collection,

your comprehensive solution to the daily dilemma of "what's for dinner?" Whether it's a quick after-school snack, a ready-in-seconds dip, a simple side dish, a no-bake dessert, or a crowd-pleasing casserole, we've got recipes and menus to suit every taste.

Need to entertain in a snap? Whip up tasty dips and small bites like 2-Minute Delicious PHILLY Dip, Bacon-Spinach Bites, VELVEETA Ultimate Queso Dip, or Tuna Cakes. Potlucks and parties are made simple with dishes like STOVE TOP Stuffed Tomatoes, White & Gold Pizza, Dressed-Up Fish Rolls for a Crowd, Fast & Easy Tiramisu, and Double-Decker OREO Cheesecake. Looking to wow your family without spending a lot of time in the kitchen? We've got classic desserts like White Chocolate-Berry Pie, No-Oven Peanut Butter Squares, and Nutty NILLA Mallow Bites, that will please everyone without a lot of cooking time or preparation. Even the kids will want to get involved in the fun, with creative treats like Aquarium Cups, Triple-Layer Peanut Butter Brownies, and Apple-Cinnamon Bun Dip.

We've collected more than 350 mouthwatering, family-pleasing favorites to enjoy year-round. So whether you're battling picky eaters or just a hectic schedule, the KRAFT Foods Recipe Collection has you covered with meal planning so easy, you'll never have to stress over dinner plans again.

HOT
APPETIZERS

corned beef & swiss appetizers

PREP: 20 min. | TOTAL: 23 min. | MAKES: 3 doz. or 18 servings, 2 appetizers each.

▶ what you need!

1 pkg. (8 oz.) PHILADELPHIA Cream Cheese, softened

2 tsp. GREY POUPON Dijon Mustard

¼ lb. corned beef, chopped

½ cup KRAFT Shredded Swiss Cheese

2 Tbsp. chopped green onion

36 slices cocktail rye bread, toasted

▶ make it!

HEAT broiler.

BEAT cream cheese and mustard in medium bowl with electric mixer on medium speed until well blended.

ADD corned beef, Swiss cheese and onion; mix well. Spread evenly onto toast slices. Place on baking sheet.

BROIL 2 to 3 min. or until lightly browned.

MAKE-AHEAD:
Prepare as directed but do not broil. Place in single layer on baking sheets. Freeze 1 hour or until firm. Place in freezer-weight resealable plastic bags. Freeze up to 1 month. When ready to serve, remove from freezer and let stand at room temperature 10 min. Then, broil as directed.

bacon-spinach bites

PREP: 10 min. | TOTAL: 30 min. | MAKES: 12 servings.

► what you need!

4 oz. (½ of 8-oz. pkg.) PHILADELPHIA Cream Cheese, softened

4 green onions, sliced

1 pkg. (10 oz.) frozen chopped spinach, thawed, squeezed dry

6 slices OSCAR MAYER Bacon, cooked, crumbled

3 Tbsp. flour

4 eggs, beaten

¼ lb. (4 oz.) VELVEETA Pasteurized Prepared Cheese Product, cut into 12 cubes

► make it!

HEAT oven to 350°F.

MIX cream cheese and onions in medium bowl. Add spinach, bacon and flour; mix well. Stir in eggs.

SPOON into 12 greased and floured muffin pan cups. Top each with 1 VELVEETA cube; press gently into center of filling.

BAKE 20 min. or until centers are set and tops are golden brown. Serve warm or chilled.

MINIATURE BACON-SPINACH BITES:
Prepare spinach mixture as directed; spoon into 24 greased and floured miniature muffin pan cups. Cut VELVEETA into 24 cubes; press 1 into batter in each cup. Bake 14 to 16 min. or until centers are set and tops are golden brown. Makes 12 servings, 2 appetizers each.

baked crab rangoon

PREP: 20 min. | TOTAL: 40 min. | MAKES: 12 servings, 1 wonton each.

► what you need!

1 can (6 oz.) white crabmeat, drained, flaked

4 oz. (½ of 8-oz. pkg.) PHILADELPHIA Neufchâtel Cheese, softened

¼ cup thinly sliced green onions

¼ cup KRAFT Mayo Light Mayonnaise

12 wonton wrappers

► make it!

HEAT oven to 350°F.

MIX crabmeat, Neufchâtel, onions and mayo.

SPRAY 12 (2½-inch) muffin cups with cooking spray. Gently place 1 wonton wrapper in each cup, allowing edges of wrappers to extend above sides of cups. Fill evenly with crabmeat mixture.

BAKE 18 to 20 min. or until edges are golden brown and filling is heated through. Serve warm. Garnish with sliced green onions, if desired.

FOOD FACTS:
Wonton wrappers are usually found in the grocery store in the refrigerated section of the produce department.

MINI CRAB RANGOON:
Use 24 wonton wrappers. Gently place 1 wonton wrapper in each of 24 miniature muffin cups sprayed with cooking spray. Fill evenly with crabmeat mixture and bake as directed. Makes 12 servings, 2 appetizers each.

cheese & bacon
jalapeño rellenos

PREP: 20 min. | TOTAL: 30 min. | MAKES: 18 servings.

▶ what you need!

4 oz. (½ of 8-oz. pkg.) PHILADELPHIA Cream Cheese, softened

1 cup KRAFT Shredded Cheddar Cheese

4 slices OSCAR MAYER Bacon, cooked, crumbled

2 Tbsp. finely chopped onions

2 Tbsp. chopped cilantro

1 clove garlic, minced

18 jalapeño peppers, cut lengthwise in half, seeds and membranes removed

▶ make it!

HEAT oven to 375°F.

MIX all ingredients except peppers until well blended.

SPOON into peppers. Place, filled-sides up, on baking sheet.

BAKE 10 min. or until cheese is melted.

SUBSTITUTE:
Substitute 3 large red, yellow or green bell peppers, each cut into 6 triangles, for the jalapeño pepper halves. Top with cheese mixture before baking as directed.

SPECIAL EXTRA:
Add ¼ tsp. ground red pepper (cayenne) to the cream cheese mixture before spooning into jalapeño peppers.

SUBSTITUTE:
Prepare using KRAFT Shredded Monterey Jack Cheese.

HOW TO HANDLE FRESH CHILE PEPPERS:
When handling fresh chile peppers, be sure to wear disposable rubber or clear plastic gloves to avoid irritating your skin. Never touch your eyes, nose or mouth when handling the peppers. If you've forgotten to wear the gloves and feel a burning sensation in your hands, apply a baking soda and water paste to the affected area. After rinsing the paste off, you should feel some relief.

cream cheese-bacon crescents

PREP: 15 min. | TOTAL: 30 min. | MAKES: 16 servings.

▶ what you need!

1 tub (8 oz.) PHILADELPHIA Chive & Onion Cream Cheese Spread

3 slices OSCAR MAYER Bacon, cooked, crumbled

2 cans (8 oz. each) refrigerated crescent dinner rolls

▶ make it!

HEAT oven to 375°F.

MIX cream cheese spread and bacon until well blended.

SEPARATE each can of dough into 8 triangles. Cut each triangle lengthwise in half. Spread each dough triangle with 1 generous tsp. cream cheese mixture. Roll up, starting at shortest side of triangle; place, point-sides down, on baking sheet.

BAKE 12 to 15 min. or until golden brown. Serve warm.

VARIATION:
For a sweet version, prepare using PHILADELPHIA Strawberry Cream Cheese Spread and substituting chopped PLANTERS Walnuts for the bacon.

KRAFT parmesan bruschetta

PREP: 15 min. | TOTAL: 19 min. | MAKES: 18 servings, 1 appetizer each.

▶ what you need!

1 large tomato, chopped

½ cup KRAFT Grated Parmesan Cheese

2 cloves garlic, minced

⅓ cup olive oil, divided

¼ cup sliced fresh basil leaves

1 loaf French bread (1 lb.), cut into 18 slices

▶ make it!

HEAT broiler.

COMBINE tomatoes, Parmesan, garlic, 2 Tbsp. oil and basil.

BRUSH remaining oil onto both sides of bread slices.

BROIL, 6 inches from heat, 2 min. on each side or until golden brown. Top with tomato mixture.

SUBSTITUTE:
Substitute 1 tsp. dried basil leaves for the fresh basil leaves.

SUBSTITUTE:
Prepare using KRAFT Shredded Parmesan Cheese or KRAFT Shredded Parmesan, Romano and Asiago Cheese.

Hot Appetizers | 13

heavenly ham roll-ups

PREP: 15 min. | TOTAL: 35 min. | MAKES: 15 servings.

▶ what you need!

1 pkg. (9 oz.) OSCAR MAYER Deli Fresh Shaved Smoked Ham

5 Tbsp. PHILADELPHIA Neufchâtel Cheese

15 fresh asparagus spears (about 1 lb.), trimmed

▶ make it!

HEAT oven to 350°F.

FLATTEN ham slices; pat dry. Stack ham in piles of 2 slices each; spread each stack with 1 tsp. Neufchâtel.

PLACE 1 asparagus spear on one long side of each ham stack; roll up. Place, seam-sides down, in 13×9-inch baking dish.

BAKE 15 to 20 min. or until heated through.

NO BAKE HEAVENLY HAM ROLL-UPS:
Substitute frozen asparagus spears, cooked as directed on package, or canned asparagus spears, heated if desired, for the fresh asparagus. Assemble roll-ups as directed. Serve immediately. Or, cover and refrigerate until ready to serve.

FOOD FACTS:
Asparagus spears should be a bright green color and free of blemishes. Choose stalks that are straight, uniformly sized (either all thick or all thin) and firm. Stand fresh asparagus spears upright in a container filled with an inch of water. Cover with a plastic bag and refrigerate up to 3 days.

MAKE AHEAD:
Assemble roll-ups as directed. Refrigerate up to 24 hours before uncovering and baking as directed.

SUBSTITUTE:
Prepare as directed, using 1 pkg. (6 oz.) OSCAR MAYER Thin Sliced Smoked Ham. Substitute 1 slice of ham for every 2 slices of the shaved ham.

speedy spicy quesadillas

PREP: 5 min. | TOTAL: 8 min. | MAKES: 8 servings.

▶ what you need!

½ lb. (8 oz.) Mild Mexican VELVEETA Pasteurized Prepared Cheese Product with Jalapeño Peppers, cut into 8 slices

8 flour tortillas (6 inch)

▶ make it!

PLACE 1 VELVEETA slice on each tortilla. Fold tortillas in half. Place 2 tortillas on microwaveable plate.

MICROWAVE on HIGH 30 to 45 sec. or until VELVEETA is melted. Repeat with remaining tortillas.

CUT in half to serve.

SUBSTITUTE:
Prepare as directed, using VELVEETA Made With 2% Milk Reduced Fat Pasteurized Prepared Cheese Product.

FOOD FACTS:
Flour tortillas, often used as soft taco shells, come in many colors and sizes. Look for them in the dairy case or grocery aisle of the supermarket. You'll also find them seasoned with herbs, tomatoes, spinach or sesame seeds.

SPECIAL EXTRA:
Garnish with chopped fresh tomatoes and green onions.

VELVEETA double-decker nachos

PREP: 15 min. | TOTAL: 15 min. | MAKES: 6 servings.

▶ what you need!

6 oz. tortilla chips (about 7 cups)

1 can (15 oz.) chili with beans

½ lb. (8 oz.) VELVEETA Pasteurized Prepared Cheese Product, cut into ½-inch cubes

1 medium tomato, finely chopped

¼ cup sliced green onions

⅓ cup BREAKSTONE'S or KNUDSEN Sour Cream

▶ make it!

ARRANGE half of the chips on large microwaveable platter; top with layers of half each of the chili and VELVEETA. Repeat layers.

MICROWAVE on HIGH 3 to 5 min. or until VELVEETA is melted.

TOP with remaining ingredients.

SIZE-WISE:
Enjoy your favorite foods while keeping portion size in mind.

SUBSTITUTE:
Prepare as directed, using Mild Mexican VELVEETA Pasteurized Prepared Cheese Product with Jalapeño Peppers.

spinach-stuffed mushrooms

PREP: 15 min. | TOTAL: 35 min. | MAKES: 40 servings.

▶ what you need!

    1 pkg. (6 oz.) STOVE TOP Stuffing Mix for Chicken

1½ cups hot water

  40 fresh mushrooms (about 2 lbs.)

    2 Tbsp. butter

    2 cloves garlic, minced

    1 pkg. (10 oz.) frozen chopped spinach, thawed, well drained

    1 cup KRAFT Shredded Low-Moisture Part-Skim Mozzarella Cheese

    1 cup KRAFT Grated Parmesan Cheese

▶ make it!

HEAT oven to 400°F.

MIX stuffing mix and hot water in large bowl; set aside. Remove stems from mushrooms; chop stems. Melt butter in skillet on medium heat. Add chopped stems and garlic; cook and stir until tender. Add to prepared stuffing with spinach and cheeses; mix well.

SPOON into mushroom caps. Place, filled-sides up, in shallow pan.

BAKE 20 min. or until mushrooms are tender and filling is heated through.

stuffing balls

PREP: 15 min. | TOTAL: 35 min. | MAKES: 8 servings.

▶ what you need!

- 1 lb. ground pork
- 1 pkg. (6 oz.) STOVE TOP Stuffing Mix for Chicken
- ¾ cup cranberry sauce
- 1 egg
- 1 cup water
- 2 Tbsp. butter, melted

▶ make it!

HEAT oven to 325°F.

COOK meat in large skillet until cooked through, stirring frequently; drain. Place in large bowl; cool slightly. Stir in stuffing mix.

ADD cranberry sauce, egg and water; mix well. Shape into 16 balls; place on foil-covered baking sheet. Brush with butter.

BAKE 20 min. or until done.

SIZE-WISE:
Enjoy your favorite foods while keeping portion size in mind.

MAKE AHEAD:
Prepare and shape stuffing balls as directed. Freeze in airtight container up to 1 month. Thaw in refrigerator, then bake as directed.

tuna cakes

PREP: 25 min. | TOTAL: 25 min. | MAKES: 6 servings.

▶ what you need!

2 cans (5 oz. each) light tuna in water, drained, flaked

1 pkg. (6 oz.) STOVE TOP Stuffing Mix for Chicken

1 cup KRAFT Shredded Mild Cheddar Cheese

¾ cup water

1 carrot, shredded

⅓ cup KRAFT Real Mayo Mayonnaise

2 Tbsp. CLAUSSEN Sweet Pickle Relish

▶ make it!

MIX all ingredients. Refrigerate 10 min.

HEAT large nonstick skillet sprayed with cooking spray on medium heat. Use ice cream scoop to add ⅓-cup portions of tuna mixture, in batches, to skillet.

FLATTEN into patties with back of spatula. Cook 6 min. or until golden brown on both sides, carefully turning patties over after 3 min.

FOR EASIER HANDLING IN THE SKILLET:
Mix all ingredients. Shape into patties as directed. Place in single layer on baking sheet. Refrigerate 1 hour before cooking as directed.

quick & easy crab cakes

PREP: 10 min. | TOTAL: 20 min. | MAKES: 6 servings.

▶ what you need!

1 cup boiling water

1 pkg. (6 oz.) STOVE TOP Cornbread Stuffing Mix

3 eggs

2 cans (6 oz. each) crabmeat, drained, flaked

¼ cup butter or margarine

1 lemon, cut into 6 wedges

▶ make it!

ADD boiling water to stuffing mix; stir just until moistened. Let stand 5 min.

BEAT eggs in large bowl. Add crabmeat; mix lightly. Stir in stuffing. Shape into 6 patties.

MELT butter in large skillet on medium heat. Add patties; cook 5 min. on each side or until heated through and lightly browned on both sides. Serve with lemon wedges.

SPECIAL EXTRA:
Add ¼ cup chopped red bell peppers and 2 Tbsp. chopped onions to the crabmeat mixture before shaping into patties.

COLD
APPETIZERS

easy appetizer bites

PREP: 10 min. | TOTAL: 1 hour 10 min. | MAKES: 12 servings.

► what you need!

1 pkg. (9 oz.) OSCAR MAYER VARIETY-PAK Ham and Turkey

5 CLAUSSEN Bread 'N Butter or Kosher Dill Sandwich Slices, cut in half lengthwise

1 tub (8 oz.) PHILADELPHIA Garden Vegetable Cream Cheese Spread

► make it!

PAT meat and pickle slices dry with paper towels.

SPREAD each meat slice with about 1 Tbsp. cream cheese spread. Top each with 1 pickle slice; roll up. (Note: You will have 1 pickle slice left over. Enjoy it as an extra snack.) Wrap tightly in plastic wrap.

REFRIGERATE at least 1 hour or overnight. Cut each roll-up into 4 pieces to serve; secure each with toothpick.

SUBSTITUTE:
Prepare as directed, using plain PHILADELPHIA Cream Cheese Spread.

cucumber roulades

PREP: 10 min. | TOTAL: 10 min. | MAKES: 1 doz. or 6 servings, 2 topped cucumber slices each.

▶ what you need!

  1 seedless cucumber, peeled

  ¼ cup PHILADELPHIA Chive & Onion Cream Cheese Spread

  1 oz. smoked salmon, thinly sliced, cut into 12 pieces

12 sprigs fresh dill

▶ make it!

CUT cucumber crosswise into 12 slices. Use a melon baller to scoop out indentation in center of each cucumber round.

FILL evenly with cream cheese spread. Top with salmon and dill.

SUBSTITUTE:
Substitute 12 canned baby shrimp for the salmon.

deviled ham finger sandwiches

PREP: 15 min. | TOTAL: 15 min. | MAKES: 18 servings, 4 sandwich quarters each.

▶ what you need!

1 pkg. (8 oz.) PHILADELPHIA Cream Cheese, softened

1 can (4.25 oz.) deviled ham

¼ cup KRAFT Mayo Real Mayonnaise

10 small stuffed green olives, finely chopped

36 slices white bread, crusts removed

▶ make it!

MIX cream cheese, ham, mayo and olives until well blended.

SPREAD each of 18 of the bread slices with about 2 Tbsp. of the cream cheese mixture. Cover with remaining bread slices to make 18 sandwiches.

CUT each sandwich into quarters.

MAKE AHEAD:
Prepare cream cheese mixture as directed. Cover and refrigerate up to 5 days. Spread onto bread slices and continue as directed. For easier spreading, mix 1 Tbsp. milk with chilled cream cheese mixture before spreading onto bread slices. Or prepare sandwiches as directed, but do not cut into quarters. Wrap in plastic wrap. Refrigerate until ready to serve. Cut into quarters just before serving.

SUBSTITUTE:
Substitute MIRACLE WHIP Dressing for the mayo.

favorite topped deviled eggs

PREP: 15 min. | TOTAL: 15 min. | MAKES: 24 servings.

▶ what you need!

12 hard-cooked eggs

4 oz. (½ of 8-oz. pkg.) PHILADELPHIA Neufchâtel Cheese, softened

3 Tbsp. KRAFT Light Mayo Reduced Fat Mayonnaise

2 tsp. GREY POUPON Dijon Mustard

2 tsp. white vinegar

1 tsp. sugar

⅛ tsp. paprika

▶ make it!

CUT eggs lengthwise in half. Remove yolks; place in medium bowl. Add all remaining ingredients except paprika; mix well.

SPOON into resealable plastic bag. Cut small corner from bottom of bag; pipe filling into egg whites. Sprinkle with paprika.

ADD Toppings, if desired. (See Tips.)

TOPPING VARIATIONS:
COUNTRY FAVORITE: Top with 10 slices cooked and crumbled OSCAR MAYER Bacon and 2 finely chopped green onions.
IT'S ITALIAN: Top with ½ cup thinly sliced drained jarred sun-dried tomatoes packed in oil and ¼ cup thinly sliced fresh basil.
FIESTA TIME: Top with 6 Tbsp. finely chopped red bell peppers and 1 Tbsp. chopped fresh cilantro.
COASTAL DELIGHT: Top with ½ cup drained canned baby shrimp and 2 Tbsp. chopped fresh dill.

MAKE AHEAD:
Prepare as directed. Store in tightly covered container in refrigerator until ready to serve.

herb-and-nut cream cheese log

PREP: 10 min. | TOTAL: 10 min. | MAKES: 12 servings, 2 Tbsp. cheese spread and 5 crackers each.

► what you need!

1 pkg. (8 oz.) PHILADELPHIA Cream Cheese, softened

⅓ cup KRAFT Grated Parmesan Cheese

½ cup chopped toasted PLANTERS Pecans, divided

¼ cup chopped fresh parsley

RITZ Crackers or RITZ Snowflake Crackers

► make it!

MIX cream cheese, Parmesan and ¼ cup nuts.

SHAPE into 8-inch log. Roll in combined remaining nuts and parsley; press gently into log to secure.

SERVE with crackers.

HOW TO WRAP FOR GIFT-GIVING:
Place cheese log and small knife on decorative platter or cutting board. Wrap with colorful cellophane and ribbon. After serving the cheese log at the holiday party, the hostess will have a lovely gift to remember the occasion by!

mini shrimp cocktail bites

PREP: 10 min. | TOTAL: 10 min. | MAKES: 8 servings, 2 topped crackers each.

▶ what you need!

16 RITZ or Holiday RITZ Crackers

⅓ cup PHILADELPHIA Whipped Cream Cheese Spread

⅓ cup KRAFT Cocktail Sauce

16 cleaned large fresh shrimp, cooked

⅓ cup finely chopped green onions

▶ make it!

SPREAD each cracker with 1 tsp. of the cream cheese spread.

TOP evenly with the cocktail sauce, shrimp and onions.

KEEPING IT SAFE:
Frozen shrimp can also be used to prepare these appetizers. To thaw the shrimp, place the bag of frozen shrimp in the refrigerator and let stand until thawed. Or, place the sealed bag of shrimp in a bowl of cold water and let stand until thawed, changing the water every 10 min. Never thaw the shrimp on the countertop.

party cheese ball

PREP: 15 min. | TOTAL: 3 hours 15 min. | MAKES: 24 servings, 2 Tbsp. each.

▶ what you need!

2 pkg. (8 oz. each) PHILADELPHIA Cream Cheese, softened

1 pkg. (8 oz.) KRAFT Shredded Sharp Cheddar Cheese

1 Tbsp. finely chopped onions

1 Tbsp. chopped red bell peppers

2 tsp. Worcestershire sauce

1 tsp. lemon juice

Dash ground red pepper (cayenne)

Dash salt

1 cup chopped PLANTERS Pecans

▶ make it!

BEAT cream cheese and Cheddar in small bowl with electric mixer on medium speed until well blended.

MIX in all remaining ingredients except nuts cover. Refrigerate several hours or overnight.

SHAPE into ball; roll in nuts. Serve with assorted NABISCO Crackers.

VARIATION:
Mix cream cheese mixture as directed; shape into log or 24 small balls, each about 1 inch in diameter. Roll in nuts until evenly coated. Serve as directed.

SUBSTITUTE:
Substitute pimientos for the red bell peppers.

roasted red pepper-basil spread

PREP: 15 min. | TOTAL: 1 hour 15 min. | MAKES: 1½ cups or 12 servings, 2 Tbsp. spread and 5 crackers each.

▶ what you need!

1 tub (12 oz.) PHILADELPHIA Cream Cheese Spread

¼ cup lightly packed fresh basil leaves

1 clove garlic, peeled

¼ cup drained roasted red peppers

5 pitted black olives, chopped

2 Tbsp. PLANTERS Sliced Almonds, toasted

RITZ Crackers

▶ make it!

PLACE cream cheese spread in blender; set aside. Wash tub; line with plastic wrap, with ends of wrap extending over side of tub. Set aside.

ADD basil and garlic to cream cheese in blender; cover. Blend using pulsing action until well blended; set aside. Cut a star shape from one of the peppers, using ½-inch star-shaped cutter; set star aside for later use. Chop pepper trimmings and remaining peppers; combine with the olives. Spoon ½ cup of the cream cheese mixture into prepared tub. Cover with the chopped pepper mixture; press lightly into cream cheese mixture. Top with the remaining cream cheese mixture; cover. Refrigerate 1 hour.

UNMOLD cheese spread onto serving plate; remove and discard plastic wrap. Top cheese spread with the almonds and pepper star. Serve as a spread with the crackers.

JAZZ IT UP:
For a holiday flair, serve with RITZ SIMPLY SOCIALS Crackers.

blt dip

PREP: 15 min. | TOTAL: 15 min. | MAKES: 2 cups or 16 servings, 2 Tbsp. each.

▶ what you need!

1 pkg. (8 oz.) PHILADELPHIA Cream Cheese, softened

¾ cup shredded or chopped romaine lettuce

2 plum tomatoes, seeded, chopped

4 slices OSCAR MAYER Bacon, crisply cooked, drained and crumbled

▶ make it!

SPREAD cream cheese onto bottom of 9-inch pie plate.

TOP with lettuce and tomatoes; sprinkle with bacon.

SERVE with WHEAT THINS Original Snacks or assorted cut-up fresh vegetables.

VARIATION:
Prepare as directed, using PHILADELPHIA Neufchâtel Cheese and LOUIS RICH Turkey Bacon.

sweet pepper-ham wraps

PREP: 10 min. | TOTAL: 10 min. | MAKES: 1 doz. or 4 servings, 3 wrapped peppers each.

► what you need!

1 each red and green bell pepper

2 Tbsp. PHILADELPHIA Neufchâtel Cheese, softened

12 slices OSCAR MAYER Deli Fresh Shaved Smoked Ham

► make it!

CUT peppers lengthwise in half; remove and discard seeds. Cut each piece into 3 lengthwise strips.

DRY insides with paper towel; spread evenly with Neufchâtel.

PLACE 1 pepper strip on each ham slice; wrap ham around pepper. Secure with wooden toothpicks.

SUBSTITUTE:
Substitute OSCAR MAYER Light Bologna for the ham.

MAKE AHEAD:
Wraps can be stored, tightly covered, in refrigerator up to 2 days.

spiced-cherry cheese ball

PREP: 15 min. | TOTAL: 2 hours 15 min. | MAKES: 3 cups spread or 24 servings, 2 Tbsp. spread and 5 crackers each.

▶ what you need!

1 pkg. (8 oz.) PHILADELPHIA Cream Cheese, softened

1 pkg. (10 oz.) CRACKER BARREL Vermont Sharp-White Cheddar Cheese, shredded

½ cup dried cherries, chopped

¼ tsp. pumpkin pie spice

½ cup finely chopped PLANTERS Pecans, toasted

RITZ Crackers

▶ make it!

MIX cream cheese and Cheddar until blended. Stir in cherries and pumpkin pie spice.

SHAPE into ball; wrap in plastic wrap. Refrigerate at least 2 hours.

ROLL in nuts just before serving. Serve with crackers.

SIZE-WISE:
Savor every bite of this tasty spread. Each 2 Tbsp. serving goes a long way on flavor.

VARIATIONS:
Prepare as directed, using one of the following flavor options: **ITALIAN:** Substitute 1 pkg. (8 oz.) KRAFT Shredded Mozzarella Cheese for the Cheddar, ¼ cup sliced drained oil-packed sun-dried tomatoes for the cherries and ½ tsp. each Italian seasoning and garlic powder for the pumpkin pie spice. **SMOKY BACON:** Omit pumpkin pie spice. Mix ingredients as directed, substituting 1 pkg. (8 oz.) KRAFT Shredded Cheddar Cheese for the shredded CRACKER BARREL Cheese and 2 Tbsp. OSCAR MAYER Real Bacon Bits for the cherries. Stir in 2 sliced green onions, then shape into ball. **HERBED:** Omit pumpkin pie spice. Prepare as directed, substituting 1 pkg. (8 oz.) KRAFT Shredded Mozzarella Cheese for the Cheddar and 1 clove minced garlic and 2 Tbsp. each chopped fresh parsley, fresh basil and chives for the cherries.

HOW TO WRAP FOR GIFT-GIVING:
Place cheese ball and knife on decorative platter or cutting board. Wrap with colorful cellophane and ribbon. After serving the cheese ball at the holiday party, the hostess will have a lovely gift to remember the occasion by!

DIPS &
SPREADS

2-minute delicious PHILLY dip

PREP: 5 min. | TOTAL: 5 min. | MAKES: ½ cup dip or 4 servings, 2 Tbsp. dip and 3 crackers each.

▶ what you need!

¼ cup PHILADELPHIA Cream Cheese Spread

1 Tbsp. KRAFT CATALINA Dressing

2 Tbsp. sliced black olives

TRISCUIT Thin Crisps

▶ make it!

MIX first 3 ingredients until well blended.

SERVE with crackers.

VARIATION:
Serve with celery sticks instead of/in addition to the crackers.

SUBSTITUTE:
Prepare using green olives.

baked triple-veggie dip

PREP: 15 min. | TOTAL: 50 min. | MAKES: 4½ cups or 36 servings, 2 Tbsp. each.

▶ what you need!

1½ cups KRAFT Grated Parmesan Cheese, divided

1 can (1 lb. 3 oz.) asparagus spears, drained, chopped

1 pkg. (10 oz.) frozen chopped spinach, thawed, drained

1 can (8½ oz.) artichoke hearts, drained, chopped

1 container (8 oz.) PHILADELPHIA Chive & Onion Cream Cheese Spread

½ cup KRAFT Real Mayo Mayonnaise

▶ make it!

HEAT oven to 375°F.

MIX 1¼ cups Parmesan with all remaining ingredients.

SPOON into 2-qt. baking dish; top with remaining Parmesan.

BAKE 35 min. or until dip is heated through and top is lightly browned.

VARIATION:
Prepare as directed, using KRAFT Reduced Fat Parmesan Style Grated Topping, PHILADELPHIA Chive & Onion ⅓ Less Fat than Cream Cheese and KRAFT Mayo with Olive Oil Reduced Fat Mayonnaise.

NUTRITION BONUS:
The spinach is a good source of vitamin A in this tasty baked dip.

cheesy pizza dip

PREP: 10 min. | TOTAL: 15 min. | MAKES: 2½ cups or 20 servings, 2 Tbsp. each.

▶ what you need!

1 lb. (16 oz.) VELVEETA Pasteurized Prepared Cheese Product, cut into ½-inch cubes

1 tomato, chopped

1½ oz. pepperoni, chopped

▶ make it!

COMBINE ingredients in 1½-qt. microwaveable bowl.

MICROWAVE on HIGH 4 to 5 min. or until VELVEETA is completely melted, stirring every 2 min.

SERVE hot with breadsticks or assorted cut-up fresh vegetables.

CREATIVE LEFTOVERS:
Cover and refrigerate any leftover dip. Reheat and drizzle over hot baked potatoes or cooked pasta for an easy cheesy sauce.

cheesy spinach and bacon dip

PREP: 10 min. | TOTAL: 15 min. | MAKES: 4 cups or 32 servings, 2 Tbsp. each.

▶ what you need!

1 pkg. (10 oz.) frozen chopped spinach, thawed, drained

1 lb. (16 oz.) VELVEETA Pasteurized Prepared Cheese Product, cut into ½-inch cubes

4 oz. (½ of 8-oz. pkg.) PHILADELPHIA Cream Cheese, cut up

1 can (10 oz.) RO*TEL Diced Tomatoes & Green Chilies, undrained

8 slices OSCAR MAYER Bacon, crisply cooked, drained and crumbled

▶ make it!

MICROWAVE all ingredients in microwaveable bowl on HIGH 5 min. or until VELVEETA is completely melted and mixture is well blended, stirring after 3 min.

SERVE with tortilla chips and cut-up fresh vegetables.

VARIATION:
Prepare as directed, using VELVEETA Made With 2% Milk Reduced Fat Pasteurized Prepared Cheese Product and PHILADELPHIA Neufchâtel Cheese.

HOW TO CUT UP VELVEETA:
Cut VELVEETA loaf into ½-inch-thick slices. Then cut each slice crosswise in both directions to make cubes.

USE YOUR SLOW COOKER:
When serving this dip at a party, pour the prepared dip into a small slow cooker set on LOW. This will keep the dip warm and at the ideal consistency for several hours. For best results, stir the dip occasionally to prevent hot spots.

*RO*TEL is a registered trademark of ConAgra Foods, Inc.*

fiesta baked cheese dip

PREP: 20 min. | **TOTAL:** 40 min. | **MAKES:** 4 cups or 32 servings, 2 Tbsp. each.

▶ what you need!

2 pkg. (8 oz. each) PHILADELPHIA Cream Cheese, softened

1 pkg. (8 oz.) KRAFT Mexican Style Finely Shredded Four Cheese, divided

1 can (4 oz.) chopped green chilies, undrained

1¼ cups BREAKSTONE'S or KNUDSEN Sour Cream, divided

¼ to ½ tsp. ground red pepper (cayenne)

▶ make it!

HEAT oven to 350°F.

BEAT cream cheese in large bowl with mixer until creamy. Reserve ¼ cup shredded cheese. Add remaining shredded cheese to cream cheese with chilies, ½ cup sour cream and ground red pepper; mix well.

SPOON into 10-inch pie plate or quiche dish.

BAKE 20 min. or until edge is lightly browned. Top with remaining sour cream and shredded cheese. Serve with tortilla chips.

SUBSTITUTE:
Substitute KRAFT Shredded Colby & Monterey Jack Cheese for Mexican Style Shredded Cheese.

SPECIAL EXTRA:
Assemble dip and bake as directed. Top with 2 Tbsp. chopped green onions or chopped fresh cilantro.

five-layer italian dip

PREP: 10 min. | TOTAL: 25 min. | MAKES: 2 cups or 16 servings, 2 Tbsp. each.

▶ what you need!

1 pkg. (8 oz.) PHILADELPHIA
Cream Cheese, softened

¼ cup KRAFT Grated Parmesan
Cheese

⅓ cup pesto

½ cup roasted red peppers,
drained, chopped

1 cup KRAFT Shredded Mozzarella
Cheese

▶ make it!

HEAT oven to 350°F.

MIX cream cheese and Parmesan. Spread onto bottom of 9-inch pie plate or quiche dish.

LAYER remaining ingredients over cream cheese mixture.

BAKE 15 min. or until heated through. Serve hot with assorted NABISCO Crackers or sliced
Italian bread.

SPECIAL EXTRA:
Garnish with sliced pitted ripe olives and fresh basil leaves.

VELVEETA southwestern chicken dip

PREP: 10 min. | TOTAL: 17 min. | MAKES: 3½ cups or 28 servings, 2 Tbsp. each.

▶ what you need!

- 1 lb. (16 oz.) VELVEETA Pasteurized Prepared Cheese Product, cut into ½-inch cubes
- 1 can (10 oz.) diced tomatoes & green chilies, drained
- 1 pkg. (6 oz.) OSCAR MAYER Southwestern Seasoned or Grilled Chicken Breast Strips, chopped
- 2 green onions, chopped

▶ make it!

MIX all ingredients in microwaveable bowl.

MICROWAVE on HIGH 6 to 7 min. or until VELVEETA is completely melted and mixture is well blended, stirring every 3 min.

SERVE with tortilla chips or assorted cut-up fresh vegetables.

SUBSTITUTE:
Substitute ½ lb. ground beef, cooked and drained, for the chopped chicken breast strips.

garden vegetable dip

PREP: 10 min. | TOTAL: 3 hours 10 min. | MAKES: 20 servings, 2 Tbsp. each.

▶ what you need!

2 pkg. (8 oz. each) PHILADELPHIA Cream Cheese, softened

½ cup KRAFT Blue Cheese Dressing

½ cup finely chopped broccoli

1 medium carrot, shredded

▶ make it!

MIX cream cheese and dressing until well blended. Stir in vegetables; cover.

REFRIGERATE several hours or until chilled.

SERVE with assorted NABISCO Crackers.

BEST OF SEASON:
Take advantage of the fresh seasonal vegetables that are available. Cut up zucchini, cucumbers and bell peppers to serve as dippers with this creamy dip.

VARIATION:
Prepare as directed, using PHILADELPHIA Neufchâtel Cheese and KRAFT Light Blue Cheese Reduced Fat Dressing.

hot broccoli dip

PREP: 30 min. | TOTAL: 30 min. | MAKES: 2½ cups or 20 servings, 2 Tbsp. each.

▶ what you need!

1 loaf (1½ lb.) round sourdough bread

½ cup chopped celery

½ cup chopped red bell peppers

¼ cup chopped onions

2 Tbsp. butter or margarine

1 lb. (16 oz.) VELVEETA Pasteurized Prepared Cheese Product, cut into ½-inch cubes

1 pkg. (10 oz.) frozen chopped broccoli, thawed, drained

¼ tsp. dried rosemary leaves, crushed

Few drops hot pepper sauce

▶ make it!

HEAT oven to 350°F.

CUT slice from top of bread loaf; remove center, leaving 1-inch-thick shell. Cut removed bread into bite-sized pieces. Cover shell with top of bread; place on baking sheet with bread pieces. Bake 15 min. Cool slightly.

MEANWHILE, cook and stir celery, bell peppers and onions in butter in medium saucepan on medium heat until tender. Reduce heat to low. Add VELVEETA cook until melted, stirring frequently. Add broccoli, rosemary and hot pepper sauce; mix well. Cook until heated through, stirring constantly.

SPOON into bread loaf. Serve hot with toasted bread pieces, NABISCO Crackers and/or assorted cut-up fresh vegetables.

USE YOUR MICROWAVE:
Mix celery, bell peppers, onions and butter in 2-qt. microwaveable bowl. Microwave on HIGH 1 min. Add VELVEETA, broccoli, rosemary and hot pepper sauce; mix well. Microwave 5 to 6 min. more or until VELVEETA is melted, stirring after 3 min.

VARIATION:
Omit bread loaf. Spoon dip into serving bowl. Serve with crackers and assorted cut-up fresh vegetables as directed.

SUBSTITUTE:
Prepare as directed, using VELVEETA Made With 2% Milk Reduced Fat Pasteurized Prepared Cheese Product.

last-minute cheesy hot dip

PREP: 10 min. | TOTAL: 25 min. | MAKES: 2½ cups dip or 20 servings, 2 Tbsp. dip and 4 crackers each.

▶ what you need!

  1 pkg. (8 oz.) PHILADELPHIA Cream Cheese, softened

1½ cups KRAFT Shredded Colby & Monterey Jack Cheese

  5 green onions, thinly sliced

  ⅓ cup KRAFT Real Mayo Mayonnaise

  1 Tbsp. GREY POUPON Harvest Coarse Ground Mustard

  2 Tbsp. chopped PLANTERS Smoked Almonds

    RITZ Simply Socials Golden Wheat Crackers

▶ make it!

HEAT oven to 350°F.

MIX cheeses, onions, mayo and mustard in 9-inch pie plate; top with nuts.

BAKE 15 min. Serve with crackers.

VELVEETA cheesy bean dip

PREP: 5 min. | TOTAL: 11 min. | MAKES: 3¼ cups or 26 servings, 2 Tbsp. each.

▶ what you need!

1 lb. (16 oz.) Mild Mexican VELVEETA Pasteurized Prepared Cheese Product with Jalapeño Peppers, cut into ½-inch cubes

1 can (16 oz.) TACO BELL HOME ORIGINALS Refried Beans*

½ cup TACO BELL HOME ORIGINALS Thick 'N Chunky Salsa

▶ make it!

MIX all ingredients in microwaveable bowl.

MICROWAVE on HIGH 5 to 6 min. or until VELVEETA is completely melted and mixture is well blended, stirring after 3 min.

SERVE with tortilla chips or assorted cut-up fresh vegetables.

USE YOUR STOVE:
Mix all ingredients in medium saucepan. Cook on medium-low heat until VELVEETA is completely melted and mixture is well blended, stirring frequently. Serve as directed.

BEAN DIP OLÉ:
Prepare as directed, omitting the salsa, using VELVEETA Pasteurized Prepared Cheese Product and adding 1 undrained 4-oz. can chopped green chilies.

SPECIAL EXTRA:
To serve in a bread bowl, cut a lengthwise slice from the top of 1-lb. round bread loaf. Remove center of loaf, leaving 1-inch-thick shell. Cut removed bread into bite-sized pieces to serve with dip. Fill bread bowl with hot dip just before serving.

*TACO BELL and HOME ORIGINALS are registered trademarks owned and licensed by Taco Bell Corp.

VELVEETA chili dip

▶ what you need!

1 lb. (16 oz.) VELVEETA Pasteurized Prepared Cheese Product, cut into ½-inch cubes

1 can (15 oz.) chili with or without beans

▶ make it!

MIX VELVEETA and chili in microwaveable bowl.

MICROWAVE on HIGH 5 min. or until VELVEETA is completely melted and mixture is well blended, stirring after 3 min.

SERVE hot with tortilla chips, RITZ Toasted Chips or assorted cut-up fresh vegetables.

HOW TO HALVE:
Mix ½ lb. (8 oz.) VELVEETA Pasteurized Prepared Cheese Product, cut up, and ¾ cup canned chili in 1-qt. microwaveable bowl. Microwave on HIGH 3 to 4 min. or until VELVEETA is melted, stirring after 2 min. Serve as directed. Makes 1¼ cups or 10 servings, 2 Tbsp. each.

VELVEETA salsa dip

PREP: 5 min. | TOTAL: 10 min. | MAKES: 2½ cups or 20 servings, 2 Tbsp. each.

▶ what you need!

1 lb. (16 oz.) VELVEETA Pasteurized Prepared Cheese Product, cut into ½-inch cubes

1 cup TACO BELL HOME ORIGINALS Thick 'N Chunky Salsa*

▶ make it!

MIX ingredients in microwaveable bowl.

MICROWAVE on HIGH 5 min. or until VELVEETA is completely melted and mixture is well blended, stirring after 3 min.

SERVE with tortilla chips, assorted cut-up fresh vegetables or RITZ Toasted Chips Original.

HOW TO HALVE:
Prepare cutting ingredients in half and reducing the microwave time to 3 to 4 min. or until VELVEETA is completely melted, stirring after 2 min. Makes 1½ cups or 12 servings, 2 Tbsp. each.

TACO BELL and HOME ORIGINALS are registered trademarks owned and licensed by Taco Bell Corp.

VELVEETA
hot 'n cheesy crab dip

PREP: 5 min. | TOTAL: 10 min. | MAKES: 2½ cups or 20 servings, 2 Tbsp. each.

▶ what you need!

1 lb. (16 oz.) VELVEETA Pasteurized Prepared Cheese Product, cut into ½-inch cubes

1 can (6½ oz.) crabmeat, drained, flaked

4 green onions, sliced

½ cup chopped red bell peppers

½ cup BREAKSTONE'S or KNUDSEN Sour Cream

⅛ tsp. ground red pepper (cayenne)

▶ make it!

MIX first 4 ingredients in large microwaveable bowl. Microwave on HIGH 5 min. or until VELVEETA is completely melted, stirring after 3 min.

STIR in remaining ingredients.

SERVE with WHEAT THINS Original Snacks or assorted cut-up fresh vegetables.

KEEPING IT SAFE:
Hot dips should be discarded after sitting at room temperature for 2 hours or longer.

JAZZ IT UP:
Top with additional BREAKSTONE'S or KNUDSEN Sour Cream before serving.

VELVEETA chipotle dip

PREP: 10 min. | TOTAL: 16 min. | MAKES: 3¼ cups or 26 servings, 2 Tbsp. each.

▶ what you need!

1 lb. (16 oz.) VELVEETA Pasteurized Prepared Cheese Product, cut into ½-inch cubes

2 Tbsp. chipotle peppers in adobo sauce, chopped

1 container (16 oz.) BREAKSTONE'S or KNUDSEN Sour Cream

▶ make it!

MIX VELVEETA and peppers in microwaveable bowl.

MICROWAVE on HIGH 4 to 6 min. or until VELVEETA is melted, stirring after 3 min. Stir in sour cream.

SERVE with assorted cut-up fresh vegetable dippers.

SIZE-WISE:
Savor every bite of this tasty, hot dip. Each 2 Tbsp. serving goes a long way on flavor.

TO HALVE:
Prepare as directed, cutting all ingredients in half. Makes about 1½ cups or 13 servings, about 2 Tbsp. each.

VELVEETA ranch dip

PREP: 5 min. | TOTAL: 11 min. | MAKES: 3¼ cups or 26 servings, 2 Tbsp. each.

▶ what you need!

1 lb. (16 oz.) VELVEETA Pasteurized Prepared Cheese Product, cut into ½-inch cubes

1 container (8 oz.) BREAKSTONE'S or KNUDSEN Sour Cream

1 cup KRAFT Ranch Dressing

▶ make it!

MIX all ingredients in microwaveable bowl.

MICROWAVE on HIGH 6 min. or until VELVEETA is completely melted and mixture is well blended, stirring every 2 min.

SERVE with assorted cut-up fresh vegetables or your favorite NABISCO Crackers.

VELVEETA PEPPER JACK RANCH DIP:
Prepare as directed, using VELVEETA Pepper Jack Pasteurized Prepared Cheese Product.

HOW TO SERVE IT COLD:
This versatile dip can also be served cold. Just prepare as directed; cool completely. Cover and refrigerate several hours or until chilled. Serve as directed.

VELVEETA
southwestern corn dip

PREP: 5 min. | TOTAL: 10 min. | MAKES: 3½ cups or 28 servings, 2 Tbsp. each.

▶ what you need!

1 lb. (16 oz.) VELVEETA Pasteurized Prepared Cheese Product, cut into ½-inch cubes

1 can (11 oz.) corn with red and green bell peppers, drained

3 jalapeño peppers, seeded, minced

1 red onion, finely chopped

½ cup fresh cilantro, finely chopped

½ cup BREAKSTONE'S or KNUDSEN Sour Cream

▶ make it!

MIX VELVEETA and corn in large microwaveable bowl.

MICROWAVE on HIGH 5 min. or until VELVEETA is completely melted, stirring after 3 min. Stir in remaining ingredients.

SERVE with WHEAT THINS Original Snacks or assorted cut-up fresh vegetables.

TO HALVE:
Mix ingredients as directed in 1-qt. microwaveable bowl, cutting all ingredients in half. Microwave on HIGH 3 to 4 min. or until VELVEETA is completely melted, stirring after 2 min. Serve as directed. Makes 1½ cups or 12 servings, 2 Tbsp. each.

KEEPING IT SAFE:
Hot dips should be discarded after sitting at room temperature for 2 hours or longer.

VELVEETA spicy buffalo dip

PREP: 5 min. | TOTAL: 10 min. | MAKES: 2¾ cups or 22 servings, 2 Tbsp. each.

▶ what you need!

1 lb. (16 oz.) VELVEETA Pasteurized Prepared Cheese Product, cut into ½-inch cubes

1 cup BREAKSTONE'S or KNUDSEN Sour Cream

¼ cup cayenne pepper sauce for Buffalo wings

¼ cup KRAFT Natural Blue Cheese Crumbles

2 green onions, sliced

▶ make it!

MIX VELVEETA, sour cream and pepper sauce in large microwaveable bowl.

MICROWAVE on HIGH 5 min. or until VELVEETA is completely melted, stirring after 3 min. Stir in remaining ingredients.

SERVE with celery and carrot sticks.

VARIATION:
Prepare as directed, using VELVEETA Made With 2% Milk Reduced Fat Pasteurized Prepared Cheese Product and BREAKSTONE'S Reduced Fat or KNUDSEN Light Sour Cream.

SERVE IT COLD:
This dip is also great served cold. Prepare as directed; cool. Cover and refrigerate several hours or until chilled. Serve as directed.

VELVEETA ultimate queso dip

PREP: 5 min. | TOTAL: 10 min. | MAKES: 3 cups or 24 servings, 2 Tbsp. each.

▶ what you need!

1 lb. (16 oz.) VELVEETA Pasteurized Prepared Cheese Product, cut into ½-inch cubes

1 can (10 oz.) RO*TEL Diced Tomatoes & Green Chilies, undrained

▶ make it!

MIX ingredients in microwaveable bowl.

MICROWAVE on HIGH 5 min. or until VELVEETA is completely melted, stirring after 3 min.

SERVE with assorted cut-up vegetables, WHEAT THINS Original Snacks or tortilla chips.

SIZE-WISE:
When eating appetizers at social occasions, preview your choices and decide which you'd like to try instead of taking some of each.

CREATIVE LEFTOVERS:
Refrigerate any leftover dip. Reheat and serve spooned over hot baked potatoes or cooked pasta.

SUBSTITUTE:
Prepare using Mild Mexican VELVEETA Pasteurized Prepared Cheese Product.

*RO*TEL is a registered trademark of ConAgra Foods, Inc.*

creamy coconut dip

PREP: 5 min. | TOTAL: 3 hours 5 min. | MAKES: 48 servings, 2 Tbsp. each.

▶ what you need!

1 pkg. (8 oz.) PHILADELPHIA Cream Cheese, softened

1 can (15 oz.) cream of coconut

1 tub (16 oz.) COOL WHIP Whipped Topping, thawed

▶ make it!

BEAT cream cheese and cream of coconut in large bowl with wire whisk until well blended.

ADD COOL WHIP; gently stir until well blended. Cover. Refrigerate several hours or until chilled.

SERVE with HONEY MAID Grahams Honey Sticks, HONEY MAID Honey Grahams or cut-up fresh fruit.

JAZZ IT UP:
Garnish with toasted BAKER'S ANGEL FLAKE Coconut just before serving.

ENTRÉES

eggplant parmesan

PREP: 10 min. | TOTAL: 50 min. | MAKES: 6 servings.

▶ what you need!

　　1 eggplant (1 lb.), sliced

　　½ lb. sliced fresh mushrooms

　　½ cup KRAFT Grated Parmesan Cheese, divided

　　1½ cups KRAFT 2% Milk Shredded Mozzarella Cheese, divided

　　1 jar (26 oz.) spaghetti sauce

▶ make it!

HEAT oven to 400°F.

PLACE ½ <u>each</u> of the eggplant and mushrooms in 13×9-inch baking pan sprayed with cooking spray; top with ⅓ of <u>each</u> cheese. Repeat layers.

TOP with sauce; cover with foil.

BAKE 35 min. Sprinkle with remaining cheeses. Bake, uncovered, 5 min. or until mozzarella is melted.

SERVING SUGGESTION:
Serve with a mixed green salad, tossed with your favorite KRAFT Dressing.

foil-wrapped fish with creamy parmesan sauce

PREP: 10 min. | TOTAL: 22 min. | MAKES: 4 servings.

▶ what you need!

4 orange roughy fillets (1 lb.), thawed if frozen

¼ cup KRAFT Mayonnaise

¼ cup KRAFT Grated Parmesan Cheese

⅛ tsp. ground red pepper (cayenne)

2 zucchini, sliced

½ of a red bell pepper, cut into strips

▶ make it!

HEAT grill to medium-high.

SPRAY 4 (18×12-inch) sheets of heavy-duty foil with cooking spray; place 1 fillet in center of each. Spread with mayo; top with Parmesan, ground red pepper and vegetables.

BRING up foil sides. Double fold top and ends to seal each packet, leaving room for heat circulation inside. Place on grill rack; cover grill with lid.

GRILL 10 to 12 min. or until fish flakes easily with fork.

SPECIAL EXTRA:
Garnish each serving with lemon wedges.

USE YOUR OVEN:
Heat oven to 450°F. Assemble foil packets as directed; place on baking sheet. Bake 18 to 22 min. or until fish flakes easily with fork.

country salisbury steak

▶ what you need!

1½ lb. extra lean ground beef

1 pkg. (6 oz.) STOVE TOP Stuffing Mix for Chicken

1½ cups water, divided

¾ cup chopped onions

1 pkg. (8 oz.) fresh mushrooms, sliced

½ cup KRAFT Original Barbecue Sauce

▶ make it!

HEAT oven to 375°F.

MIX meat, stuffing mix, 1¼ cups water and onions until well blended. Shape into 6 (½-inch-thick) oval patties. Place on 15×10×1-inch pan.

BAKE 25 min. or until patties are done.

MEANWHILE, spray large nonstick skillet with cooking spray. Add mushrooms; cook on medium-high heat 5 min. or until lightly browned, stirring occasionally. Add sauce and remaining water; simmer on low heat 1 to 2 min. or until sauce is heated through. Serve over meat patties.

MAKEOVER—HOW WE DID IT:
We have taken a classic comfort food and made it over by preparing it with extra lean ground beef and cooking the mushrooms in a nonstick skillet instead of in a regular skillet with butter. These changes will save you 15 grams of fat per serving.

SUBSTITUTE:
Prepare using KRAFT Hickory Smoke Barbecue Sauce.

easy chicken pot pie

PREP: 10 min. | TOTAL: 40 min. | MAKES: 6 servings.

▶ what you need!

1⅔ cups hot water

1 pkg. (6 oz.) STOVE TOP Lower Sodium
   Stuffing Mix for Chicken

3 cups chopped cooked chicken

1 pkg. (10 oz.) frozen mixed vegetables

1 can (10¾ oz.) less sodium condensed
   cream of chicken soup

1 cup milk

▶ make it!

HEAT oven to 375°F.

ADD hot water to stuffing mix; stir just until moistened.

COMBINE chicken and vegetables in 2-qt. casserole. Mix soup and milk; pour over chicken mixture. Top with stuffing.

BAKE 30 min. or until hot and bubbly.

SHORTCUT:
Prepare using 2 pkg. (6 oz. each) OSCAR MAYER Deli Fresh Oven Roasted Chicken Breast Cuts.

SPECIAL EXTRA:
Add ¼ tsp. dried thyme leaves to chicken mixture before topping with soup mixture.

STOVE TOP one-dish chicken skillet

PREP: 5 min. | TOTAL: 25 min. | MAKES: 6 servings.

▶ what you need!

1½ cups hot water

¼ cup butter or margarine, melted

1 pkg. (6 oz.) STOVE TOP Stuffing Mix for Chicken

6 small boneless skinless chicken breast halves (1½ lb.)

1 can (10¾ oz.) condensed cream of mushroom soup

⅓ cup BREAKSTONE'S or KNUDSEN Sour Cream

▶ make it!

MIX hot water, butter and stuffing mix; set aside.

SPRAY nonstick skillet with cooking spray. Add chicken; cook on medium heat 5 min. on each side.

MIX soup and sour cream; pour over chicken. Top with stuffing; cover. Cook on low heat 10 min. or until chicken is done.

SERVING SUGGESTION:
Serve with a mixed green salad tossed with your favorite KRAFT Light Dressing.

bruschetta 'n cheese-stuffed chicken breasts

PREP: 15 min. | TOTAL: 1 hour | MAKES: 8 servings.

► what you need!

1 can (14½ oz.) Italian-style diced tomatoes, undrained

1¼ cups KRAFT Shredded Low-Moisture Part-Skim Mozzarella Cheese, divided

¼ cup chopped fresh basil

1 pkg. (6 oz.) STOVE TOP Stuffing Mix for Chicken

8 small boneless skinless chicken breast halves (2 lb.)

⅓ cup KRAFT Roasted Red Pepper Italian with Parmesan Dressing

► make it!

HEAT oven to 350°F.

MIX tomatoes, ½ cup mozzarella and basil in medium bowl. Add stuffing mix; stir just until moistened.

PLACE 2 chicken breasts in large freezer-weight resealable plastic bag. Pound with meat mallet or side of heavy can until chicken is ¼-inch thick. Remove from bag; place, top-sides down, on cutting board. Repeat with remaining chicken. Spread chicken with stuffing mixture. Starting at 1 narrow end, tightly roll up each breast. Place, seam-sides down, in 13×9-inch baking dish. Drizzle with dressing.

BAKE 40 min. or until chicken is done. Sprinkle with remaining mozzarella; bake 5 min. or until melted.

baked italian-style meatballs

PREP: 10 min. | TOTAL: 30 min. | MAKES: 8 servings.

▶ what you need!

2 lb. ground beef

1 pkg. (6 oz.) STOVE TOP Stuffing Mix for Chicken

1¼ cups water

2 eggs, beaten

2 cloves garlic, minced

⅓ cup KRAFT Grated Parmesan Cheese

4 cups pasta, uncooked

1 cup spaghetti sauce

▶ make it!

HEAT oven to 400°F.

MIX first 6 ingredients until well blended. Shape into 24 meatballs, using about ¼ cup for each. Place in foil-lined 15×10×1-inch pan.

BAKE 20 min. or until done. Meanwhile, cook pasta as directed on package and heat sauce.

DRAIN pasta. Serve topped with sauce and meatballs.

cheese & chicken fajita quesadillas

PREP: 15 min. | TOTAL: 32 min. | MAKES: 6 servings, 1 quesadilla each.

▶ what you need!

- ½ lb. boneless skinless chicken breasts, cut into thin strips

- ¾ cup <u>each</u> sliced onions and red bell pepper strips

- ½ cup salsa

- ½ cup drained canned black beans, rinsed

- 6 flour tortillas (6 inch)

- 1½ cups KRAFT 2% Milk Shredded Sharp Cheddar Cheese

▶ make it!

COOK chicken in large skillet sprayed with cooking spray on medium-high heat 5 min., stirring frequently.

ADD onions and peppers; cook 4 to 5 min. or until crisp-tender. Stir in salsa and beans; cook 3 min. or until heated through, stirring occasionally.

TOP tortillas with chicken mixture and Cheddar; fold in half. Spray second large skillet with cooking spray. Heat on medium heat. Add quesadillas, in batches; cook 2 min. on each side or until evenly browned. Cut in half or into quarters to serve, if desired.

VARIATION:
Prepare as directed, substituting ½ cup drained canned corn for the black beans. Serve topped with shredded romaine lettuce, chopped fresh tomatoes and chopped cilantro.

SPECIAL EXTRA:
Top each serving with 1 Tbsp. BREAKSTONE'S Reduced Fat or KNUDSEN Light Sour Cream.

NOTE:
If you have only 1 large skillet, cook chicken mixture in skillet as directed, then transfer to bowl; cover to keep warm. Wipe out skillet, then spray with additional cooking spray and use to cook quesadillas as directed.

dressed-up fish
rolls for a crowd

PREP: 10 min. | TOTAL: 35 min. | MAKES: 10 servings.

▶ what you need!

1 pkg. (6 oz.) STOVE TOP Cornbread Stuffing Mix

¾ cup KRAFT Zesty Italian Dressing

¼ cup chopped fresh parsley

½ tsp. garlic powder

¼ tsp. paprika

10 whitefish fillets (2½ lb.)

▶ make it!

HEAT oven to 425°F.

PREPARE stuffing as directed on package; set aside. Mix dressing, parsley and seasonings until well blended; brush half onto fish.

SPOON stuffing onto one end of each fish fillet; roll up. Place, seam-sides down, in 13×9-inch baking dish sprayed with cooking spray. Pour remaining dressing mixture over fish.

BAKE 20 to 25 min. or until fish flakes easily with fork.

COOKING KNOW-HOW:
For best results, use thin flounder or sole fillets.

easy cheesy stuffed chicken

PREP: 30 min. | TOTAL: 1 hour 25 min. | MAKES: 8 servings.

▶ what you need!

- 2 Tbsp. butter or margarine
- 2 zucchini, shredded (about 2 cups)
- 1 onion, chopped
- 1 pkg. (6 oz.) STOVE TOP Stuffing Mix for Chicken
- 1 cup KRAFT Finely Shredded Italian Five Cheese Blend
- 2 chickens (5 lb.), quartered
- ¾ cup KRAFT Honey Barbecue Sauce

▶ make it!

HEAT oven to 400°F.

MELT butter in medium saucepan on medium heat. Add zucchini and onions; cook and stir 2 min. or until tender. Remove from heat. Stir in stuffing mix and cheese until well blended.

INSERT fingers carefully between the meat and skin of each chicken quarter to form a pocket. Fill pockets with stuffing mixture. Place, skin-sides up, in large roasting pan.

BAKE 45 min. or until chicken is done. Brush with sauce. Bake 5 to 10 min. or until heated through.

SIZE-WISE:
Serve this simple main dish for your friends and family at your next dinner party.

SUBSTITUTE:
This recipe can easily be turned into a Mexican-style chicken dish by preparing with KRAFT Mexican Style Finely Shredded Four Cheese.

easy parmesan-garlic chicken

PREP: 5 min. | TOTAL: 30 min. | MAKES: 6 servings, 1 chicken breast each.

▶ what you need!

½ cup KRAFT Grated Parmesan Cheese

1 env. GOOD SEASONS Italian Salad Dressing & Recipe Mix

½ tsp. garlic powder

6 boneless skinless chicken breast halves (2 lb.)

▶ make it!

HEAT oven to 400°F.

MIX Parmesan, dressing mix and garlic powder.

MOISTEN chicken with water; coat with Parmesan mixture. Place in single layer in shallow baking dish.

BAKE 20 to 25 min. or until chicken is cooked through (165°F).

SERVING SUGGESTION:
Serve with a mixed green salad, tossed with your favorite KRAFT Dressing.

STOVE TOP sweet citrus chicken

PREP: 10 min. | TOTAL: 40 min. | MAKES: 6 servings.

▶ what you need!

1⅔ cups hot water

1 pkg. (6 oz.) STOVE TOP Stuffing Mix for Chicken

6 small boneless skinless chicken breast halves (1½ lb.), pounded to ½-inch thickness

⅔ cup orange juice

⅓ cup packed brown sugar

3 Tbsp. butter or margarine, melted

▶ make it!

HEAT oven to 400°F.

ADD hot water to stuffing mix; stir just until moistened.

PLACE chicken in 13×9-inch baking dish. Mix juice, sugar and butter until blended; pour over chicken. Top with stuffing.

BAKE 30 min. or until chicken is done.

SUBSTITUTE:
Substitute honey for the brown sugar.

french onion-pork chop skillet

PREP: 10 min. | TOTAL: 35 min. | MAKES: 6 servings.

▶ what you need!

- 6 boneless pork chops (1½ lb.), ½-inch thick
- 2 onions, thinly sliced
- 2 Tbsp. Worcestershire sauce
- 1 pkg. (6 oz.) STOVE TOP Stuffing Mix for Chicken
- 1½ cups hot water
- 1 cup KRAFT Shredded Low-Moisture Part-Skim Mozzarella Cheese

▶ make it!

HEAT large nonstick skillet sprayed with cooking spray on medium-high heat. Add chops and onions; cook 10 min. or until chops are done, turning chops and stirring onions after 5 min. Remove chops from skillet. Cook and stir onions 5 min. or until golden brown.

STIR in Worcestershire sauce. Return chops to skillet; top with onion mixture.

MIX stuffing mix and hot water; spoon around edge of skillet. Top with mozzarella; cover. Cook 5 min. or until cheese is melted.

SERVING SUGGESTION:
Serve with hot steamed broccoli or green beans.

jumbo meatballs

PREP: 10 min. | TOTAL: 40 min. | MAKES: 4 servings.

▶ what you need!

- 1 pkg. (6 oz.) STOVE TOP Stuffing Mix for Chicken
- ½ cup hot water
- 1 egg
- ¼ cup KRAFT Ranch Dressing
- 1 lb. lean ground beef
- 1 cup KRAFT Shredded Cheddar Cheese
- ⅓ cup ketchup

▶ make it!

HEAT oven to 375°F.

COMBINE first 4 ingredients in large bowl. Add meat and Cheddar; mix well. Shape into 8 (2-inch) meatballs.

PLACE on greased baking sheet; spread with ketchup.

BAKE 30 min. or until done.

SERVING SUGGESTION:
Serve with hot cooked rice and steamed broccoli.

parmesan baked salmon

PREP: 10 min. | TOTAL: 25 min. | MAKES: 4 servings.

▶ what you need!

¼ cup KRAFT Mayonnaise

2 Tbsp. KRAFT Grated Parmesan Cheese

⅛ tsp. ground red pepper (cayenne)

4 salmon fillets (1 lb.), skin removed

2 tsp. lemon juice

10 RITZ Crackers, crushed

▶ make it!

HEAT oven to 400°F.

MIX mayo, Parmesan and pepper.

PLACE fish in foil-lined baking pan; top with lemon juice, mayo mixture and crumbs.

BAKE 12 to 15 min. or until fish flakes easily with fork.

SPECIAL EXTRA:
Add ¼ tsp. dill weed to the mayo mixture before spreading onto fish.

SERVING SUGGESTION:
Serve with your favorite green vegetable, such as fresh green beans.

stuffing-topped beef filets

PREP: 10 min. | TOTAL: 27 min. | MAKES: 2 servings.

▶ what you need!

- 2 beef tenderloin filets (½ lb.)
- 1 Tbsp. butter
- ½ cup shredded zucchini
- ⅓ cup finely chopped onions
- ¾ cup STOVE TOP Stuffing Mix for Chicken
  in the Canister
- ½ cup KRAFT Shredded Cheddar Cheese

▶ make it!

HEAT broiler.

HEAT ovenproof skillet on medium heat. Add meat; cook 6 min. on each side or until medium doneness. Remove from skillet; cover to keep warm.

MELT butter in same skillet on medium-high heat. Add zucchini and onions; cook and stir 2 min. or until crisp-tender. Transfer to large bowl; stir in stuffing mix and Cheddar. Add meat to skillet; top with stuffing mixture.

BROIL, 6 inches from heat source, 5 min. or until stuffing is lightly browned.

SUBSTITUTE:
If you are a blue cheese lover, substitute ¼ cup ATHENOS Crumbled Blue Cheese for the ½ cup Cheddar.

easy pleasing meatloaf

PREP: 10 min. | TOTAL: 1 hour 10 min. | MAKES: 8 servings.

▶ what you need!

2 lb. lean ground beef

1 pkg. (6 oz.) STOVE TOP Stuffing Mix
  for Chicken

1 cup water

2 eggs, beaten

½ cup KRAFT Original Barbecue Sauce,
  divided

▶ make it!

HEAT oven to 375°F.

PLACE meat, stuffing mix, water, eggs and ¼ cup sauce in bowl.

MIX just until blended.

SHAPE into loaf in 13×9-inch baking dish.

TOP with remaining sauce. Bake 1 hour or until done.

TO DOUBLE:
Mix meat mixture as directed, doubling all ingredients. Shape into 2 loaves. Place, side-by-side, in 13×9-inch baking dish. Bake at 375°F for 1 hour and 25 min. or until done. Refrigerate leftover meatloaf; use to make sandwiches.

super crunch chicken

PREP: 10 min. | TOTAL: 40 min. | MAKES: 4 servings.

▶ what you need!

8 boneless skinless chicken thighs (1 lb.)

¼ cup MIRACLE WHIP Light Dressing

1 pkg. (6 oz.) STOVE TOP Stuffing Mix for Chicken

¼ cup KRAFT Grated Parmesan Cheese

▶ make it!

HEAT oven to 375°F.

SPREAD chicken with dressing.

MIX stuffing mix and Parmesan in pie plate. Add chicken, 1 piece at a time; turn to evenly coat. Place on foil-covered baking sheet. Discard any leftover stuffing mixture.

BAKE 25 to 30 min. or until chicken is done.

SERVING SUGGESTION:
Serve with fresh vegetable sticks, such as carrots, celery and cucumbers, and a fresh fruit salad.

PASTA &
CASSEROLES

cheesy chicken & broccoli bake

PREP: 10 min. | TOTAL: 50 min. | MAKES: 6 servings.

▶ what you need!

1 pkg. (6 oz.) STOVE TOP Stuffing Mix for Chicken

1½ lb. boneless skinless chicken breasts, cut into bite-size pieces

1 pkg. (16 oz.) frozen broccoli florets, thawed, drained

1 can (10¾ oz.) reduced-sodium condensed cream of chicken soup

½ lb. (8 oz.) VELVEETA Pasteurized Prepared Cheese Product, cut into ½-inch cubes

▶ make it!

HEAT oven to 400°F.

PREPARE stuffing as directed on package; set aside.

COMBINE remaining ingredients; spoon into 13×9-inch baking dish. Top with stuffing.

BAKE 40 min. or until chicken is done.

CHICKEN & GREEN BEAN BAKE:
Omit VELVEETA. Prepare as directed, using STOVE TOP Traditional Sage Stuffing Mix and substituting frozen green beans for the broccoli.

bruschetta chicken bake

PREP: 10 min. | TOTAL: 40 min. | MAKES: 6 servings.

▶ what you need!

- 1 can (14½ oz.) diced tomatoes, undrained
- 1 pkg. (6 oz.) STOVE TOP Stuffing Mix for Chicken
- ½ cup water
- 2 cloves garlic, minced
- 1½ lb. boneless skinless chicken breasts, cut into bite-size pieces
- 1 tsp. dried basil leaves
- 1 cup KRAFT 2% Milk Shredded Mozzarella Cheese

▶ make it!

HEAT oven to 400°F.

MIX tomatoes, stuffing mix, water and garlic just until stuffing mix is moistened.

LAYER chicken, basil and mozzarella in 3-qt. casserole or 13×9-inch baking dish.

TOP with stuffing. Bake 30 min. or until chicken is done.

MAKE AHEAD:
Prepare and bake as directed; cool. Refrigerate up to 24 hours. To reheat, spoon each serving onto microwaveable plate. Microwave on HIGH 2 to 3 min. or until heated through.

STOVE TOP
one-dish chicken bake

PREP: 10 min. | TOTAL: 40 min. | MAKES: 6 servings.

▶ what you need!

1⅔ cups hot water

1 pkg. (6 oz.) STOVE TOP Stuffing Mix
for Chicken

1½ lb. boneless skinless chicken breasts,
cut into bite-size pieces

1 can (10¾ oz.) condensed cream of
mushroom soup

⅓ cup BREAKSTONE'S or KNUDSEN
Sour Cream

▶ make it!

HEAT oven to 400°F.

ADD hot water to stuffing mix; stir just until moistened.

PLACE chicken in 13×9-inch baking dish or 2-qt. casserole. Mix soup and sour cream until
well blended; pour over chicken. Top with stuffing.

BAKE 30 min. or until chicken is done.

SERVING SUGGESTION:
Serve with a steamed green vegetable, such as broccoli, and a glass of fat-free milk.

SPECIAL EXTRA:
Prepare as directed, topping chicken with 1 cup frozen mixed vegetables before covering with soup
mixture.

STORAGE KNOW-HOW:
Package boneless skinless chicken breast halves in recipe-size portions in the freezer. Thaw only the
amount needed for a recipe.

baked cheese-stuffing casserole

PREP: 5 min. | TOTAL: 30 min. | MAKES: 8 servings.

▶ what you need!

2 cups water

1 Tbsp. margarine or butter

1 pkg. (6 oz.) STOVE TOP Savory Herbs Stuffing Mix

1 egg, beaten

¾ cup KRAFT Mexican Style Finely Shredded Four Cheese, divided

▶ make it!

HEAT oven to 375°F.

BRING water and margarine to boil in large saucepan. Stir in stuffing mix; cover. Remove from heat; let stand 5 min.

STIR egg and ½ cup cheese into stuffing mixture until blended. Spoon into greased 9-inch pie plate. Sprinkle with remaining cheese.

BAKE 20 min. or until casserole is heated through and cheese is melted.

SPECIAL EXTRA:
For a more rounded side dish, stir ¾ cup cooked broccoli florets or chopped cooked mixed vegetables into stuffing mixture before spooning into pie plate.

SUBSTITUTE:
Prepare using KRAFT Mexican Style 2% Milk Finely Shredded Four Cheese.

better-than-ever cheesy meat lasagna

PREP: 30 min. | TOTAL: 1 hour 10 min. | MAKES: 9 servings.

 what you need!

¾ lb. extra lean ground beef

3 cloves garlic, minced

1½ tsp. dried oregano leaves

1 jar (26 oz.) spaghetti sauce

1 large tomato, chopped

1 egg, beaten

1 container (16 oz.) BREAKSTONE'S or KNUDSEN Low Fat Cottage Cheese

¼ cup KRAFT Grated Parmesan Cheese

9 lasagna noodles, cooked, drained

2 cups KRAFT 2% Milk Shredded Mozzarella Cheese, divided

make it!

HEAT oven to 375°F.

BROWN meat with garlic and oregano in medium saucepan. Stir in sauce; simmer 5 min., stirring occasionally. Remove from heat; stir in tomatoes.

MIX egg, cottage cheese and Parmesan; spread ½ cup onto bottom of 13×9-inch baking dish. Top with layers of 3 noodles, 1 cup cottage cheese mixture, ½ cup mozzarella cheese and 1 cup of the remaining spaghetti sauce mixture. Repeat layers. Top with remaining noodles and spaghetti sauce mixture. Cover with foil.

BAKE 30 min. or until heated through. Top with remaining mozzarella. Bake, uncovered, 5 min. or until mozzarella is melted. Let stand 5 min.

MAKE AHEAD:
Assemble lasagna as directed; cover. Refrigerate up to 24 hours. When ready to serve, bake, covered, at 375°F for 40 min. or until heated through.

cheesy italian pasta bake

PREP: 25 min. | TOTAL: 45 min. | MAKES: 6 servings, 1½ cups each.

▶ what you need!

1½ cups wagon wheel pasta, uncooked

1 lb. extra lean ground beef

1 large carrot, shredded (about 1 cup)

1 large zucchini, shredded (about 1 cup)

1 red bell pepper, chopped

1 can (8 oz.) pizza sauce

½ lb. (8 oz.) VELVEETA 2% Milk Pasteurized Prepared Cheese Product, cut into ½-inch cubes

½ cup KRAFT Grated Parmesan Cheese

▶ make it!

HEAT oven to 350°F.

COOK pasta as directed on package. Meanwhile, brown meat in large nonstick skillet on medium-high heat; drain. Stir in vegetables and sauce; cook 5 min. or until vegetables are tender. Drain pasta. Add to meat mixture along with VELVEETA; mix well.

SPOON into 8-inch square baking dish sprayed with cooking spray; sprinkle with Parmesan.

BAKE 15 to 20 min. or until heated through.

SUBSTITUTE:
Prepare using any other bite-size pasta.

chicken and spinach risotto

PREP: 10 min. | TOTAL: 30 min. | MAKES: 4 servings.

▶ what you need!

1 lb. boneless skinless chicken breasts, cut into bite-size pieces

1 Tbsp. oil

4 cups baby spinach leaves, cleaned

1½ cups instant white rice, uncooked

1 cup grape or cherry tomatoes

1 can (10½ oz.) condensed chicken broth

½ cup water

¼ cup KRAFT Grated Parmesan Cheese

▶ make it!

COOK chicken in hot oil in large deep nonstick skillet on medium heat 10 min. or until cooked through, stirring frequently.

ADD spinach, rice, tomatoes, broth and water; mix well. Bring to boil. Reduce heat to low; cover. Simmer 5 min., stirring occasionally.

STIR in Parmesan.

SUBSTITUTE:
Substitute dry white wine for ½ cup broth.

SUBSTITUTE:
Prepare using KRAFT Grated Three Cheese Blend.

easy baked manicotti

PREP: 25 min. | TOTAL: 1 hour 5 min. | MAKES: 6 servings, 2 manicotti each.

▶ what you need!

2 cups spaghetti sauce, divided

1 egg, beaten

1¾ cups POLLY-O Original Ricotta Cheese

1½ cups KRAFT Shredded Mozzarella Cheese

½ cup KRAFT Grated Parmesan Cheese

¼ cup pesto

12 manicotti shells, cooked, rinsed in cold water

▶ make it!

HEAT oven to 350°F.

SPREAD ¾ cup sauce onto bottom of 13×9-inch baking dish. Mix egg, cheeses and pesto; spoon into resealable plastic bag. Cut small hole in bottom corner of bag; use to squeeze cheese mixture into both ends of each shell.

PLACE in dish; top with remaining sauce. Cover with foil.

BAKE 40 min. or until heated through.

SIZE-WISE:
Enjoy your favorite foods on occasion, but keep portion size in mind. This recipe makes enough to serve 6.

MAKE AHEAD:
Cook manicotti shells up to 1 day ahead. Place on greased tray, cover with plastic wrap and refrigerate until ready to fill.

SUBSTITUTE:
Substitute BREAKSTONE'S or KNUDSEN Cottage Cheese for the ricotta cheese and/or KRAFT Grated Romano Cheese for the Parmesan cheese.

fettuccine alfredo

PREP: 5 min. | TOTAL: 20 min. | MAKES: 4 servings, about 1 cup each.

▶ what you need!

4 oz. (½ of 8-oz. pkg.) PHILADELPHIA Cream Cheese, cubed

½ cup KRAFT Grated Parmesan Cheese

¾ cup milk

¼ cup butter or margarine

¼ tsp. white pepper

⅛ tsp. garlic powder

8 oz. fettuccine, cooked, drained

⅛ tsp. ground nutmeg

▶ make it!

PLACE cream cheese, Parmesan, milk, butter, white pepper and garlic powder in medium saucepan; cook and stir on low heat until cream cheese is melted.

TOSS with hot fettuccine. Sprinkle with nutmeg.

SERVING SUGGESTION:
Try serving with Italian bread and a mixed green salad tossed with your favorite KRAFT Dressing, such as Balsamic Vinaigrette.

SPECIAL EXTRA:
Prepare as directed, heating 1 pkg. (6 oz.) OSCAR MAYER Grilled or Italian Style Chicken Breast Strips with the sauce before tossing with pasta.

SUBSTITUTE:
Prepare using PHILADELPHIA Neufchâtel Cheese.

garden-fresh pasta salad

PREP: 20 min. | TOTAL: 1 hour 30 min. | MAKES: 14 servings, ¾ cup each.

▶ what you need!

1 pkg. (1 lb.) farfalle (bow-tie pasta), uncooked

2 cups broccoli florets

1 small red onion, thinly sliced

1 red bell pepper, chopped

1 cup halved cherry tomatoes

1 bottle (8 oz.) KRAFT Sun-Dried Tomato Dressing

½ cup KRAFT Grated Parmesan Cheese

▶ make it!

COOK pasta as directed on package, adding broccoli for the last 3 min. Drain; rinse under cold water. Drain well; place in large bowl.

ADD onions, peppers and tomatoes; mix lightly. Toss with dressing.

REFRIGERATE 1 hour. Stir before serving; sprinkle with Parmesan.

SUBSTITUTE:
Substitute 1-inch asparagus pieces for the broccoli.

SUBSTITUTE:
Prepare using KRAFT Shredded Parmesan Cheese or KRAFT Shredded Parmesan, Romano and Asiago Cheese.

gram's chicken pot pie updated

PREP: 15 min. | TOTAL: 45 min. | MAKES: 6 servings.

▶ what you need!

- 1 lb. boneless skinless chicken breasts, cut into bite-size pieces

- 2 Tbsp. KRAFT Light Zesty Italian Dressing

- 2 cups frozen mixed vegetables

- 1 can (10¾ oz.) reduced-sodium condensed cream of chicken soup

- ¼ lb. (4 oz.) VELVEETA 2% Milk Pasteurized Prepared Cheese Product, cut into ½-inch cubes

- 1 sheet frozen puff pastry (½ of 17.3-oz. pkg.), thawed

- 1 egg, beaten

▶ make it!

HEAT oven to 400°F.

COOK and stir chicken in dressing in large skillet on medium heat 5 min. or until done. Stir in vegetables, soup and VELVEETA. Spoon into greased 9-inch square baking dish.

UNFOLD pastry sheet; place over chicken mixture. Fold under edges of pastry; press onto top of baking dish to seal. Brush with egg. Cut several slits in crust to permit steam to escape. Place on baking sheet.

BAKE 30 min. or until crust is deep golden brown. Let stand 5 min.

HOW TO THAW PASTRY SHEETS:
Remove pastry sheet from freezer; cover with plastic wrap. Thaw at room temperature for 30 min. or in refrigerator for 4 hours. Thawed wrapped pastry sheets can be stored in refrigerator up to 2 days before using as desired.

ham and cheese stuff'n puff

PREP: 5 min. | TOTAL: 1 hour 10 min. | MAKES: 6 servings.

▶ what you need!

- 5 eggs
- 1 cup milk
- ½ cup BREAKSTONE'S or KNUDSEN Sour Cream
- 1 pkg. (10 oz.) frozen chopped broccoli, thawed, drained
- 1 pkg. (6 oz.) STOVE TOP Stuffing Mix for Chicken
- 1½ pkg. (6 oz. each) OSCAR MAYER Smoked Ham, chopped
- 1 cup KRAFT Shredded Cheddar Cheese, divided

▶ make it!

HEAT oven to 375°F.

BEAT eggs, milk and sour cream in large bowl with whisk until well blended. Add broccoli, stuffing mix, ham and ½ cup Cheddar; mix lightly.

POUR into 2-qt. casserole; cover loosely with foil.

BAKE 1 hour. Uncover. Sprinkle with remaining Cheddar; bake 5 min. or until Cheddar is melted and broccoli mixture is heated through.

SUBSTITUTE:
Use whatever frozen vegetables and shredded cheese you have on hand, such as peas and KRAFT Shredded Mozzarella Cheese.

jude's chicken casserole

PREP: 5 min. | TOTAL: 35 min. | MAKES: 6 servings.

▶ what you need!

- 1 pkg. (6 oz.) STOVE TOP Stuffing Mix for Chicken

- 2 cups chopped cooked chicken

- 1 can (10¾ oz.) condensed cream of chicken soup

- ½ lb. (8 oz.) VELVEETA Pasteurized Prepared Cheese Product, cut into ½-inch cubes

▶ make it!

HEAT oven to 350°F.

PREPARE stuffing as directed on package. Combine remaining ingredients in large bowl. Add stuffing; mix lightly.

SPOON into 2-qt. casserole.

BAKE 30 min. or until heated through.

SPECIAL EXTRA:
Prepare as directed, adding ½ cup chopped celery and/or red bell peppers to chicken mixture before baking.

layered enchilada bake

PREP: 25 min. | TOTAL: 1 hour 10 min. | MAKES: 8 servings.

▶ what you need!

- 1 lb. lean ground beef
- 1 large onion, chopped
- 2 cups TACO BELL HOME ORIGINALS Thick 'N Chunky Salsa*
- 1 can (15 oz.) black beans, drained, rinsed
- ¼ cup KRAFT Zesty Italian Dressing
- 2 Tbsp. TACO BELL HOME ORIGINALS Taco Seasoning Mix
- 6 flour tortillas (8 inch)
- 1 cup BREAKSTONE'S or KNUDSEN Sour Cream
- 1 pkg. (8 oz.) KRAFT Mexican Style Shredded Four Cheese

*TACO BELL and HOME ORIGINALS are registered trademarks owned and licensed by Taco Bell Corp.

▶ make it!

HEAT oven to 400°F.

BROWN meat with onions in large skillet on medium-high heat; drain. Stir in salsa, beans, dressing and seasoning mix.

PLACE 3 tortillas in single layer on bottom of 13×9-inch baking dish; cover with layers of ½ each meat mixture, sour cream and cheese. Repeat layers. Cover with foil.

BAKE 30 min. Remove foil. Bake 10 min. or until casserole is heated through and cheese is melted. Let stand 5 min.

MAKE AHEAD:
Line 13×9-inch baking dish with foil, with ends of foil extending over sides of dish. Assemble recipe in prepared dish as directed. Cover with foil. Freeze up to 3 months. When ready to serve, heat oven to 400°F. Bake, covered, 1 hour. Remove foil. Bake an additional 15 to 20 min. or until casserole is heated through and cheese is melted. Let stand 5 min. before cutting to serve. To decrease the baking time, thaw casserole in refrigerator overnight, then bake, uncovered, 45 min. or until casserole is heated through and cheese is melted.

SERVING SUGGESTION:
Top with chopped tomatoes, shredded lettuce and cilantro just before serving.

FAMILY FUN:
Set out bowls of chopped lettuce, tomatoes and avocados so everyone can help themselves to their favorite toppings.

mexican tortilla stack

PREP: 15 min. | TOTAL: 45 min. | MAKES: 6 servings, 1¼ cups each.

▶ what you need!

1½ lb. lean ground beef

½ lb. (8 oz.) VELVEETA 2% Milk Pasteurized Prepared Cheese Product, cut into ½-inch cubes

3 cups frozen corn

1 jar (16 oz.) TACO BELL HOME ORIGINALS Thick 'N Chunky Medium Salsa*

12 corn tortillas, cut into quarters

*TACO BELL and HOME ORIGINALS are registered trademarks owned and licensed by Taco Bell Corp.

▶ make it!

HEAT oven to 400°F.

BROWN meat in large skillet; drain. Add VELVEETA; cook and stir until melted. Stir in corn and salsa.

SPREAD ¼ of meat mixture onto bottom of 13×9-inch baking dish; top with 16 tortilla pieces. Repeat layers 2 times. Top with remaining meat mixture; cover tightly with foil.

BAKE 30 min.

SPECIAL EXTRA:
Top each serving with 1 Tbsp. BREAKSTONE'S or KNUDSEN Sour Cream.

new-look scalloped potatoes and ham

PREP: 30 min. | TOTAL: 1 hour | MAKES: 16 servings, about 1 cup each.

▶ what you need!

4½ lb. red potatoes, cut into ¼-inch-thick slices

1 container (16 oz.) BREAKSTONE'S FREE or KNUDSEN FREE Fat Free Sour Cream

¾ lb. (12 oz.) VELVEETA 2% Milk Pasteurized Prepared Cheese Product, cut into ½-inch cubes

½ lb. (½ of 1-lb. pkg.) OSCAR MAYER Smoked Ham, chopped

4 green onions, sliced

¼ cup KRAFT Grated Parmesan Cheese

▶ make it!

HEAT oven to 350°F.

COOK potatoes in boiling water in covered large saucepan 10 to 12 min. or just until potatoes are tender; drain. Place ¾ of potatoes in large bowl. Add sour cream; mash until smooth. Stir in VELVEETA, ham and onions. Add remaining potatoes; mix lightly.

SPOON into 13×9-inch baking dish sprayed with cooking spray; sprinkle with Parmesan.

BAKE 30 min. or until heated through.

PURCHASING POTATOES:
Look for firm, smooth, well-shaped potatoes that are free of wrinkles, cracks and blemishes. Avoid any with green-tinged skins or sprouting "eyes" or buds.

SIZE-WISE:
Enjoy your favorite foods on occasion, but keep portion size in mind.

taco bake

PREP: 15 min. | TOTAL: 35 min. | MAKES: 6 servings, 1 cup each.

▶ what you need!

1 pkg. (14 oz.) KRAFT Deluxe Macaroni & Cheese Dinner

1 lb. ground beef

1 pkg. TACO BELL HOME ORIGINALS Taco Seasoning Mix*

¾ cup BREAKSTONE'S or KNUDSEN Sour Cream

1½ cups KRAFT Shredded Cheddar Cheese

1 cup TACO BELL HOME ORIGINALS Thick 'N Chunky Salsa

*TACO BELL and HOME ORIGINALS are registered trademarks owned and licensed by Taco Bell Corp.

▶ make it!

HEAT oven to 400°F.

PREPARE Dinner as directed on package. While Macaroni is cooking, cook meat with taco seasoning mix as directed on package.

STIR sour cream into prepared Dinner; spoon ½ into 8-inch square baking dish. Top with layers of meat mixture, 1 cup Cheddar and remaining Dinner mixture; cover with foil.

BAKE 15 min. Top with salsa and remaining Cheddar. Bake, uncovered, 5 min. or until Cheddar is melted.

VARIATION:
Prepare using BREAKSTONE'S Reduced Fat or KNUDSEN Light Sour Cream, and KRAFT 2% Milk Shredded Cheddar Cheese.

SERVING SUGGESTION:
Serve with your favorite hot cooked vegetable, such as broccoli.

turkey-parmesan casserole

PREP: 20 min. | TOTAL: 50 min. | MAKES: 6 servings, 1⅓ cups each.

▶ what you need!

8 oz. spaghetti, broken in half, uncooked

1 can (10¾ oz.) condensed cream of
    mushroom soup

¾ cup BREAKSTONE'S or KNUDSEN Sour
    Cream

¼ cup milk

⅓ cup KRAFT Grated Parmesan Cheese

¼ tsp. black pepper

3 cups frozen broccoli florets, thawed

2 cups chopped cooked turkey

▶ make it!

HEAT oven to 350°F.

COOK spaghetti as directed on package; drain.

MIX soup, sour cream, milk, Parmesan and pepper in large bowl. Add spaghetti, broccoli
and turkey; mix lightly. Spoon into 2-qt. casserole dish.

BAKE 25 to 30 min. or until heated through.

SUBSTITUTE:
Substitute frozen cut green beans or peas for broccoli.

SUBSTITUTE:
Prepare using KRAFT Grated Parmesan and Romano Cheese.

vegetable & stuffing bake

PREP: 10 min. | TOTAL: 35 min. | MAKES: 6 servings.

▶ what you need!

¾ cup MIRACLE WHIP Dressing

½ cup milk

1 pkg. (6 oz.) STOVE TOP Stuffing Mix for Chicken

1 pkg. (16 oz.) frozen broccoli florets, thawed, drained

1 cup KRAFT Shredded Cheddar Cheese

▶ make it!

HEAT oven to 350°F.

MIX dressing and milk in large bowl until blended. Add remaining ingredients; mix lightly.

SPOON into 8-inch square baking dish.

BAKE 20 to 25 min. or until heated through.

MAKE AHEAD:
Assemble casserole as directed. Refrigerate up to 24 hours. When ready to serve, uncover and bake at 350°F for 25 to 30 min. or until heated through.

SPECIAL EXTRA:
Add 2 cups chopped turkey or chicken for a heartier dish.

chicken & stuffing florentine

PREP: 10 min. | TOTAL: 40 min. | MAKES: 4 servings.

▶ what you need!

2 cups STOVE TOP Stuffing Mix for Chicken in the Canister

1 cup hot water

¼ cup KRAFT Grated Parmesan Cheese

4 small boneless skinless chicken breast halves (1 lb.)

1 can (10¾ oz.) condensed cream of chicken soup

1 pkg. (10 oz.) frozen chopped spinach, thawed, well drained

▶ make it!

HEAT oven to 400°F.

MIX stuffing mix, hot water and Parmesan just until stuffing mix is moistened.

PLACE chicken in 13×9-inch baking dish. Mix soup and spinach; spoon over chicken. Top with stuffing mixture.

BAKE 30 min. or until chicken is done.

SUBSTITUTE:
Prepare using 3 cups chopped fresh spinach.

SIDE DISHES

apple, cranberry
& pecan stuffing

PREP: 10 min. | TOTAL: 15 min. | MAKES: 8 servings.

▶ what you need!

1½ cups apple juice

2 Tbsp. butter or margarine

1 small apple, chopped

½ cup cranberries

1 pkg. (6 oz.) STOVE TOP Stuffing Mix for Chicken

¼ cup PLANTERS Pecan Pieces, toasted

▶ make it!

BRING juice and butter to boil in medium saucepan on high heat. Stir in apples, cranberries and stuffing mix; cover.

REMOVE from heat. Let stand 5 min.

STIR in nuts.

SUBSTITUTE:
Prepare using dried cranberries.

FEEDING A CROWD:
Prepare as directed, doubling all ingredients.

zesty grilled veggies

PREP: 10 min. | TOTAL: 20 min. | MAKES: 8 servings.

▶ what you need!

4 zucchini (1½ lb.), cut diagonally into ½-inch-thick slices

3 <u>each</u> red and yellow bell peppers (1¾ lb.), cut into ½-inch-wide strips

¼ cup KRAFT Zesty Italian Dressing

¼ cup KRAFT Grated Parmesan Cheese

▶ make it!

HEAT grill to medium.

PLACE vegetables in grill basket.

GRILL 10 min. or until crisp-tender, turning occasionally. Place in large bowl.

ADD dressing; toss to coat. Sprinkle with Parmesan.

COOKING KNOW-HOW:
Don't have a grill basket? Cover grill grate with large sheet of heavy-duty foil before heating as directed.
Spread vegetables onto foil. Grill as directed, stirring occasionally.

HOW TO BUY PEPPERS:
Look for bell peppers with very bright colors and a firm, thick flesh. Refrigerate unwashed bell peppers
in a plastic bag for up to 2 weeks.

broccoli & cauliflower supreme

PREP: 25 min. | TOTAL: 25 min. | MAKES: 6 servings.

► what you need!

4 oz. (½ of 8-oz. pkg.) PHILADELPHIA
   Fat Free Cream Cheese, cubed

¼ cup KRAFT FREE Peppercorn Ranch
   Dressing

1 Tbsp. GREY POUPON Dijon Mustard

1½ bunches broccoli, cut into florets
   (about 6 cups), steamed, drained

½ head cauliflower, cut into florets
   (about 3 cups), steamed, drained

12 RITZ Reduced Fat Crackers, crushed

► make it!

MICROWAVE cream cheese, dressing and mustard in medium microwaveable bowl on HIGH 30 to 45 sec. or until cream cheese is softened and mixture is hot. Stir until well blended.

TOSS hot cooked broccoli and cauliflower with hot cream cheese mixture.

SPOON into serving bowl; sprinkle with crushed crackers.

SUBSTITUTE:
If you'd prefer, use equal amounts of frozen broccoli and cauliflower.

NUTRITION BONUS:
Delight your family with this creamy and delicious, yet low-fat, side dish that is high in vitamins A and C from the broccoli.

broccoli polonaise

PREP: 15 min. | TOTAL: 15 min. | MAKES: 4 servings.

► what you need!

1 bunch broccoli, cut into florets (about 4 cups)

1 cup STOVE TOP Stuffing Mix for Chicken in the Canister

2 hard-cooked eggs, chopped

¼ cup butter or margarine, melted

¼ cup KRAFT Grated Parmesan Cheese

► make it!

COOK broccoli in boiling water 5 to 10 min. or until crisp-tender.

MEANWHILE, mix remaining ingredients.

DRAIN broccoli; spoon into serving dish. Top with stuffing mixture; cover. Let stand 5 min.

SERVING SUGGESTION:
Enjoy a serving of this vegetable dish at your next get-together along with a serving of your favorite grilled lean meat.

MAKE AHEAD:
Cook broccoli as directed; spoon into casserole. Mix stuffing mix, eggs, butter and cheese; spoon over broccoli. Refrigerate. When ready to serve, bake, uncovered, at 350°F for 10 min. or until heated through.

cheesy broccoli casserole

PREP: 10 min. | TOTAL: 40 min. | MAKES: 8 servings.

▶ what you need!

1 pkg. (6 oz.) STOVE TOP Stuffing Mix for Chicken

2 pkg. (10 oz. each) frozen broccoli florets, thawed, drained

1 can (10¾ oz.) condensed cream of mushroom soup

1 cup CHEEZ WHIZ Cheese Dip

▶ make it!

HEAT oven to 350°F.

PREPARE stuffing as directed on package, using only 3 Tbsp. margarine.

MIX remaining ingredients in 2-qt. baking dish; top with stuffing.

BAKE 30 min. or until heated through.

MAKE AHEAD:
Assemble casserole as directed. Refrigerate up to 24 hours. When ready to serve, bake, uncovered, at 350°F for 45 to 50 min. or until heated through.

cheesy green bean casserole

PREP: 10 min. | TOTAL: 40 min. | MAKES: 14 servings.

▶ what you need!

2 bags (16 oz. each) frozen French cut green beans, thawed

1 can (10¾ oz.) condensed cream of mushroom soup

1 cup CHEEZ WHIZ Cheese Dip

1½ cups hot water

¼ cup margarine

1 pkg. (6 oz.) STOVE TOP Stuffing Mix for Chicken

▶ make it!

HEAT oven to 350°F.

COMBINE beans, soup and CHEEZ WHIZ in 2-qt. casserole.

ADD hot water to margarine in medium bowl; stir until melted. Stir in stuffing mix just until moistened. Spoon over bean mixture.

BAKE 30 min. or until heated through.

MAKE AHEAD:
Assemble casserole as directed. Refrigerate up to 24 hours. When ready to serve, bake, uncovered, at 350°F for 45 to 50 min. or until heated through.

cheesy chipotle vegetable bake

PREP: 15 min. | TOTAL: 50 min. | MAKES: 10 servings, ¾ cup each.

▶ what you need!

- 4 cups small cauliflower florets
- 4 large zucchini, sliced
- 3 medium carrots, sliced
- 2 Tbsp. chopped chipotle peppers in adobo sauce
- ¼ cup KRAFT Zesty Italian Dressing
- ½ lb. (8 oz.) VELVEETA Pasteurized Prepared Cheese Product, thinly sliced
- 20 RITZ Crackers, crushed
- 2 Tbsp. butter or margarine, melted

▶ make it!

HEAT oven to 375°F.

COMBINE first 5 ingredients; spoon into 13×9-inch baking dish. Top with VELVEETA.

MIX cracker crumbs and butter; sprinkle over vegetable mixture.

BAKE 30 to 35 min. or until vegetables are tender and casserole is heated through.

MAKE AHEAD:
Assemble casserole as directed. Store in refrigerator until ready to bake as directed.

cheesy red beans & rice

PREP: 10 min. | TOTAL: 1 hour | MAKES: 6 servings, 1 cup each.

▶ what you need!

1 can (15½ oz.) kidney beans, drained, rinsed

1 can (10 oz.) RO*TEL Diced Tomatoes & Green Chilies, undrained

2 cups instant white rice, uncooked

2 cups water

7 oz. (½ of 14-oz. pkg.) OSCAR MAYER Turkey Smoked Sausage, sliced, halved

6 oz. VELVEETA Pasteurized Prepared Cheese Product, cut into ½-inch cubes

1 small onion, chopped

2 tsp. chili powder

*RO*TEL is a registered trademark of ConAgra Foods, Inc.*

▶ make it!

HEAT oven to 350°F.

COMBINE all ingredients.

SPOON into 13×9-inch baking dish sprayed with cooking spray.

BAKE 45 to 50 min. or until rice is tender and mixture is heated through.

SUBSTITUTE:
Prepare using VELVEETA 2% Milk Pasteurized Prepared Cheese Product.

corn souffle

PREP: 15 min. | TOTAL: 55 min. | MAKES: 16 servings.

▶ what you need!

2 Tbsp. butter

1 pkg. (8 oz.) PHILADELPHIA Cream Cheese, cubed

1 can (15¼ oz.) whole kernel corn, drained

1 can (14.75 oz.) cream-style corn

1 pkg. (8.5 oz.) corn muffin mix

2 eggs, lightly beaten

1 cup KRAFT Shredded Cheddar Cheese

▶ make it!

HEAT oven to 350°F.

MICROWAVE butter in medium microwaveable bowl on HIGH 30 sec. or until melted. Add cream cheese; continue microwaving 15 sec. or until cream cheese is softened; stir until well blended. Add both corns, muffin mix and eggs; mix well.

POUR into greased 13×9-inch baking pan; sprinkle with Cheddar.

BAKE 40 min. or until golden brown. Cool slightly.

SERVING SUGGESTION:
This dish is versatile enough to pair with your favorite barbecued meat, beef stew, chicken soup or even chili.

SPECIAL EXTRA:
Add ¼ cup sliced green onions along with the corn, muffin mix and eggs.

creamy vegetable bake

PREP: 20 min. | TOTAL: 50 min. | MAKES: 10 servings.

▶ what you need!

1 pkg. (8 oz.) PHILADELPHIA Cream Cheese, softened

⅓ cup milk

¼ cup KRAFT Grated Parmesan Cheese

1 tsp. dried basil leaves

4 large carrots, diagonally sliced

½ lb. sugar snap peas

½ lb. fresh asparagus, cut into 1-inch lengths

1 large red bell pepper, chopped

1 pkg. (6 oz.) STOVE TOP Stuffing Mix for Chicken

▶ make it!

HEAT oven to 350°F.

MICROWAVE cream cheese and milk in large microwaveable bowl on HIGH 1 min. or until cream cheese is melted and mixture is blended when stirred. Add Parmesan and basil; stir until blended. Add vegetables; toss to coat.

SPOON into greased 13×9-inch baking dish. Prepare stuffing as directed on package; spoon over vegetable mixture.

BAKE 30 min. or until golden brown.

SUBSTITUTE:
Prepare using PHILADELPHIA Neufchâtel Cheese.

creamy veggies

PREP: 5 min. | TOTAL: 18 min. | MAKES: 5 servings.

▶ what you need!

- 1 pkg. (16 oz.) frozen mixed vegetables (California mix)
- ¼ lb. (4 oz.) VELVEETA 2% Milk Pasteurized Prepared Cheese Product, cut into ½-inch cubes
- 4 oz. (½ of 8-oz. pkg.) PHILADELPHIA Fat Free Cream Cheese, cubed

▶ make it!

LAYER ingredients in 1½-qt. microwaveable dish; cover with waxed paper.

MICROWAVE on HIGH 13 min. or until heated through, turning dish after 7 min.

STIR until well blended.

USE YOUR OVEN:
Layer ingredients in 1½-qt. casserole. Bake at 350°F for 55 min. or until heated through. Stir until well blended.

NUTRITION BONUS:
This low-fat side dish is a delicious way to eat your vegetables. Not only are the vegetables a good source of both vitamins A and C, but the cheese also provides calcium.

easy cheesy mashed potatoes

PREP: 25 min. | TOTAL: 25 min. | MAKES: 8 servings, ½ cup each.

▶ what you need!

2 lb. Yukon gold potatoes (about 5), cubed

¼ cup milk

2 oz. VELVEETA Pasteurized Prepared Cheese Product, cut into ½-inch cubes

¼ tsp. garlic powder

1 green onion, thinly sliced

▶ make it!

COOK potatoes in large saucepan of boiling water 15 min. or until tender. Drain potatoes; return to saucepan.

MASH potatoes until light and fluffy, gradually adding milk alternately with the VELVEETA.

STIR in garlic powder. Top with onions.

SPECIAL EXTRA:
For a change of pace, stir ¼ cup OSCAR MAYER Real Bacon Bits into mashed potatoes with garlic powder.

crispy-topped creamy spinach

PREP: 10 min. | TOTAL: 35 min. | MAKES: 12 servings.

▶ what you need!

2 pkg. (10 oz. each) frozen chopped spinach, thawed, well drained

1 container (8 oz.) PHILADELPHIA Chive & Onion Cream Cheese Spread

½ cup KRAFT Ranch Dressing

2 eggs, lightly beaten

1½ cups KRAFT Shredded Cheddar Cheese, divided

1 cup crushed RITZ Crackers, divided

▶ make it!

HEAT oven to 375°F.

MIX spinach, cream cheese spread, dressing, eggs and ¾ cup Cheddar in large bowl. Stir in ½ cup of the crushed crackers.

SPOON spinach mixture evenly into greased 2-qt. ovenproof casserole dish. Sprinkle with remaining ½ cup crushed crackers and remaining ¾ cup Cheddar.

BAKE 20 to 25 min. or until heated through and Cheddar on top is melted.

HOW TO THAW FROZEN SPINACH:
Thaw frozen spinach in refrigerator overnight or unwrap; place in microwaveable bowl and thaw in microwave as directed on package. Be sure to squeeze well after thawing to remove as much water as possible.

easy cheesy
scalloped potatoes

PREP: 30 min. | TOTAL: 1 hour 30 min. | MAKES: 15 servings, ¾ cup each.

▶ what you need!

- 1 pkg. (8 oz.) PHILADELPHIA Cream Cheese, softened

- ½ cup BREAKSTONE'S or KNUDSEN Sour Cream

- 1 cup chicken broth

- 3 lb. red potatoes (about 9), thinly sliced

- 1 pkg. (6 oz.) OSCAR MAYER Smoked Ham, chopped

- 1 pkg. (8 oz.) KRAFT Shredded Cheddar Cheese, divided

- 1 cup frozen peas

▶ make it!

HEAT oven to 350°F.

MIX cream cheese, sour cream and broth in large bowl until well blended. Add potatoes, ham, 1¾ cups Cheddar and peas; stir gently to coat all ingredients.

SPOON into 13×9-inch baking dish sprayed with cooking spray. Sprinkle with remaining Cheddar.

BAKE 1 hour or until casserole is heated through and potatoes are tender.

SERVING SUGGESTION:
Balance this creamy, indulgent side dish by serving it alongside cooked lean meat or fish and a steamed green vegetable.

easy cheesy potatoes

PREP: 15 min. | TOTAL: 1 hour 10 min. | MAKES: 10 servings, ½ cup each.

▶ what you need!

1 lb. russet potatoes (about 4 medium), cut into ½-inch chunks

½ lb. (8 oz.) VELVEETA Pasteurized Prepared Cheese Product, cut up

½ cup chopped onions

¼ cup KRAFT Real Mayo Mayonnaise

4 slices OSCAR MAYER Bacon, cooked, drained and crumbled (about ¼ cup)

▶ make it!

HEAT oven to 375°F.

COMBINE all ingredients except bacon in 8-inch square baking dish sprayed with cooking spray; cover with foil.

BAKE 45 min.

TOP with bacon; bake, uncovered, 5 to 10 min. or until potatoes are tender.

SPECIAL EXTRA:
Sprinkle with 1 Tbsp. chopped fresh parsley just before serving.

fresh vegetable medley

PREP: 10 min. | TOTAL: 25 min. | MAKES: 12 servings, 1½ cups each.

▶ what you need!

1 small onion, chopped

1 Tbsp. margarine

½ lb. (8 oz.) VELVEETA Pasteurized Prepared Cheese Product, cut into ½-inch cubes

1 can (10¾ oz.) condensed cream of mushroom soup

8 cups mixed fresh vegetables (broccoli and cauliflower florets; sliced carrots, squash and zucchini; cut-up green beans; corn)

▶ make it!

COOK and stir onions in margarine in large skillet on medium heat until crisp-tender.

ADD VELVEETA and soup; cook until VELVEETA is completely melted and mixture is well blended, stirring frequently.

STIR in remaining vegetables; cook 10 min. or until crisp-tender, stirring frequently.

SHORTCUT:
To shave even more time off this easy recipe, purchase cut-up fresh vegetables from the supermarket salad bar. Or, substitute 2 pkg. (16 oz. each) frozen mixed vegetables for the 8 cups mixed fresh vegetables.

italian bread salad with olives

PREP: 20 min. | TOTAL: 1 hour 20 min. | MAKES: 12 servings.

▶ what you need!

1 cup hot water

4 cups STOVE TOP Stuffing Mix for Chicken in the Canister

1 tomato, seeded, chopped

1 cup chopped red onions

1 cup sliced stuffed green olives

½ cup KRAFT Grated Parmesan Cheese

¾ cup prepared GOOD SEASONS Italian Dressing Mix

▶ make it!

ADD hot water to stuffing mix in large bowl; stir just until moistened. Cover; let stand 5 min.

STIR in remaining ingredients.

REFRIGERATE 1 hour.

BEST OF SEASON:
Use the freshest tomatoes and onions available from your garden or a farmer's market!

SUBSTITUTE:
Prepare using GOOD SEASONS Basil Vinaigrette Dressing Mix.

KRAFT golden parmesan potatoes

PREP: 10 min. | TOTAL: 55 min. | MAKES: 6 servings.

▶ what you need!

2 lb. new potatoes, quartered

¼ cup olive oil

1½ tsp. Italian seasoning

2 cloves garlic, minced

⅓ cup KRAFT Grated Parmesan Cheese

▶ make it!

HEAT oven to 400°F.

TOSS potatoes with oil, seasoning and garlic. Add Parmesan; mix lightly.

SPREAD into 15×10×1-inch baking pan.

BAKE 45 min. or until potatoes are tender.

SUBSTITUTE:
Prepare using KRAFT Grated Parmesan and Romano Cheese.

mini new potato bites

PREP: 20 min. | TOTAL: 1 hour 20 min. | MAKES: 15 servings.

▶ what you need!

15 new potatoes (1½ lb.)

4 oz. (½ of 8-oz. pkg.) PHILADELPHIA Cream Cheese, softened

2 Tbsp. BREAKSTONE'S or KNUDSEN Sour Cream

2 Tbsp. KRAFT Grated Parmesan Cheese

4 slices OSCAR MAYER Bacon, cooked, crumbled

2 Tbsp. snipped fresh chives

▶ make it!

COOK potatoes in boiling water in large saucepan 15 min. or until tender.

MEANWHILE, mix cream cheese, sour cream and Parmesan. Refrigerate until ready to use.

DRAIN potatoes. Cool slightly. Cut in half, then cut small piece from rounded bottom of each. Place, bottom-sides down, on platter; top with cream cheese mixture, bacon and chives.

MAKE AHEAD:
These potatoes are delicious served hot or cold.

SUBSTITUTION:
Substitute PHILADELPHIA Chive & Onion Cream Cheese Spread for the regular cream cheese for added flavor.

new potatoes in dill cream sauce

PREP: 10 min. | TOTAL: 30 min. | MAKES: 16 servings, about ½ cup each.

▶ what you need!

2½ lb. new red potatoes, quartered

1 tub (8 oz.) PHILADELPHIA Chive & Onion Cream Cheese Spread

¼ cup milk

1 green bell pepper, chopped

3 Tbsp. chopped fresh dill

▶ make it!

PLACE potatoes in large saucepan. Add enough water to cover potatoes. Bring to boil on medium-high heat. Reduce heat to medium; simmer 15 min. or until potatoes are tender. Drain.

MEANWHILE, mix cream cheese spread, milk and bell pepper in large microwaveable bowl. Microwave on HIGH 40 to 50 sec. or until cream cheese spread is melted; stir until well blended. Stir in dill.

ADD potatoes; toss to coat.

SUBSTITUTE:
Substitute chopped fresh basil leaves or 2 tsp. dill weed for the chopped fresh dill.

CREATIVE LEFTOVERS:
Cover and refrigerate any leftovers. Serve as a cold potato salad, stirring in a small amount of additional milk to thin, if necessary.

oat-topped sweet potato crisp

PREP: 20 min. | TOTAL: 1 hour | MAKES: 8 servings.

▶ what you need!

1 pkg. (8 oz.) PHILADELPHIA Cream Cheese, softened

1 can (40 oz.) cut sweet potatoes, drained

¾ cup firmly packed brown sugar, divided

¼ tsp. ground cinnamon

1 cup chopped apples

⅔ cup chopped cranberries

½ cup flour

½ cup old-fashioned or quick-cooking oats, uncooked

⅓ cup cold butter or margarine

¼ cup chopped PLANTERS Pecans

▶ make it!

HEAT oven to 350°F.

BEAT cream cheese, sweet potatoes, ¼ cup of the sugar and cinnamon with electric mixer on medium speed until well blended. Spoon into 1½-qt. casserole dish; top with apples and cranberries.

MIX flour, oats and remaining ½ cup sugar in medium bowl; cut in butter until mixture resembles coarse crumbs. Stir in nuts. Sprinkle over fruit mixture.

BAKE 35 to 40 min. or until heated through.

VARIATION:
Prepare as directed, substituting 10×6-inch baking dish for the 1½-qt. casserole dish.

savory apple stuffing

PREP: 5 min. | TOTAL: 15 min. | MAKES: 6 servings.

▶ what you need!

1 pkg. (6 oz.) STOVE TOP Stuffing Mix for Pork

1 apple, chopped

¼ cup cooked chopped onions

▶ make it!

PREPARE stuffing as directed on package, adding apples and onions with the stuffing mix.

spinach mushroom stuffing

PREP: 10 min. | TOTAL: 10 min. | MAKES: 6 servings.

▶ what you need!

1 pkg. (6 oz.) STOVE TOP Stuffing Mix for Chicken

1 cup packed baby spinach leaves

1 cup sliced fresh mushrooms

2 green onions, sliced

▶ make it!

PREPARE stuffing as directed on package, adding spinach and vegetables with the stuffing mix.

SPECIAL EXTRA:
Sprinkle with 2 slices crumbled cooked OSCAR MAYER Bacon before serving.

savory corn spoon bread

PREP: 10 min. | TOTAL: 55 min. | MAKES: 8 servings.

▶ what you need!

2 cups hot milk

3 Tbsp. butter or margarine, cut into pieces

2 cups STOVE TOP Cornbread Stuffing Mix in the Canister

1 cup frozen corn, thawed

2 eggs, beaten

1 green onion, chopped

2 tsp. sugar

▶ make it!

HEAT oven to 350°F.

ADD milk to butter in 1½-qt. casserole; stir until butter is melted.

STIR in remaining ingredients.

BAKE 45 min. or until knife inserted in center comes out clean.

SPECIAL EXTRA:
Add ¼ cup OSCAR MAYER Real Bacon Bits with stuffing mix.

HOW TO LIGHTLY BEAT EGGS:
For lightly beaten eggs, use a wire whisk or fork to break up yolks and barely combine yolks and whites.
For well beaten eggs, mix vigorously to combine yolks and whites until mixture is light and frothy.

vegetables in cream sauce

PREP: 10 min. | TOTAL: 23 min. | MAKES: 6 servings, ½ cup each.

▶ what you need!

1 pkg. (16 oz.) frozen broccoli, cauliflower and carrot blend

¼ lb. (4 oz.) VELVEETA 2% Milk Pasteurized Prepared Cheese Product, cut into ½-inch cubes

4 oz. (½ of 8-oz. pkg.) PHILADELPHIA Neufchâtel Cheese, cubed

▶ make it!

LAYER ingredients in microwaveable 1½-qt. casserole; cover.

MICROWAVE on HIGH 13 min. or until vegetables are heated through, stirring after 7 min.

USE YOUR OVEN:
Heat oven to 350°F. Layer ingredients in 1-qt. casserole. Bake 55 min. or until vegetables are heated through; stir.

STOVE TOP spinach balls

PREP: 15 min. | TOTAL: 35 min. | MAKES: 20 servings.

▶ what you need!

1 pkg. (6 oz.) STOVE TOP Savory Herbs Stuffing Mix

1⅔ cups hot water

¼ cup butter or margarine

2 pkg. (10 oz. each) frozen chopped spinach, thawed, well drained and patted dry

1 cup KRAFT Grated Parmesan Cheese

1 cup chopped fresh mushrooms

1 small onion, finely chopped

4 eggs

▶ make it!

HEAT oven to 400°F.

MIX stuffing mix, hot water and butter in large bowl until well blended.

ADD remaining ingredients; mix lightly. Shape into 60 (1-inch) balls. Place in single layer in 2 (15×10×1-inch) pans sprayed with cooking spray.

BAKE 15 to 20 min. or until lightly browned.

MAKE AHEAD:
Prepare and bake spinach balls as directed; cool completely. Place in freezer-weight resealable plastic bags; freeze up to 3 months. When ready to serve, thaw in refrigerator. Place on baking sheets and bake at 400°F for 10 to 15 min. or until heated through.

STOVE TOP stuffed tomatoes

PREP: 10 min. | TOTAL: 30 min. | MAKES: 6 servings.

▶ what you need!

6 tomatoes

1 cup hot water

¼ cup spread or margarine, cut up

1 pkg. (6 oz.) STOVE TOP Savory Herbs Stuffing Mix

▶ make it!

HEAT oven to 400°F.

CUT tops off tomatoes; remove seeds and pulp, leaving ¼-inch-thick shells. Chop pulp; drain. Set aside for later use. Discard tomato tops and seeds. Invert shells on paper towels to drain.

MEANWHILE, combine hot water and spread in large bowl. Stir in stuffing mix and reserved pulp. Let stand 5 min. Place tomato shells in greased shallow baking dish; fill with stuffing mixture.

BAKE 20 min. or until tomatoes are tender and stuffing is heated through.

SPECIAL EXTRA:
Assemble as directed, adding ¼ cup KRAFT Shredded Mozzarella Cheese to stuffing mixture before spooning into tomato shells. Sprinkle with ¼ cup KRAFT Grated Parmesan Cheese, then bake as directed.

SANDWICHES
& SOUPS

beef wrap melt

PREP: 5 min. | TOTAL: 6 min. | MAKES: 1 serving.

▶ what you need!

- 1 tsp. KRAFT Light Mayo Reduced Fat Mayonnaise
- 1 tsp. KRAFT Prepared Horseradish
- 1 whole wheat tortilla (10 inch)
- 6 slices OSCAR MAYER Deli Fresh Shaved Roast Beef
- 1 slice VELVEETA 2% Milk Pasteurized Prepared Cheese Product (½ oz.)
- 12 baby spinach leaves
- 2 Tbsp. chopped tomatoes

▶ make it!

MIX mayo and horseradish; spread onto tortilla.

TOP with remaining ingredients; roll up. Place on microwaveable plate.

MICROWAVE on HIGH 1 min. or until VELVEETA is melted.

SUBSTITUTE:
Omit mayo. Substitute KRAFT Horseradish Sauce for the prepared horseradish.

cheesy chicken ranch sandwiches

PREP: 10 min. | TOTAL: 24 min. | MAKES: 6 servings.

▶ what you need!

- 6 small boneless skinless chicken breast halves (1½ lb.)
- ⅔ cup KRAFT Ranch Dressing, divided
- 6 oz. VELVEETA Pasteurized Prepared Cheese Product, sliced
- 6 French bread rolls, split
- 6 large lettuce leaves

▶ make it!

HEAT broiler.

PLACE chicken on rack of broiler pan sprayed with cooking spray. Brush with ⅓ cup of the dressing.

BROIL, 3 to 4 inches from heat, 5 to 6 min. on each side or until chicken is cooked through (165°F). Top with VELVEETA; broil 2 min. or until melted.

SPREAD rolls with remaining dressing; fill with lettuce and chicken.

SERVING SUGGESTION:
Serve with your favorite fresh fruit.

KEEPING IT SAFE:
Use a visual test to ensure boneless chicken breasts are thoroughly cooked. Cut small slit in thickest part of chicken breast. If meat is totally white with no pink color, it is safe to eat.

STORAGE KNOW-HOW:
Seal chicken in freezer-safe resealable plastic bag. Uncooked chicken can be kept frozen for up to 6 months; cooked chicken for up to 3 months.

cheesy shrimp bisque

PREP: 10 min. | TOTAL: 30 min. | MAKES: 5 servings, 1 cup each.

▶ what you need!

½ cup sliced celery

1 Tbsp. butter or margarine

1 pkg. (8 oz.) PHILADELPHIA Cream
 Cheese, cubed

1 cup milk

½ lb. (8 oz.) VELVEETA Pasteurized
 Prepared Cheese Product, cut up

1 pkg. (6 oz.) frozen cooked tiny shrimp,
 thawed, drained

⅓ cup dry white wine

¼ tsp. dill weed

▶ make it!

COOK and stir celery in butter in 2-qt. saucepan on medium heat until tender. Reduce heat to low.

STIR in cream cheese and milk; cook until cream cheese is completely melted, stirring occasionally.

ADD VELVEETA, shrimp and wine; cook until VELVEETA is completely melted and mixture is heated through, stirring occasionally. Sprinkle with dill weed.

VARIATION:
Omit wine. Increase milk to 1⅓ cups.

USE YOUR MICROWAVE:
Decrease milk to ½ cup and wine to ¼ cup. Place celery and butter in 2-qt. microwaveable bowl. Microwave on HIGH 1 to 2 min. or until celery is crisp-tender. Add milk; microwave 3 min., stirring after 2 min. Stir in cream cheese; microwave 4 to 6 min. or until cream cheese is melted, stirring every 2 min. Stir in VELVEETA, shrimp and wine; microwave 2 to 3 min. or until heated through. Sprinkle with dill weed.

santa fe chicken fajita soup

PREP: 15 min. | TOTAL: 1 hour 5 min. | MAKES: 8 servings, 1 cup each.

▶ what you need!

1 pkg. (1.4 oz.) TACO BELL HOME
   ORIGINALS Fajita Seasoning Mix*

⅓ cup water

1 lb. boneless skinless chicken breasts,
   cut into thin strips

4 large cloves garlic, minced

2 Tbsp. chopped fresh cilantro

1 large red onion, chopped

1 small green bell pepper, chopped

1 pkg. (8 oz.) PHILADELPHIA Fat Free
   Cream Cheese, cut into cubes

1 lb. (16 oz.) VELVEETA Made With 2% Milk Reduced Fat Pasteurized Prepared Cheese
   Product, cut into ½-inch cubes

2 cans (14.5 oz. each) fat-free reduced-sodium chicken broth

TACO BELL and HOME ORIGINALS are registered trademarks owned and licensed by Taco Bell Corp.

▶ make it!

COMBINE seasoning mix and water in medium bowl. Add chicken; toss to evenly coat.
Cover. Refrigerate 30 min.

COOK garlic and cilantro in large nonstick saucepan sprayed with cooking spray on
medium-high heat 1 min. Stir in chicken mixture, onions and peppers; cook 10 min. or until
chicken is done, stirring frequently.

ADD cream cheese, VELVEETA and broth; mix well. Cook on medium heat until cream
cheese and VELVEETA are completely melted and chicken mixture is heated through, stirring
occasionally.

SERVING SUGGESTION:
Serve this hearty main-dish soup with a tossed leafy green salad.

cheesy spinach soup

PREP: 15 min. | TOTAL: 25 min. | MAKES: 4 servings, about 1 cup each.

▶ what you need!

1 Tbsp. soft reduced-calorie margarine

¼ cup chopped onions

2 cups fat-free milk

½ lb. (8 oz.) VELVEETA Made With 2% Milk Reduced Fat Pasteurized Prepared Cheese Product, cut into ½-inch cubes

1 pkg. (10 oz.) frozen chopped spinach, cooked, well drained

⅛ tsp. ground nutmeg

Dash black pepper

▶ make it!

MELT margarine in medium saucepan on medium heat. Add onions; cook and stir until tender.

ADD remaining ingredients; cook on low heat until VELVEETA is melted and soup is heated through, stirring occasionally.

SIZE-WISE:
Savor the flavor of this cheesy soup while keeping portion size in mind.

SUBSTITUTE:
Prepare as directed, substituting frozen chopped broccoli for the spinach.

USE YOUR MICROWAVE:
Microwave onions and margarine in medium microwaveable bowl on HIGH 30 sec. to 1 min. or until onions are tender. Stir in remaining ingredients. Microwave 6 to 8 min. or until VELVEETA is completely melted and soup is heated through, stirring every 3 min.

cheesy turkey grill

PREP: 5 min. | TOTAL: 11 min. | MAKES: 4 servings.

▶ what you need!

8 slices whole wheat bread

2 oz. VELVEETA 2% Milk Pasteurized Prepared Cheese Product, cut into 4 slices

16 slices OSCAR MAYER Deli Fresh Shaved Oven Roasted Turkey Breast

1 Tbsp. margarine, softened

▶ make it!

FILL bread slices with VELVEETA and turkey.

SPREAD outsides of sandwiches with margarine.

COOK in large skillet on medium heat 3 min. on each side or until golden brown on both sides.

SPECIAL EXTRA:
Spread bread with GREY POUPON Dijon Mustard before filling with the VELVEETA and turkey.

quick bacon & "egg-wich"

PREP: 1 min. | TOTAL: 2 min. 10 sec. | MAKES: 1 serving.

▶ what you need!

- 1 whole wheat English muffin, split
- 1 egg
- 1 thin slice tomato
- 1 slice OSCAR MAYER Fully Cooked Bacon, cut in half
- 1 slice VELVEETA 2% Milk Pasteurized Prepared Cheese Product (½ oz.)

▶ make it!

PLACE 1 English muffin half on microwaveable plate. Carefully crack egg over muffin. Microwave on HIGH 40 sec.

TOP with tomato, bacon and VELVEETA; cover with remaining muffin half.

MICROWAVE on HIGH 30 sec. or until egg white is completely set and yolk is thickened around the edge.

TAKE ALONG:
Wrap hot sandwich in foil before heading out the door to enjoy as part of a quick grab-'n-go breakfast.

the ultimate leftover turkey sandwich

PREP: 5 min. | TOTAL: 5 min. | MAKES: 1 serving.

▶ what you need!

2 slices multi-grain bread

1 Tbsp. MIRACLE WHIP Dressing

3 oz. oven-roasted turkey breast, sliced

½ cup prepared STOVE TOP Stuffing Mix for Turkey

2 Tbsp. cranberry sauce

▶ make it!

SPREAD 1 bread slice with dressing.

FILL bread slices with remaining ingredients.

SERVING SUGGESTION:
Serve with a mixed green salad tossed with your favorite KRAFT Dressing.

SPECIAL EXTRA:
For an extra creamy treat, spread second bread slice with 1 Tbsp. PHILADELPHIA Cream Cheese Spread before adding to sandwich.

turkey-cheese pita

PREP: 10 min. | TOTAL: 18 min. | MAKES: 4 servings.

► what you need!

- 4 whole wheat pita bread rounds
- 2 tsp. GREY POUPON Hearty Spicy Brown Mustard
- 16 baby spinach leaves
- ¼ lb. (4 oz.) VELVEETA Made With 2% Milk Reduced Fat Pasteurized Prepared Cheese Product, sliced, cut into strips
- 1 pkg. (6 oz.) OSCAR MAYER Thin Sliced Oven Roasted Turkey Breast, cut into strips
- ½ cup sliced fresh mushrooms
- ½ cup slivered red onions

► make it!

SPREAD bread with mustard; top each with remaining ingredients.

MICROWAVE, 1 at a time, on microwaveable plate on HIGH 1 to 2 min. or until VELVEETA begins to melt.

SUBSTITUTE:
Prepare as directed, using your favorite flavor of OSCAR MAYER Thin Sliced Turkey or Ham.

FUN IDEA:
Prepare as directed. Roll up pitas; tie each with green onion top.

VELVEETA-bacon burgers

PREP: 10 min. | TOTAL: 24 min. | MAKES: 4 servings.

▶ what you need!

1 lb. extra lean ground beef

2 Tbsp. KRAFT Light House Italian Reduced Fat Dressing

¼ lb. (4 oz.) VELVEETA Made With 2% Milk Reduced Fat Pasteurized Prepared Cheese Product, cut into 4 slices

4 tsp. OSCAR MAYER Real Bacon Recipe Pieces

4 whole wheat hamburger buns, split

▶ make it!

SHAPE meat into 4 patties. Cook in dressing in skillet on medium-high heat 10 to 12 min. or until done (160°F), turning after 5 min.

TOP with VELVEETA and bacon; cover. Cook 1 to 2 min. or until VELVEETA begins to melt.

SERVE in buns.

SPECIAL EXTRA:
Cover bottom half of each bun with lettuce leaf before topping with burger.

COOK GROUND MEAT THOROUGHLY:
Cook ground beef thoroughly and evenly. The color of the raw ground meat can vary from bright red to light pink. Do not rely on the color of the meat to check for doneness but use an instant read thermometer instead. Ground beef should be cooked to an internal temperature of 160°F.

SERVING SUGGESTION:
Serve with bagged mixed greens tossed with cut-up fresh vegetables. Top with your favorite KRAFT Dressing, such as Light Reduced Fat Ranch.

VELVEETA salsa joe sandwich

PREP: 10 min. | TOTAL: 25 min. | MAKES: 6 servings.

▶ what you need!

1 lb. lean ground beef

¼ cup chopped onions

6 oz. VELVEETA Pasteurized Prepared
    Cheese Product, cut into ½-inch cubes

1 cup TACO BELL HOME ORIGINALS
    Thick 'N Chunky Salsa*

6 kaiser rolls, split

*TACO BELL and HOME ORIGINALS are registered
trademarks owned and licensed by Taco Bell Corp.

▶ make it!

BROWN meat with onions in large skillet on medium heat; drain. Return to skillet.

STIR in VELVEETA and salsa; cook on medium-low heat until VELVEETA is completely melted and mixture is well blended, stirring frequently.

SPOON into rolls just before serving.

VELVEETA CHEESY TACOS:
Omit rolls. Prepare meat mixture as directed; spoon into 12 TACO BELL HOME ORIGINALS Taco Shells. Top with shredded lettuce and chopped tomatoes. Makes 6 servings, 2 tacos each.

CREATIVE LEFTOVERS:
Cover and refrigerate any leftover meat mixture. Reheat, then spoon over split hot baked potatoes.

SUBSTITUTE:
Prepare as directed, using VELVEETA Made with 2% Milk Reduced Fat Pasteurized Prepared Cheese Product.

VELVEETA
sweet & cheesy panini

PREP: 10 min. | TOTAL: 16 min. | MAKES: 4 servings.

▶ what you need!

8 slices bread

¼ lb. (4 oz.) VELVEETA Pasteurized Prepared Cheese Product, cut into 8 slices

24 slices OSCAR MAYER Shaved Brown Sugar Ham

1 Granny Smith apple, thinly sliced

8 tsp. margarine, softened

2 tsp. powdered sugar

▶ make it!

FILL bread slices with VELVEETA, ham and apples.

SPREAD outsides of sandwiches with margarine.

COOK in skillet on medium heat for 3 min. on each side or until golden brown on both sides. Sprinkle with powdered sugar.

SUBSTITUTE:
Prepare as directed, using whole grain bread and VELVEETA Made With 2% Milk Reduced Fat Pasteurized Prepared Cheese Product.

VELVEETA wow! burger

PREP: 10 min. | TOTAL: 30 min. | MAKES: 6 servings.

▸ what you need!

1½ lb. extra lean ground beef

6 oz. VELVEETA 2% Milk Pasteurized Prepared Cheese Product, cut into 6 slices

6 whole wheat hamburger buns, toasted

1 can (10 oz.) RO*TEL Diced Tomatoes & Green Chilies, drained

*RO*TEL is a registered trademark of ConAgra Foods, Inc.*

▸ make it!

HEAT grill to medium heat.

SHAPE meat into 6 (¾-inch-thick) patties.

GRILL 7 to 9 min. on each side or until done (160°F). Top with VELVEETA; grill 1 to 2 min. or until melted.

PLACE cheeseburgers on bottom halves of buns; cover with tomatoes and tops of buns.

HOW TO USE YOUR STOVE:
Cook patties in skillet on medium heat 4 to 6 min. on each side or until done (160°F). Top with VELVEETA; cover with lid. Cook 1 to 2 min. or until VELVEETA is melted. Continue as directed.

VELVEETA
ultimate grilled cheese

PREP: 5 min. | TOTAL: 11 min. | MAKES: 4 servings.

► what you need!

8 slices white bread

6 oz. VELVEETA Pasteurized Prepared Cheese Product, sliced

8 tsp. soft margarine

► make it!

FILL bread slices with VELVEETA.

SPREAD outsides of sandwiches with margarine.

COOK in skillet on medium heat 3 min. on each side or until golden brown on both sides.

SUBSTITUTE:
Prepare as directed, using VELVEETA Made With 2% Milk Reduced Fat Pasteurized Prepared Cheese Product.

wrapped veggie sandwich

PREP: 5 min. | TOTAL: 5 min. | MAKES: 1 serving, 2 roll-ups.

▶ what you need!

2 TACO BELL HOME ORIGINALS Flour Tortillas*

2 Tbsp. PHILADELPHIA Chive & Onion Cream Cheese Spread

1 KRAFT Singles, cut in half

1 cup fresh spinach leaves

½ cup chopped, drained roasted red peppers

¼ cup shredded carrots

*TACO BELL and HOME ORIGINALS are registered trademarks owned and licensed by Taco Bell Corp.

▶ make it!

SPREAD each tortilla with 1 Tbsp. of the cream cheese spread.

TOP evenly with remaining ingredients; roll up.

SECURE with toothpicks.

PIZZA

bacon chicken alfredo pizza

PREP: 10 min. | TOTAL: 20 min. | MAKES: 6 servings.

▶ what you need!

1 pkg. (2.1 oz.) OSCAR MAYER Fully Cooked Bacon

1 ready-to-use baked pizza crust (12 inch)

½ cup refrigerated Alfredo sauce

1 pkg. (6 oz.) OSCAR MAYER Deli Fresh Oven Roasted Chicken Breast Cuts

1 cup KRAFT Pizza Shredded Mozzarella & Cheddar Cheese

¼ cup KRAFT Shredded Parmesan Cheese

½ tsp. Italian seasoning

▶ make it!

HEAT oven to 400°F.

CUT bacon slices crosswise in half; heat as directed on package. (Or, see Tip.)

PLACE pizza crust on baking sheet; spread with sauce to within 1 inch of edge. Top with bacon and remaining ingredients.

BAKE 8 to 10 min. or until cheese is melted and pizza is heated through.

HOW TO EASILY HEAT BACON:
Remove stack of bacon on parchment from package. Cut entire stack in half with clean kitchen scissors. Place on microwaveable plate or paper towel. Microwave on HIGH 30 sec. Remove bacon from paper. (Do not microwave bacon in plastic tray.)

california-style barbecue chicken pizza

PREP: 15 min. | TOTAL: 33 min. | MAKES: 6 servings.

▶ what you need!

¾ lb. boneless skinless chicken breasts, cut into thin strips

1 green bell pepper, cut into strips

¼ cup thin red onion slices

1 ready-to-use baked pizza crust (12 inch)

⅓ cup BULL'S-EYE Original Barbecue Sauce

1½ cups KRAFT Mexican Style Finely Shredded Cheddar Jack Cheese

▶ make it!

HEAT oven to 400°F.

COOK and stir chicken and vegetables in large skillet sprayed with cooking spray on medium-high heat 4 to 5 min. or until chicken is done.

SPREAD pizza crust with barbecue sauce; top with chicken mixture and cheese. Place crust directly on middle oven rack.

BAKE 15 to 18 min. or until cheese is melted.

SHORTCUT:
For a quick alternative to the cooked fresh chicken, use chopped chicken from a rotisserie chicken purchased at your local supermarket. Add to pizza along with the cooked vegetables and cheese before baking as directed.

caramelized pear, blue cheese and bacon pizza

PREP: 20 min. | TOTAL: 28 min. | MAKES: 8 servings.

▶ what you need!

2 Tbsp. butter

2 pears, cored, each cut into 12 lengthwise slices

2 Tbsp. packed brown sugar

4 ready-to-use baked pizza crusts (8 inch)

½ cup refrigerated Alfredo sauce

1 cup KRAFT Shredded Low-Moisture Part-Skim Mozzarella Cheese

¾ cup ATHENOS Crumbled Blue Cheese

¾ cup OSCAR MAYER Bacon Pieces

▶ make it!

HEAT oven to 425°F.

MELT butter in medium skillet on medium heat. Add pears; sprinkle with sugar. Cook 2 to 3 min. or until sugar is melted and pears are evenly coated with sugar mixture, stirring occasionally. Remove from heat.

PLACE pizza crusts on baking sheet; spread with Alfredo sauce. Top with half of mozzarella, blue cheese, bacon, pears and remaining mozzarella.

BAKE 6 to 8 min. or until topping is golden brown and bubbly.

SUBSTITUTE:
Substitute POLLY-O Natural Shredded Low-Moisture Part-Skim Mozzarella Cheese for KRAFT Mozzarella Cheese.

chicago-style deep-dish sausage pizza

PREP: 30 min. | TOTAL: 1 hour | MAKES: 8 servings.

▶ what you need!

1 pkg. active dry yeast

¾ cup warm water (108°F)

2 cups flour

¼ cup oil

1 tsp. salt

½ cup KRAFT Grated Parmesan Cheese, divided

1 lb. Italian sausage

¼ cup chopped onions

1 can (14½ oz.) diced tomatoes, undrained

1 can (6 oz.) tomato paste

2 tsp. dried oregano leaves

2 pkg. (6 oz. each) KRAFT Whole Milk Mozzarella Cheese Slices

▶ make it!

HEAT oven to 425°F.

DISSOLVE yeast in warm water; let stand 5 min. Add flour, oil and salt; stir until mixture forms ball. Place on lightly floured surface; knead until smooth. Sprinkle 2 Tbsp. Parmesan onto bottom of greased 12-inch deep-dish pizza pan. Press dough onto bottom and 1 inch up side of pan; set aside.

REMOVE sausage from casing. Brown sausage in large skillet; drain. Add onions; cook and stir until tender. Stir in tomatoes, tomato paste and oregano; simmer 15 min., stirring occasionally. Place half the mozzarella on bottom of crust; cover with half the meat sauce. Repeat layers of mozzarella and sauce. Sprinkle with remaining Parmesan.

BAKE 30 min. or until crust is golden brown. Let stand 10 min. before cutting to serve.

VARIATION:
Substitute 13×9-inch pan for the pizza pan. Assemble pizza as directed. Bake at 425°F for 20 min. or until crust is golden brown.

mushroom & herb pizza

PREP: 10 min. | TOTAL: 22 min. | MAKES: 6 servings.

▶ what you need!

1 cup sliced fresh mushrooms

1 Tbsp. olive oil

1 ready-to-use baked pizza crust (12 inch)

½ cup pizza sauce

1¼ cups KRAFT Shredded Low-Moisture Part-Skim Mozzarella Cheese

1 Tbsp. Italian seasoning

▶ make it!

HEAT oven to 450°F.

COOK and stir mushrooms in hot oil in skillet on medium-high heat 2 to 3 min. or until tender.

SPREAD pizza crust with sauce; top with mushrooms, mozzarella and seasoning. Place directly on middle oven rack.

BAKE 10 to 12 min. or until mozzarella is melted and crust is golden brown.

SPECIAL EXTRA:
Garnish with 1 Tbsp. small fresh oregano leaves just before serving.

pizza margherita

PREP: 10 min. | TOTAL: 22 min. | MAKES: 6 servings.

► what you need!

1½ cups KRAFT Shredded Low-Moisture Part-Skim Mozzarella Cheese, divided

1 ready-to-use baked pizza crust (12 inch)

2 large plum tomatoes, thinly sliced

2 cloves garlic, minced

¼ cup slivered red onions

8 fresh basil leaves, torn

2 Tbsp. KRAFT Grated Parmesan Cheese

► make it!

HEAT oven to 425°F.

RESERVE ½ cup mozzarella; sprinkle remaining mozzarella onto pizza crust. Top with all remaining ingredients; sprinkle with reserved mozzarella.

PLACE crust directly on middle oven rack.

BAKE 10 to 12 min. or until mozzarella is melted.

SUBSTITUTE:
Substitute drained roasted red pepper slices for the tomatoes.

taco pizza

PREP: 15 min. | TOTAL: 25 min. | MAKES: 6 servings.

▶ what you need!

- 1 lb. lean ground beef
- 1 pkg. (10.75 oz.) TACO BELL HOME ORIGINALS Taco Dinner
- 1 ready-to-use baked pizza crust (12 inch)
- 1 cup KRAFT Mexican Style Finely Shredded Four Cheese
- 1 cup shredded lettuce
- 1 large tomato, chopped

▶ make it!

HEAT oven to 400°F.

COOK meat with Taco Seasoning Mix as directed on package. Spoon onto pizza crust; top with cheese. Place directly on oven rack.

BAKE 8 to 10 min. or until crust is golden brown and cheese is melted.

TOP with lettuce and tomatoes. Crush Taco Shells; sprinkle over pizza. Drizzle with Salsa.

SUPREME IT!:
Top with green onion slices and black olive slices just before serving.

TACO BELL and HOME ORIGINALS are trademarks owned and licensed by Taco Bell Corp.

mini pizzas

PREP: 10 min. | TOTAL: 20 min. | MAKES: 4 servings.

▶ what you need!

  4 English muffins, cut in half, toasted

  ½ cup pizza sauce

24 slices OSCAR MAYER Pepperoni

  1 cup KRAFT Shredded Whole Milk Mozzarella Cheese

  ¼ cup KRAFT Grated Parmesan Cheese

▶ make it!

HEAT oven to 400°F.

PLACE muffin halves on parchment or foil-covered baking sheet; spread with pizza sauce.

TOP with remaining ingredients.

BAKE 8 to 10 min. or until cheese is melted.

SERVING SUGGESTION:
Try serving with a quick bagged salad tossed with your favorite KRAFT Dressing, such as Zesty Italian.

shrimp pizza squares

PREP: 10 min. | TOTAL: 35 min. | MAKES: 36 servings.

▶ what you need!

1 can (13.8 oz.) refrigerated pizza crust

1 lb. uncooked deveined peeled medium shrimp

3 cloves garlic, minced

2 Tbsp. KRAFT Zesty Italian Dressing

4 oz. (½ of 8-oz. pkg.) PHILADELPHIA Cream Cheese, softened

1 cup KRAFT Shredded Italian Mozzarella-Parmesan Cheese Blend*

1 cup roasted red pepper strips

¼ cup chopped fresh basil

*Made with quality cheeses crafted in the USA.

▶ make it!

HEAT oven to 425°F.

UNROLL dough onto baking sheet sprayed lightly with cooking spray; press into 13×9-inch rectangle. Bake 12 to 15 min. or until lightly browned.

MEANWHILE, cook shrimp and garlic in dressing in large skillet on medium-high heat 3 to 5 min. or until shrimp turn pink, stirring frequently. Remove from heat; drain.

SPREAD cream cheese onto pizza crust, leaving ¼-inch border around sides. Top with shrimp, shredded cheese and peppers. Bake 10 min. or until shredded cheese is melted. Sprinkle with basil.

SUBSTITUTE:
For variety, top pizza with sliced fresh mushrooms and/or chopped artichoke hearts instead of the roasted peppers.

SPECIAL EXTRA:
Sprinkle pizza with ½ tsp. crushed red pepper, or more to taste, before baking as directed.

spinach-garlic pizza

PREP: 10 min. | TOTAL: 22 min. | MAKES: 6 servings.

▶ what you need!

1 Tbsp. olive oil

1 clove garlic, minced

1 ready-to-use baked pizza crust (12 inch)

1 pkg. (10 oz.) frozen chopped spinach, thawed, squeezed dry

1 cup KRAFT Shredded Whole Milk Mozzarella Cheese

1 small tomato, cut into thin slices

1 pkg. (4 oz.) ATHENOS Crumbled Feta Cheese with Garlic & Herb

1 tsp. chopped fresh rosemary

▶ make it!

HEAT oven to 450°F.

MIX oil and garlic in small microwaveable bowl. Microwave on HIGH 30 sec.

PLACE pizza crust on baking sheet; brush with oil mixture. Top with remaining ingredients.

BAKE 10 to 12 min. or until cheese is melted and crust is golden brown.

SUBSTITUTE:
Prepare using ATHENOS Crumbled Feta Cheese with Basil & Tomato or ATHENOS Traditional Crumbled Feta Cheese.

white & gold pizza

PREP: 10 min. | TOTAL: 43 min. | MAKES: 6 servings.

▶ what you need!

3 Tbsp. olive oil, divided

1 large sweet onion, thinly sliced

1 lb. frozen pizza dough, thawed

1 large clove garlic, minced

4 oz. (½ of 8-oz. pkg.) PHILADELPHIA Cream Cheese, softened

¾ cup KRAFT Shredded Mozzarella Cheese

½ cup DIGIORNO* Grated Romano Cheese

½ tsp. crushed red pepper

DIGIORNO is a registered trademark of Nestle, used under license.

▶ make it!

HEAT oven to 425°F.

HEAT 1 Tbsp. oil in large skillet on medium heat. Add onions; cook 15 to 20 min. or until tender and golden brown, stirring occasionally.

MEANWHILE, place pizza dough on lightly floured baking sheet; pat to 16×12-inch rectangle. Mix garlic and remaining oil; spread onto dough. Bake 10 min.

SPREAD cream cheese onto crust; top with remaining cheeses, onions and crushed red pepper. Bake 10 to 12 min. or until crust is golden brown.

MAKE AHEAD:
Caramelized onions can be made ahead of time. Cool, then refrigerate up to 2 days before using as directed.

SMOKED SALMON & CAPERS PIZZA:
Prepare as directed, using PHILADELPHIA Salmon Cream Cheese Spread and substituting 2 tsp. capers for the crushed red pepper.

rocky road CHIPS AHOY! "pizza"

PREP: 15 min. | TOTAL: 1 hour 15 min. | MAKES: 16 servings.

▶ what you need!

28 CHIPS AHOY! Cookies, divided

¼ cup butter or margarine, melted

4 oz. (½ of 8-oz. pkg.) PHILADELPHIA Cream Cheese, softened

2 Tbsp. powdered sugar

1 cup thawed COOL WHIP Whipped Topping

⅓ cup PLANTERS COCKTAIL Peanuts, chopped

⅔ cup JET-PUFFED Miniature Marshmallows

1 square BAKER'S Semi-Sweet Chocolate, melted

▶ make it!

LINE 9-inch round pan with plastic wrap. Finely crush 24 cookies; mix with butter. Press onto bottom of prepared pan. Chop remaining cookies; set aside.

MIX cream cheese and sugar in medium bowl until well blended. Gently stir in COOL WHIP; spread onto crust. Top with nuts, marshmallows and chopped cookies; press lightly into cream cheese layer. Drizzle with chocolate.

REFRIGERATE 1 hour or until firm. Lift pizza from pan using plastic wrap. Remove plastic wrap and cut into slices.

NOTE:
For best results, spray bottom and side of round pan with cooking spray before lining with plastic wrap. This will help the plastic wrap stay in place making it easier to press the cookie crumbs onto bottom of pan.

HOLIDAY
CELEBRATION

irish cream
chocolate mousse

PREP: 10 min. | TOTAL: 30 min. | MAKES: 6 servings, ½ cup each.

▸ what you need!

1 pkg. (3.9 oz.) JELL-O Chocolate Instant Pudding

1¼ cups cold milk

¼ cup Irish cream liqueur

2 cups thawed COOL WHIP Whipped Topping, divided

½ cup fresh raspberries

▸ make it!

BEAT dry pudding mix, milk and liqueur in medium bowl with whisk 2 min. Stir in 1½ cups COOL WHIP.

SPOON into dessert dishes. Refrigerate 20 min.

TOP with remaining COOL WHIP and berries.

SPECIAL EXTRA:
Top with grated BAKER'S Semi-Sweet Chocolate.

american berry no-bake cheesecake

PREP: 15 min. | TOTAL: 3 hours 15 min. | MAKES: 8 servings.

▶ what you need!

2 pkg. (8 oz. each) PHILADELPHIA Cream Cheese, softened

⅓ cup sugar

2 cups thawed COOL WHIP Whipped Topping

1 HONEY MAID Graham Pie Crust (6 oz.)

1 pt. (2 cups) strawberries, halved

⅓ cup blueberries

▶ make it!

BEAT cream cheese and sugar in large bowl with electric mixer on medium speed until well blended. Gently stir in COOL WHIP.

SPOON into crust.

REFRIGERATE 3 hours or until set. Arrange strawberries and blueberries in rows on top of cheesecake to resemble flag. (Or arrange fruit in other desired design on top of cheesecake.) Store leftover cheesecake in refrigerator.

BEST OF SEASON:
Omit strawberries and blueberries. Prepare cheesecake as directed. Top with 2⅓ cups combined fresh raspberries and sliced peaches.

bit-of-irish cheesecake

PREP: 20 min. | TOTAL: 5 hours 25 min. | MAKES: 16 servings.

▶ what you need!

1½ cups finely chopped PLANTERS Pecans

2 Tbsp. sugar

3 Tbsp. butter or margarine, melted

4 pkg. (8 oz. each) PHILADELPHIA Cream Cheese, softened

1 cup sugar

3 Tbsp. flour

1 cup BREAKSTONE'S or KNUDSEN Sour Cream

¼ cup Irish cream liqueur

4 eggs

▶ make it!

HEAT oven to 325°F if using a silver 9-inch springform pan (or to 300°F if using a dark nonstick 9-inch springform pan).

MIX nuts, 2 Tbsp. sugar and the butter; press firmly onto bottom of pan. Bake 10 min.

BEAT cream cheese, 1 cup sugar and the flour in large bowl with electric mixer on medium speed until well blended. Add sour cream and liqueur; mix well. Add eggs, 1 at a time, mixing on low speed after each addition just until blended. Pour over crust.

BAKE 1 hour 5 min. or until center is almost set. Run small knife or metal spatula around rim of pan to loosen cake; cool before removing rim of pan. Refrigerate 4 hours or overnight. Store leftover cheesecake in refrigerator.

FUN IDEA:
Celebrate St. Patrick's Day by garnishing chilled cheesecake with green colored sugar just before serving. Or, sprinkle the green colored sugar over a clover-shaped template placed on top of chilled cheesecake to resemble a shamrock.

classic s'mores

PREP: 10 min. | TOTAL: 10 min. | MAKES: 4 servings.

▶ what you need!

4 HONEY MAID Honey Grahams, broken in half (8 squares)

1 HERSHEY'S® Milk Chocolate Bar (1.55 oz.), quartered

4 JET-PUFFED Marshmallows

▶ make it!

TOP 4 graham squares with chocolate.

TOAST marshmallows over hot campfire or grill using long-handled fork. Use second fork to carefully slide marshmallows onto chocolate.

COVER with remaining graham squares. Press together gently to secure.

USE YOUR MICROWAVE:
Make indoor s'mores! Top each of 4 graham squares with 1 chocolate piece and 1 untoasted marshmallow. Place on microwaveable plate. Microwave on HIGH 15 to 20 sec. or until marshmallows puff. Cover each with a second graham square to make sandwich.

NOTE:
Be sure to supervise the kids if they are toasting the marshmallows.

HERSHEY'S® trademark and trade dress are used with permission from The Hershey Company.

JELL-O holiday jigglers

PREP: 10 min. | TOTAL: 3 hours 10 min. | MAKES: 2 doz. or 24 servings, 1 JIGGLERS each.

► what you need!

2½ cups boiling water

4 pkg. (3 oz. each) JELL-O Gelatin

► make it!

ADD boiling water to dry gelatin mixes; stir 3 min. until completely dissolved.

POUR into 13×9-inch pan. Refrigerate 3 hours or until firm.

DIP bottom of pan in warm water 15 sec. Cut gelatin into shapes using JELL-O Holiday JIGGLERS Cutters.

KEEP KIDS SAFE:
For children under 6 years of age, cut JIGGLERS into small bite-size pieces. Children should always be seated and supervised while eating. For more information, visit www.KraftKidsSafe.com.

cream cheese flan

PREP: 20 min. | TOTAL: 4 hours 20 min. | MAKES: 8 servings.

▶ what you need!

2 cups sugar, divided

1 can (12 oz.) evaporated milk

1 pkg. (8 oz.) PHILADELPHIA Cream Cheese, cubed, softened

5 eggs

1 tsp. vanilla

Dash salt

▶ make it!

HEAT oven to 350°F.

COOK 1 cup sugar in small heavy saucepan on medium heat until sugar is melted and deep golden brown, stirring constantly. Pour into 9-inch round pan; tilt pan to evenly cover bottom with syrup.

BLEND evaporated milk and cream cheese in blender until smooth. Add remaining sugar, eggs, vanilla and salt; blend just until smooth. Pour over syrup in pan. Place filled pan in larger pan; add enough hot water to larger pan to come halfway up side of smaller pan.

BAKE 50 min. to 1 hour or until knife inserted near center comes out clean. Cool slightly. Carefully remove flan from water. Cool completely on wire rack. Refrigerate several hours or until chilled. Unmold onto plate just before serving. Garnish as desired.

FLAVOR VARIATIONS:
Prepare as directed. Choose one of the following options: **GUAVA:** Add ½ cup guava paste, cut into pieces, or ½ cup canned guava shells in heavy syrup to cream cheese batter before pouring into prepared pan. **LIME:** Add zest from 1 lime to boiling sugar mixture; remove from syrup before sugar caramelizes. Pour into prepared pan as directed. **CAJETA:** Add ¼ cup cajeta (Mexican goat milk caramel) to cream cheese batter before pouring into prepared pan. **CHOCOLATE-ORANGE:** Add 2 squares BAKER'S Semi-Sweet Chocolate, melted and cooled, and 1 Tbsp. orange zest to cream cheese batter before pouring into prepared pan. **COCONUT:** Omit vanilla and add ¼ cup BAKER'S ANGEL FLAKE Coconut or ½ cup coconut milk and 1 Tbsp. rum to cream cheese batter before pouring into prepared pan.

drummer boy cake

PREP: 20 min. | TOTAL: 1 hour 20 min. | MAKES: 18 servings.

▶ what you need!

- 1 tub (8 oz.) COOL WHIP Whipped Topping (Do not thaw.), divided
- 1 pkg. (2-layer size) chocolate cake mix
- 1 pkg. (3.9 oz.) JELL-O Chocolate Instant Pudding
- ¼ cup plus 2 Tbsp. powdered sugar, divided
- ½ tsp. milk
- 11 NILLA Wafers
- 4 squares BAKER'S Semi-Sweet Chocolate, chopped
- 1 pkg. (8 oz.) PHILADELPHIA Cream Cheese, softened
- 1 jar (10 oz.) maraschino cherries, well drained, chopped
- 1 strip peelable red licorice
- 2 JET-PUFFED Marshmallows
- 2 pretzel rods

▶ make it!

HEAT oven to 350°F.

REFRIGERATE ⅓ of the COOL WHIP. Return remaining COOL WHIP to freezer. Prepare cake batter; blend in dry pudding mix. Bake as directed on package for 2 (9-inch) round layers. Cool cakes in pans 10 min. Invert onto wire racks and cool completely.

MEANWHILE, mix 2 Tbsp. powdered sugar and milk. Brush onto wafers. Microwave frozen COOL WHIP and chopped chocolate on HIGH 1½ min. or until chocolate is melted, stirring after 1 min. Cool 15 min. to thicken.

BEAT cream cheese and remaining sugar with whisk until well blended. Stir in cherries and thawed COOL WHIP. Stack cake layers on plate, filling with cream cheese mixture. Frost with chocolate mixture. Decorate with wafers and remaining ingredients to resemble a drum and sticks. Refrigerate leftovers.

s'more brownies

PREP: 15 min. | TOTAL: 52 min. | MAKES: 36 servings.

▶ what you need!

10 HONEY MAID Honey Grahams, broken in half (20 squares), divided

¾ cup butter or margarine

4 squares BAKER'S Unsweetened Chocolate

2 cups sugar

3 eggs

1 tsp. vanilla

1 cup flour

2½ cups JET-PUFFED Miniature Marshmallows

1 cup BAKER'S Semi-Sweet Chocolate Chunks

▶ make it!

HEAT oven to 350°F.

LINE 13×9-inch pan with foil, with ends of foil extending over sides of pan; spray with cooking spray. Place 15 squares in pan, with sides overlapping slightly. Break remaining grahams into pieces.

MICROWAVE butter and chocolate squares in large microwaveable bowl on HIGH 2 min.; stir until chocolate is completely melted. Add sugar, eggs and vanilla; mix well. Stir in flour. Pour over grahams in pan.

BAKE 30 to 32 min. or until toothpick inserted in center comes out with fudgy crumbs. (Do not overbake.) Sprinkle with marshmallows and chocolate chunks. Bake 3 to 5 min. or until marshmallows begin to puff. Press reserved graham pieces gently into marshmallows. Cool. Use foil to lift brownies from pan before cutting to serve.

HOW TO EASILY CUT BROWNIES:
For ease in cutting, dip knife in warm water and wipe dry between cuts.

eggnog eclair dessert

PREP: 30 min. | TOTAL: 3 hours 30 min. | MAKES: 12 servings.

▶ what you need!

1 pkg. (8 oz.) PHILADELPHIA Cream Cheese, softened

2 cups cold milk

1 pkg. (3.4 oz.) JELL-O Vanilla Flavor Instant Pudding

½ tsp. rum extract

¼ tsp. ground nutmeg

1 tub (8 oz.) COOL WHIP Whipped Topping, thawed, divided

78 NILLA Wafers

2 squares BAKER'S Semi-Sweet Chocolate

▶ make it!

BEAT cream cheese in large bowl with mixer until creamy. Gradually beat in milk. Add dry pudding mix, extract and nutmeg; beat 2 min. Gently stir in 1½ cups COOL WHIP.

LINE 9×5-inch loaf pan with plastic wrap. Arrange 15 wafers, top-sides down, on bottom of pan; cover with ¼ of the pudding mixture. Repeat layers 3 times. Top with 15 of the remaining wafers. Refrigerate 3 hours.

INVERT dessert onto plate; remove plastic wrap. Microwave chocolate and 1 cup of the remaining COOL WHIP in microwaveable bowl on HIGH 25 sec.; stir until chocolate is completely melted and mixture is well blended. Cool 1 min. Pour over dessert. Garnish with remaining COOL WHIP and wafers.

VARIATION:
Omit rum extract and substitute eggnog for the milk.

firecracker bites

PREP: 40 min. | TOTAL: 2 hours 30 min. | MAKES: 14 servings, 3 wafer sandwiches each.

▶ what you need!

- 1 pkg. (8 oz.) PHILADELPHIA Cream Cheese, softened
- 1 cup cold milk
- 1 pkg. (3.4 oz.) JELL-O Vanilla Flavor Instant Pudding
- 1½ cups thawed COOL WHIP Whipped Topping, divided
- 1 pkg. (12 oz.) NILLA Wafers
- ½ cup mixed red, white and blue sprinkles
- 42 pieces red string licorice (1 inch)

▶ make it!

BEAT cream cheese in large bowl with mixer until creamy. Gradually beat in milk. Add dry pudding mix; beat 2 min. Whisk in 1 cup COOL WHIP.

SPOON about 1½ Tbsp. pudding mixture onto each of half the wafers; cover with remaining wafers to make sandwiches. Freeze 2 hours or until filling is firm.

SPREAD tops of wafer sandwiches with remaining COOL WHIP. Dip in sprinkles. Insert licorice piece into top of each for the fuse. Freeze until ready to serve.

SPECIAL EXTRA:
Divide COOL WHIP into thirds. Color one portion with 4 drops red food coloring and second portion with 4 drops blue food coloring. Leave remaining portion white. Spread onto wafers and continue as directed.

HOW TO FILL SANDWICHES:
Spoon pudding mixture into resealable plastic bag; seal bag. Cut off small corner from bottom of bag; use to pipe pudding onto wafers. Cover with remaining wafers and continue as directed.

NOTE:
If you have any pudding mixture left over or choose to not make all 42 wafer sandwiches, layer remaining pudding mixture in parfait glasses with fresh fruit, such as strawberries and blueberries. Top each parfait with a dollop of the remaining COOL WHIP.

holiday cheesecake presents

PREP: 10 min. | TOTAL: 4 hours 10 min. | MAKES: 32 servings.

▶ what you need!

1½ cups HONEY MAID Graham Cracker Crumbs

⅓ cup butter, melted

3 Tbsp. sugar

3 pkg. (8 oz. each) PHILADELPHIA Cream Cheese, softened

¾ cup sugar

1 tsp. vanilla

3 eggs

Suggested decorations: decorating gels, colored sprinkles

▶ make it!

HEAT oven to 350°F.

MIX graham crumbs, butter and 3 Tbsp. sugar; press onto bottom of 13×9-inch pan.

BEAT cream cheese, ¾ cup sugar and vanilla with mixer until well blended. Add eggs; mix just until blended. Pour over crust.

BAKE 30 min. or until center is almost set. Cool. Refrigerate 3 hours. Cut into bars. Decorate with gels and sprinkles to resemble presents.

SIZE-WISE:
Sweets can add enjoyment to a balanced diet, but remember to keep an eye on portions.

VARIATION:
Substitute 50 NILLA Wafers, crushed (about 1½ cups), and ¼ cup butter, melted, for the HONEY MAID Graham Cracker Crumbs and ⅓ cup butter, melted.

key lime margarita pie

PREP: 15 min. | TOTAL: 6 hours 15 min. | MAKES: 10 servings.

▶ what you need!

1¼ cups crushed pretzels

¼ cup sugar

6 Tbsp. butter or margarine, melted

1 can (14 oz.) sweetened condensed milk

½ cup lime juice

1 envelope KOOL-AID Lemon Lime Unsweetened Soft Drink Mix

1 tub (8 oz.) COOL-WHIP Whipped Topping, thawed, divided

▶ make it!

MIX crushed pretzels, sugar and butter. Press onto bottom and up side of 9-inch pie plate. Refrigerate until ready to fill.

MIX next 3 ingredients in large bowl. Whisk in 2½ cups COOL WHIP. Pour into crust.

FREEZE 6 hours. Remove from freezer 15 min. before serving; let stand at room temperature until slightly softened. Top with remaining COOL WHIP.

JAZZ IT UP:
For added lime flavor, stir in 2 Tbsp. grated lime zest with lime juice.

MAKE IT EASY:
For easy serving, dip pie plate into warm water, just to rim, for 30 seconds before removing pie slice.

turtle pumpkin pie

PREP: 15 min. | TOTAL: 1 hour 15 min. | MAKES: 10 servings.

▶ what you need!

¼ cup plus 2 Tbsp. caramel ice cream topping, divided

1 HONEY MAID Graham Pie Crust (6 oz.)

½ cup plus 2 Tbsp. chopped PLANTERS Pecans, divided

2 pkg. (3.4 oz. each) JELL-O Vanilla Flavor Instant Pudding

1 cup cold milk

1 cup canned pumpkin

1 tsp. ground cinnamon

½ tsp. ground nutmeg

1 tub (8 oz.) COOL WHIP Whipped Topping, thawed, divided

▶ make it!

POUR ¼ cup caramel topping into crust; sprinkle with ½ cup nuts.

BEAT dry pudding mixes, milk, pumpkin and spices with whisk until blended. Stir in 1½ cups COOL WHIP. Spoon into crust.

REFRIGERATE 1 hour. Top with remaining COOL WHIP, 2 Tbsp. caramel topping and nuts just before serving.

OREO turkey

PREP: 30 min. | TOTAL: 30 min. | MAKES: 6 servings.

▶ what you need!

- 6 OREO Cookies
- 1 square BAKER'S Semi-Sweet Chocolate, melted
- 30 pieces candy corn
- 6 chocolate malted milk balls
- 6 cinnamon red hot candies

▶ make it!

SEPARATE each cookie, leaving all the cream filling on 1 half of each. Set filling-topped halves aside.

USE small amount of melted chocolate to attach 5 candy corn pieces, pointed-sides down, to each plain cookie half for the turkey's tail. Refrigerate 5 min. or until chocolate is firm.

ATTACH malted milk ball to center of each filling-topped cookie half with melted chocolate for the turkey's body. Use dot of melted chocolate to attach cinnamon candy to each body for the head.

ATTACH turkey tails to bodies with remaining melted chocolate. Refrigerate until firm.

HOW TO EASILY SEPARATE COOKIES:
Refrigerate cookies for 15 min. before carefully twisting top from bottom so that the cream remains entirely on 1 half of the cookie. Use a knife to smooth filling if necessary.

patriotic fruit pizza

PREP: 20 min. | TOTAL: 1 hour 6 min. | MAKES: 16 servings.

▶ what you need!

1 pkg. (16.5 oz.) refrigerated sliceable sugar cookies, sliced

1 pkg. (3.4 oz.) JELL-O Vanilla Flavor Instant Pudding

1¼ cups cold milk

3 cups JET-PUFFED Miniature Marshmallows, divided

1 cup thawed COOL WHIP Whipped Topping

2 cups cut-up fresh fruit, such as strawberries, raspberries and blueberries

▶ make it!

HEAT oven to 350°F.

LINE 12-inch pizza pan with foil; spray with cooking spray. Arrange dough slices in pan; press together to form crust. Bake 14 to 16 min. or until lightly browned. Cool completely. Remove cookie from pan and foil; place on plate.

BEAT dry pudding mix and milk in large bowl with whisk 2 min. Let stand 5 min. Stir in 2 cups marshmallows and COOL WHIP; spread onto crust.

TOP with fruit and remaining marshmallows.

SUBSTITUTE:
Substitute other fruits, such as seedless grapes, orange sections, banana slices and/or peeled kiwi slices for the strawberries, raspberries and blueberries.

VARIATION:
If pizza pan is not available, trace a 12-inch circle on parchment paper or foil; place on baking sheet. Press cookie dough onto circle. Bake as directed.

PHILADELPHIA chocolate cheesecakes for two

PREP: 10 min. | TOTAL: 2 hours 10 min. | MAKES: 2 servings.

▶ what you need!

2 oz. (¼ of 8-oz. pkg.) PHILADELPHIA Cream Cheese, softened

1 Tbsp. sugar

1 square BAKER'S Semi-Sweet Chocolate, melted

½ cup thawed COOL WHIP Whipped Topping

2 OREO Cookies

▶ make it!

BEAT cream cheese, sugar and chocolate in medium bowl with wire whisk until well blended. Add COOL WHIP; mix well.

PLACE 1 cookie on bottom of each of 2 paper-lined medium muffin cups; fill evenly with cream cheese mixture.

REFRIGERATE 2 hours or overnight. (Or, if you are in a hurry, place in the freezer for 1 hour.)

JAZZ IT UP:
Dust surface with cocoa powder. Top with heart-shaped stencil; dust with powdered sugar.

sparkling tree cakes

PREP: 20 min. | TOTAL: 1 hour 20 min. | MAKES: 16 servings, 1 tree each.

▶ what you need!

1 pkg. (2-layer size) yellow cake mix

¼ tsp. green food coloring

1 pkg. (8 oz.) PHILADELPHIA Cream Cheese, softened

1 cup powdered sugar

1½ cups thawed COOL WHIP Whipped Topping

16 peppermint sticks (3 inches each)

½ cup BAKER'S ANGEL FLAKE Coconut

2 squares BAKER'S Semi-Sweet Chocolate, chopped

¼ cup PLANTERS Dry Roasted Peanuts, chopped

Assorted Christmas candies and colored sugar

▶ make it!

HEAT oven to 350°F.

GREASE and flour 2 (9-inch) round cake pans; set aside. Prepare cake batter as directed on package; tint with food coloring. Pour evenly into prepared pans.

BAKE as directed on package. Cool in pans 10 min.; remove to wire racks. Cool completely.

BEAT cream cheese and powdered sugar with electric mixer on medium speed until well blended. Stir in COOL WHIP with wire whisk. Spread onto tops and sides of cakes.

CUT each cake into 8 wedges to resemble Christmas trees. Insert peppermint stick into curved side of each cake for the tree trunk. Decorate with remaining ingredients. Store in refrigerator.

SIZE-WISE:
With their built-in portion control, these cakes make great holiday treats!

spider web pumpkin cheesecake

PREP: 15 min. | TOTAL: 5 hours 10 min. | MAKES: 16 servings.

▶ what you need!

18 OREO Cookies, finely crushed (about 1½ cups)

2 Tbsp. butter or margarine, melted

3 pkg. (8 oz. each) PHILADELPHIA Cream Cheese, softened

¾ cup sugar

1 can (15 oz.) pumpkin

1 Tbsp. pumpkin pie spice

3 eggs

1 cup BREAKSTONE'S or KNUDSEN Sour Cream

1 square BAKER'S Semi-Sweet Chocolate

1 tsp. butter or margarine

▶ make it!

HEAT oven to 350°F.

MIX cookie crumbs and 2 Tbsp. butter; press onto bottom of 9-inch springform pan.

BEAT cream cheese and sugar in large bowl with electric mixer on medium speed until well blended. Add pumpkin and pumpkin pie spice; mix well. Add eggs, 1 at a time, mixing on low speed after each addition just until blended. Pour over crust.

BAKE 50 to 55 min. or until center is almost set; cool slightly. Carefully spread sour cream over top of cheesecake. Run knife or metal spatula around rim of pan to loosen cake; cool before removing rim of pan.

PLACE chocolate and 1 tsp. butter in small microwaveable bowl. Microwave on MEDIUM (50%) 30 sec.; stir chocolate until completely melted; drizzle over cheesecake in spiral pattern. Starting at center of cheesecake, pull a toothpick through lines from center of cheesecake to outside edge to resemble a spider's web. Refrigerate 4 hours.

triple layer eggnog pie

PREP: 15 min. | TOTAL: 3 hours 15 min. | MAKES: 10 servings.

▶ what you need!

10 KRAFT Caramels

1 cup cold milk, divided

1 HONEY MAID Graham Pie Crust (6 oz.)

½ cup chopped PLANTERS Pecans, toasted

2 pkg. (3.4 oz. each) JELL-O Vanilla Flavor Instant Pudding

1 cup cold eggnog

1 tub (8 oz.) COOL WHIP Whipped Topping, thawed, divided

▶ make it!

MICROWAVE caramels and 1 Tbsp. of the milk in microwaveable bowl on MEDIUM (50%) 30 sec. or until caramels are completely melted when stirred. Pour into crust; sprinkle with nuts.

BEAT dry pudding mixes, eggnog and remaining milk with whisk 2 min; spoon 1½ cups over the nuts. Stir half the COOL WHIP into remaining pudding; spread over pudding layer in crust. Top with remaining COOL WHIP.

REFRIGERATE 3 hours.

JAZZ IT UP:
Sprinkle pie with ground nutmeg or ground cinnamon just before serving.

OREO baseball dessert

PREP: 15 min. | TOTAL: 24 hours 15 min. | MAKES: 10 servings.

▶ what you need!

    1 pkg. (3.9 oz.) JELL-O Chocolate Instant Pudding

    2 cups cold milk

   35 OREO Cookies, divided

   1½ cups thawed COOL WHIP Whipped Topping

    1 piece red string licorice (36 inches)

▶ make it!

BEAT dry pudding mix and milk with whisk 2 min. Let stand 5 min. or until thickened.

LINE 8-inch round pan with plastic wrap. Arrange 14 cookies on bottom of pan, cutting to fit if necessary; cover with 1 cup pudding. Repeat layers. Cover with plastic wrap. Refrigerate 24 hours.

UNCOVER dessert. Invert onto serving plate; remove plastic wrap. Frost dessert with COOL WHIP. Cut remaining cookies in half; arrange around edge of dessert. Cut licorice into 2 (8-inch) pieces and 20 (1-inch) pieces. Use licorice to decorate top of dessert to resemble a baseball.

HOW TO EASILY CUT COOKIES IN HALF:
Refrigerate OREO Cookies first for about 15 min. Then, use a serrated knife to cut in half.

CAKES & PIES

chocolate indulgence cake

PREP: 15 min. | TOTAL: 1 hour | MAKES: 12 servings.

▶ what you need!

1 pkg. (6 squares) BAKER'S Bittersweet Chocolate

¾ cup butter

4 eggs

1 cup sugar

½ cup flour

▶ make it!

HEAT oven to 350°F.

MICROWAVE chocolate and butter in large microwaveable bowl on HIGH 2 min. or until butter is melted. Stir until chocolate is completely melted; cool.

BEAT eggs and sugar in large bowl with mixer until well blended. Whisk in chocolate mixture. Stir in flour until well blended. Pour into greased and floured 9-inch round pan.

BAKE 30 min. or until center is set. Cool 5 min.; remove from pan to wire rack. Cool completely.

SIZE-WISE:
Enjoy this indulgent dessert on occasion. One serving goes a long way on chocolate flavor.

banana-sour cream cake

PREP: 15 min. | TOTAL: 1 hour 50 min. | MAKES: 16 servings.

▶ what you need!

1 pkg. (2-layer size) yellow cake mix

3 eggs

1 cup mashed ripe bananas (about 3)

1 cup BREAKSTONE'S or KNUDSEN Sour Cream

¼ cup oil

1 pkg. (8 oz.) PHILADELPHIA Cream Cheese, softened

½ cup butter, softened

1 pkg. (16 oz.) powdered sugar

1 cup finely chopped PLANTERS Walnuts

▶ make it!

HEAT oven to 350°F.

BEAT first 5 ingredients with mixer on low speed just until moistened, stopping frequently to scrape bottom and side of bowl. Beat on medium speed 2 min. Pour into greased and floured 13×9-inch pan.

BAKE 35 min. or until toothpick inserted in center comes out clean. Cool completely.

BEAT cream cheese and butter with mixer until well blended. Gradually add sugar, beating well after each addition.

REMOVE cake from pan. Carefully cut cake crosswise in half using serrated knife. Place 1 cake half, top-side down, on plate; spread with some of the cream cheese frosting. Top with remaining cake half, top-side up. Spread top and sides with remaining frosting. Press nuts into sides. Keep refrigerated.

SUBSTITUTE:
Prepare using BREAKSTONE'S Reduced Fat or KNUDSEN Light Sour Cream.

HOW TO NEATLY FROST THE CAKE:
Freeze cake layers about 20 min. before frosting. This helps to set the crumbs on the cut edges of the cake layers so they don't pull up into the frosting. And don't worry if the frosting does not look perfect on the sides of the cake—the nuts will cover any imperfections.

triple-chocolate bliss cake

▶ what you need!

- 1 pkg. (2-layer size) chocolate cake mix
- 1 cup BREAKSTONE'S or KNUDSEN Sour Cream
- 1 pkg. (3.9 oz.) JELL-O Chocolate Instant Pudding
- 4 eggs
- ½ cup oil
- ½ cup water
- 3 cups thawed COOL WHIP Whipped Topping
- 1 pkg. (8 squares) BAKER'S Semi-Sweet Chocolate
- 1½ cups raspberries

▶ make it!

HEAT oven to 350°F.

LIGHTLY grease 12-cup fluted tube pan or 10-inch tube pan; set aside. Beat all ingredients except COOL WHIP, chocolate and raspberries in large bowl with electric mixer on low speed just until moistened. Beat on medium speed 2 min. Pour into prepared pan.

BAKE 50 min. to 1 hour or until wooden toothpick inserted near center comes out clean. Cool in pan 10 min. Loosen cake from side of pan with knife or metal spatula. Invert cake onto serving plate. Gently remove pan. Cool cake completely. Transfer to serving plate.

MICROWAVE COOL WHIP and chocolate in microwaveable bowl on HIGH 1½ to 2 min. or until chocolate is completely melted and mixture is well blended, stirring after each min. Drizzle over cake. Let stand until firm. Spoon raspberries into center of cake. Store leftover cake in refrigerator.

chocolate ganache layered torte

PREP: 40 min. | TOTAL: 1 hour 15 min. | MAKES: 16 servings, 1 slice each.

▶ what you need!

1 pkg. (2-layer size) chocolate cake mix

1 pkg. (8 squares) BAKER'S Semi-Sweet Chocolate, melted

⅔ cup whipping cream

½ cup strawberry preserves

1½ cups sliced strawberries

Powdered sugar

Additional sliced strawberry (optional)

▶ make it!

HEAT oven to 350°F.

LIGHTLY grease 2 (9-inch) round cake pans. Prepare cake batter as directed on package; pour evenly into prepared pans. Bake 30 to 35 min. or until wooden toothpick inserted in centers comes out clean. Cool in pans 10 min. on wire racks. Loosen cakes from sides of pans with spatula or knife. Invert cakes onto racks; gently remove pans. Cool cakes completely.

MEANWHILE, place chocolate in small saucepan. Add cream; cook on low heat just until chocolate is melted, stirring frequently. Remove from heat; let stand 15 min. or until completely cooled. (Ganache will thicken as it cools.)

CUT each cake horizontally in half with serrated knife to make 2 layers. Place 1 of the cake layers on serving plate; spread with about 3 Tbsp. of the preserves. Top with ½ cup of the strawberries and ⅓ cup of the ganache, spreading ganache to completely cover cake layer. Repeat layers 2 times; top with the remaining cake layer. Sprinkle with powdered sugar just before serving. Garnish with additional sliced strawberry.

VARIATION:
Prepare as directed, using raspberry preserves and substituting fresh raspberries for the sliced strawberries.

chocolate mousse torte

PREP: 20 min. | TOTAL: 3 hours 20 min. | MAKES: 16 servings.

▶ what you need!

37 NILLA Wafers, divided

4 squares BAKER'S Semi-Sweet Chocolate, divided

2 pkg. (3.9 oz. each) JELL-O Chocolate Instant Pudding

2 cups plus 2 Tbsp. cold milk, divided

1 tub (8 oz.) COOL WHIP Whipped Topping, thawed, divided

1 pkg. (8 oz.) PHILADELPHIA Cream Cheese, softened

¼ cup sugar

¾ cup fresh raspberries

▶ make it!

STAND 16 wafers around inside edge of 9-inch round pan lined with plastic wrap. Melt 3 chocolate squares as directed on package.

BEAT dry pudding mixes and 2 cups milk in medium bowl with whisk 2 min. Add melted chocolate; mix well. Stir in 1 cup COOL WHIP; pour into prepared pan.

BEAT cream cheese, sugar and remaining milk with mixer until well blended. Stir in 1 cup of the remaining COOL WHIP; spread over pudding. Top with remaining wafers. Refrigerate 3 hours.

INVERT torte onto plate. Remove pan and plastic wrap. Shave remaining chocolate square into curls. Top torte with remaining COOL WHIP, berries and chocolate curls.

chocolate truffle pie

PREP: 10 min. | TOTAL: 45 min. | MAKES: 10 servings, 1 slice each.

▶ what you need!

  10 squares (1¼ pkg.) BAKER'S Semi-Sweet Chocolate

  ½ cup whipping cream

  4 eggs

  ½ cup sugar

  ¼ cup flour

  1 cup thawed COOL WHIP Whipped Topping

▶ make it!

HEAT oven to 325°F.

PLACE chocolate squares in large microwaveable bowl. Add whipping cream. Microwave on HIGH 2 min. or until chocolate is almost melted. Stir until chocolate is completely melted; cool slightly.

ADD eggs, sugar and flour; beat with wire whisk until well blended. Pour into lightly greased 9-inch pie plate.

BAKE 35 min. or until outer half of pie is puffed but center is still slightly soft; cool. Top each slice with a dollop of COOL WHIP just before serving.

chocolate-caramel creme pie

PREP: 30 min. | TOTAL: 3 hours 30 min. | MAKES: 8 servings.

▶ what you need!

4 oz. (½ of 8-oz. pkg.) PHILADELPHIA Cream Cheese, softened

2 Tbsp. caramel ice cream topping

1 cup thawed COOL WHIP Whipped Topping

1 OREO Pie Crust (recipe follows)

1 pkg. (3.9 oz.) JELL-O Chocolate Instant Pudding

1½ cups cold milk

▶ make it!

MIX cream cheese and caramel topping in medium bowl until well blended. Gently stir in COOL WHIP; spread onto bottom of OREO Pie Crust.

BEAT dry pudding mix and milk with whisk 2 min.; pour over cream cheese layer. Refrigerate 3 hours.

OREO Pie Crust

PREP: 15 min. | TOTAL: 15 min. | MAKES: 1 (9-inch) pie crust.

▶ what you need!

18 OREO Cookies

3 Tbsp. butter or margarine, melted

▶ make it!

PLACE cookies in large resealable plastic bag; press bag to remove excess air, then seal bag. Use rolling pin to crush cookies to form fine crumbs.

ADD butter; squeeze bag to evenly moisten crumbs.

PRESS crumb mixture onto bottom and up side of 9-inch pie plate sprayed with cooking spray. Refrigerate until ready to fill.

HOW TO EASILY SERVE CRUMB CRUST PIES:
When serving a crumb-crust pie, dip filled pie plate in warm water for 10 sec., being careful to dip pie plate to just below rim. This will help loosen the crust to make it easier to serve the cut pieces.

dark molten chocolate cakes

PREP: 15 min. | TOTAL: 30 min. | MAKES: 12 servings, 1 cake half each.

▶ what you need!

1 pkg. (6 squares) BAKER'S Bittersweet Chocolate

10 Tbsp. butter

1½ cups powdered sugar

½ cup flour

3 whole eggs

3 egg yolks

Additional powdered sugar and raspberries (optional)

▶ make it!

HEAT oven to 425°F.

GREASE 6 (6-oz.) custard cups or soufflé dishes. Place on baking sheet.

MICROWAVE chocolate and butter in large microwaveable bowl on HIGH 2 min. or until butter is melted. Stir until chocolate is completely melted. Add powdered sugar and flour; mix well. Add whole eggs and egg yolks; stir with wire whisk until well blended. Divide batter evenly among prepared custard cups.

BAKE 14 to 15 min. or until cakes are firm around the edges but soft in the centers. Let stand 1 min. Run small knife around cakes to loosen. Immediately invert cakes onto serving plates. Sprinkle lightly with additional powdered sugar and garnish with raspberries. Cut each cake in half to serve.

fudgy walnut pie

PREP: 20 min. | TOTAL: 1 hour 45 min. | MAKES: 12 servings.

▶ what you need!

½ pkg. (15 oz.) ready-to-bake pie crusts (1 crust)

1 pkg. (8 squares) BAKER'S Semi-Sweet Chocolate

¼ cup butter, softened

¾ cup firmly packed brown sugar

3 eggs

1 tsp. vanilla

¼ cup flour

1 cup chopped PLANTERS Walnuts

½ cup PLANTERS Walnut Halves

▶ make it!

POSITION oven rack in lower third of oven. Heat oven to 375°F.

PREPARE pie crust as directed on package, using 9-inch pie plate; set aside. Microwave chocolate in large microwaveable bowl on HIGH 2 min. Stir until chocolate is completely melted; set aside.

BEAT butter and sugar in large bowl with electric mixer on medium speed until light and fluffy. Add eggs, 1 at a time, beating well after each addition. Blend in melted chocolate and vanilla. Add flour; mix well. Stir in chopped nuts. Pour into crust. Arrange nut halves over filling.

BAKE 25 min. or until center of filling is set. Cool completely. Refrigerate at least 1 hour before serving.

intensely chocolate mousse cake

PREP: 20 min. | TOTAL: 6 hours 5 min. | MAKES: 12 servings.

▶ what you need!

¾ cup cold water

½ cup light corn syrup

½ cup sugar

¼ cup cornstarch

1½ pkg. (6 squares each) BAKER'S Bittersweet Chocolate (9 squares), coarsely chopped

¼ tsp. salt

¼ cup butter or margarine

3 eggs, beaten

1 cup whipping cream

Boiling water

▶ make it!

HEAT oven to 350°F.

MIX first 4 ingredients in large saucepan; cook on low heat until sugar is dissolved, stirring constantly with whisk. Add chocolate and salt; bring just to a boil on medium heat, stirring constantly. Remove from heat. Add butter; stir until melted. Pour into large bowl. Refrigerate 15 min. or until cooled, stirring occasionally. (Mixture can still be slightly warm to the touch.) Add eggs; mix well.

BEAT whipping cream in small bowl with mixer on high speed until soft peaks form. Add to chocolate mixture; stir gently until well blended. Spoon into greased and floured 9-inch springform pan. Place pan in larger shallow pan, then place on center oven rack. Carefully pour boiling water into larger pan to come halfway up side of springform pan.

BAKE 45 min. or until center is set. (Top will feel slightly firm to the touch.) Remove springform pan to wire rack. Run knife around rim of pan to loosen cake; cool before removing rim. Refrigerate 4 hours.

SPECIAL EXTRA:
Garnish with powdered sugar and raspberries.

red velvet cake

▶ what you need!

- 1 pkg. (2-layer size) white cake mix
- 2 squares BAKER'S Unsweetened Chocolate, melted
- 1 Tbsp. red food coloring
- 1 pkg. (8 oz.) PHILADELPHIA Cream Cheese, softened
- ½ cup butter or margarine, melted
- 1 pkg. (16 oz.) powdered sugar (about 4 cups)
- ½ cup chopped PLANTERS Pecans

▶ make it!

PREPARE and bake cake mix as directed on package for 2 (9-inch) round cake layers, adding chocolate and food coloring with water, eggs and oil; cool completely.

BEAT cream cheese and butter with electric mixer on medium speed until well blended. Gradually add sugar, beating well after each addition. Stir in nuts.

FILL and frost cake layers with cream cheese frosting.

NILLA tortoni "cake"

PREP: 20 min. | TOTAL: 4 hours 20 min. | MAKES: 16 servings, 1 wedge each.

▶ what you need!

1 pkg. (12 oz.) NILLA Wafers (about 88 wafers), coarsely crushed (about 5 cups)

1 cup PLANTERS Slivered Almonds, toasted

1¾ qt. (7 cups) vanilla ice cream, softened

½ cup caramel ice cream topping

▶ make it!

SPRINKLE 1 cup wafer crumbs and ⅓ cup nuts onto bottom of 9-inch springform pan; cover with half of the ice cream. Repeat layers. Top with remaining crumbs and nuts; press into ice cream with back of spoon to secure.

FREEZE 4 hours.

REMOVE side of pan before cutting dessert into wedges to serve. Drizzle with caramel topping.

SUBSTITUTE:
Prepare as directed, substituting your favorite flavor ice cream.

HOW TO TOAST NUTS:
Spread almonds into single layer in shallow baking pan. Bake at 350°F for 5 to 7 min. or until lightly toasted, stirring occasionally.

slow-cooker chocolate pudding cake

PREP: 10 min. | TOTAL: 4 hours 10 min. | MAKES: 16 servings.

▶ what you need!

1 pkg. (3.9 oz.) JELL-O Chocolate Instant Pudding

3 cups cold milk

1 pkg. (2-layer size) chocolate fudge chocolate cake mix

2 squares BAKER'S Semi-Sweet Chocolate, coarsely chopped

2 cups thawed COOL WHIP Whipped Topping

▶ make it!

BEAT dry pudding mix and milk in 3½- or 4½-qt. slow cooker sprayed with cooking spray with whisk 2 min.

PREPARE cake batter as directed on package; slowly pour over pudding in slow cooker. (Do not stir.) Cover.

COOK on LOW 2½ to 3 hours (or on HIGH 1½ to 2 hours) or until toothpick inserted in cake comes out clean. Top with chopped chocolate. Turn off heat. Let slow cooker stand, covered, 30 min. or until pudding is thickened. Serve topped with COOL WHIP.

SPECIAL EXTRA:
Serve with assorted toppings, such as chopped PLANTERS Nuts, toasted BAKER'S ANGEL FLAKE Coconut, chocolate chips or crushed peppermint candies.

SLOW COOKER VARIABILITY:
Since slow cookers cook differently, begin checking for doneness at the shorter cooking time and increase time if necessary.

texas sheet cake

PREP: 25 min. | TOTAL: 45 min. | MAKES: 24 servings, 1 square each.

▶ what you need!

CAKE

- 2 cups flour
- 2 cups granulated sugar
- ¼ tsp. salt
- 1 cup plus 2 Tbsp. water
- ¾ cup butter
- 2 squares BAKER'S Unsweetened Chocolate
- ½ cup buttermilk
- 2 eggs
- 1 tsp. baking soda
- 1 tsp. vanilla

FROSTING

- 6 Tbsp. butter
- 2 squares BAKER'S Unsweetened Chocolate
- 6 Tbsp. milk
- 1 pkg. (1 lb.) powdered sugar
- 1 tsp. vanilla

▶ make it!

HEAT oven to 400°F.

COMBINE flour, granulated sugar and salt in large bowl; set aside. Microwave water, ¾ cup butter and 2 squares chocolate in microwaveable bowl on HIGH 2 min.; stir. Continue microwaving 2 min. or until chocolate is completely melted and mixture is well blended, stirring after each min. Add to flour mixture; mix well. Add buttermilk, eggs, baking soda and 1 tsp. vanilla; beat with electric mixer on medium speed 1 min. or until well blended. Pour into greased 15×10×1-inch baking pan.

BAKE 18 to 20 min. or until wooden toothpick inserted in center comes out clean. Meanwhile, start to prepare the Frosting after 15 min.

MICROWAVE 6 Tbsp. butter, 2 squares chocolate and milk in large microwaveable bowl on HIGH 2 min. or until chocolate is completely melted and mixture is well blended, stirring after each min. Add remaining ingredients; beat with electric mixer on medium speed until well blended.

SPREAD immediately onto warm cake. Cool completely before cutting into squares to serve.

SUBSTITUTE:
Omit buttermilk. Place 1 Tbsp. white vinegar in measuring cup. Add enough 2% milk to measure ½ cup. Let stand 5 min., then use as directed.

walnut-praline cake with cream cheese frosting

PREP: 30 min. | TOTAL: 1 hour 55 min. | MAKES: 16 servings, 1 slice each.

▶ what you need!

- 1 pkg. (6 oz.) PLANTERS Walnut Pieces, divided
- 1 pkg. (2-layer size) white cake mix
- ½ cup granulated sugar
- 2 Tbsp. water
- 1 pkg. (8 oz.) PHILADELPHIA Cream Cheese, softened
- ½ cup butter, softened
- 1 pkg. (16 oz.) powdered sugar
- 3 squares BAKER'S Bittersweet Chocolate, divided

▶ make it!

HEAT oven to 350°F.

GREASE and flour 2 (9-inch) round baking pans. Process ⅔ cup nuts in food processor or blender until finely ground; set aside. Prepare cake batter as directed on package. Stir in ground nuts. Pour evenly into prepared pans. Bake 25 min. or until wooden toothpick inserted in centers comes out clean. Cool cake layers in pans 10 min. on wire racks. Remove cakes from pans; cool completely.

MEANWHILE, cover baking sheet with foil; spray with cooking spray. Mix granulated sugar and water in small saucepan. Bring to boil on medium-high heat. Reduce heat to medium-low; simmer 5 min. or until deep golden brown, stirring occasionally. Stir in remaining nuts; spread onto prepared baking sheet. Cool completely. Carefully remove nuts from foil; break into small clusters.

BEAT cream cheese and butter in large bowl with electric mixer on medium speed until well blended. Gradually add powdered sugar, beating well after each addition. Remove 2 cups of the frosting; set aside. Melt chocolate as directed on package; cool slightly. Add ⅔ of the chocolate to remaining frosting in bowl; beat until well blended.

CUT each cake layer horizontally into 2 layers. Stack cake layers on serving plate, spreading chocolate frosting between layers. Frost top and side of cake with reserved plain cream cheese frosting. Gently press nut clusters into top of cake. Drizzle with remaining melted chocolate. Store in refrigerator.

MAKE AHEAD:
Cake layers, walnut praline and cream cheese frosting can be made 1 day ahead. Keep cake layers covered at room temperature; store praline in airtight container at room temperature. Refrigerate frosting until ready to use; soften before spreading over cake.

SUBSTITUTE:
Substitute PLANTERS Slivered Almonds or Pecan Pieces for the walnuts.

PRALINE COATING COOKING TIP:
After mixing sugar and water in saucepan, brush down side of saucepan with a clean wet pastry brush. This will help prevent the sugar from caramelizing on the side of the pan. For best results, continue to brush down side of saucepan as needed with clean wet brush to ensure even cooking of the praline coating.

warm & gooey peanut butter-chocolate cake

PREP: 15 min. | TOTAL: 45 min. | MAKES: 16 servings.

▶ what you need!

1 pkg. (2-layer size) chocolate cake mix

½ cup butter, melted

4 eggs, divided

1 pkg. (8 oz.) PHILADELPHIA Cream Cheese, softened

½ cup PLANTERS Creamy Peanut Butter

2 cups powdered sugar

▶ make it!

HEAT oven to 350°F.

BEAT cake mix, butter and 2 eggs with mixer on low speed 30 sec., stopping frequently to scrape beater and side of bowl. Beat on medium speed 2 min. Spread onto bottom of 13×9-inch pan sprayed with cooking spray.

BEAT remaining ingredients until well blended; pour over batter in pan.

BAKE 30 min. or until edges are firm. Cool slightly.

KEEPING IT SAFE:
Refrigerate any leftovers.

SUBSTITUTE:
Swap in your favorite flavor of cake mix to change up the flavor.

COOKIES
& BARS

berry creamy sandwich cookies

PREP: 10 min. | TOTAL: 10 min. | MAKES: 12 servings, 1 topped cookie each.

▶ what you need!

12 SNACKWELL'S Sugar Free Lemon Creme Sandwich Cookies

¼ cup PHILADELPHIA Strawberry ⅓ Less Fat than Cream Cheese

12 fresh raspberries (about ½ cup)

½ cup fresh blueberries

▶ make it!

SPREAD cookies with cream cheese.

PLACE raspberry in center of each cookie; surround with blueberries.

MAKE AHEAD:
Cookies can be prepared ahead of time. Store in refrigerator up 1 hour before serving.

BEST OF SEASON:
When fresh strawberries are in season, substitute them for the raspberries and blueberries.

almond crescents

PREP: 20 min. | TOTAL: 35 min. | MAKES: 4½ doz. or 54 servings, 1 cookie each.

▶ what you need!

2 cups butter, softened

1 cup powdered sugar

4 cups flour

1 cup ground PLANTERS Almonds

4 squares BAKER'S Semi-Sweet Chocolate, chopped

½ cup finely chopped pistachios

▶ make it!

HEAT oven to 350°F.

MIX butter and sugar in large bowl with wooden spoon until well blended. Gradually add flour, stirring after each addition until well blended. Stir in nuts.

SHAPE into 2-inch crescents, using 1 Tbsp. dough for each. Place, 2 inches apart, on parchment- or foil-covered baking sheets.

BAKE 12 to 15 min. or until lightly browned. Cool on baking sheets 2 min. Remove to wire racks; cool completely.

MELT chocolate as directed on package. Dip 1 end of each cookie in chocolate; top with pistachios. Return to wire racks; let stand until chocolate is firm.

quick lemon-blueberry cheese bars

PREP: 20 min. | TOTAL: 4 hours | MAKES: 30 servings, 1 bar each.

▶ what you need!

1 pkg. (2-layer size) lemon cake mix

½ cup MIRACLE WHIP Dressing

3 eggs, divided

2 pkg. (8 oz. each) PHILADELPHIA Cream Cheese, softened

1 cup powdered sugar

2 Tbsp. lemon juice

1 can (21 oz.) blueberry pie filling

▶ make it!

HEAT oven to 350°F.

MIX dry cake mix, dressing and 1 of the eggs until well blended; press firmly onto bottom of greased 13×9-inch baking pan.

BEAT cream cheese in small bowl with electric mixer on medium speed until creamy. Add remaining 2 eggs, the sugar and juice; mix well. Pour over crust.

BAKE 35 to 40 min. or until center is almost set and edges are lightly browned. Cool. Top with the pie filling. Refrigerate 3 hours or overnight. Cut into 30 bars to serve. Store leftover bars in refrigerator.

HOW TO SOFTEN CREAM CHEESE:
Place completely unwrapped package of cream cheese in microwaveable bowl. Microwave on HIGH 10 sec. or just until softened. Add 15 sec. for each additional package of cream cheese.

cappuccino bars

▶ what you need!

15 HONEY MAID Honey Grahams

2 pkg. (8 oz. each) PHILADELPHIA Cream Cheese, softened

3½ cups cold milk, divided

3 pkg. (3.9 oz. each) JELL-O Chocolate Instant Pudding

1 Tbsp. MAXWELL HOUSE Instant Coffee

¼ tsp. ground cinnamon

1 tub (8 oz.) COOL WHIP Whipped Topping, thawed, divided

1 square BAKER'S Semi-Sweet Chocolate, grated or 3 Tbsp. chocolate sprinkles

▶ make it!

ARRANGE half of the grahams in bottom of 13×9-inch pan, cutting grahams to fit if necessary.

BEAT cream cheese in large bowl with electric mixer on low speed until creamy. Gradually add 1 cup of the milk, beating until well blended. Add remaining 2½ cups milk, dry pudding mixes, coffee granules and cinnamon. Beat 1 to 2 min. or until well blended. (Mixture will be thick.) Gently stir in 2 cups COOL WHIP.

SPREAD half of the pudding mixture over grahams in pan; arrange remaining grahams over pudding. Cover with remaining pudding mixture; top with remaining COOL WHIP. Sprinkle with grated chocolate. Freeze 3 hours or overnight. Cut into 32 bars to serve. Store leftover bars in freezer.

SIZE-WISE:
Serve this easy frozen treat at your next celebration.

HOW TO THAW COOL WHIP:
Place unopened 8-oz. tub of whipped topping in the refrigerator for 4 hours. Do not thaw in the microwave.

big-batch kris kringle cookies

PREP: 20 min. | TOTAL: 31 min. | MAKES: 6 doz. or 72 servings, 1 cookie each.

▶ what you need!

1 cup butter, softened

1 cup granulated sugar

½ cup packed brown sugar

2 eggs

1 tsp. vanilla

2¼ cups flour

1 tsp. baking soda

½ tsp. salt

2 pkg. (6 squares each) BAKER'S White Chocolate, chopped

2 cups chopped PLANTERS Pecans, toasted

2 cups dried cranberries

▶ make it!

HEAT oven to 375°F.

BEAT butter and sugars in large bowl with mixer until light and fluffy. Blend in eggs and vanilla. Add flour, baking soda and salt; mix well. Stir in chocolate, nuts and cranberries.

DROP rounded tablespoonfuls of dough, 1½ inches apart, onto baking sheets.

BAKE 9 to 11 min. or until lightly browned. Cool on baking sheets 3 min.; remove to wire racks. Cool completely.

FREEZING COOKIE DOUGH:
Enjoy homemade cookies anytime by preparing and freezing cookie dough in advance.

CHIPS AHOY! sweetheart valentine's cookies

PREP: 30 min. | TOTAL: 30 min. | MAKES: 2 doz. or 24 servings.

▶ what you need!

24 CHIPS AHOY! Cookies

4 squares BAKER'S Semi-Sweet Chocolate, melted

Assorted decorations (colored sprinkles, colored sugars and assorted small candies)

Decorating icings or gels

▶ make it!

DIP bottoms of cookies in chocolate; place on waxed paper-covered baking sheets. Let stand until chocolate is firm.

ADD decorations, attaching to cookies with icings or remaining melted chocolate.

WRITE messages on cookies with icings.

HOW TO MAKE A COOKIE BOUQUET:
Make your cookies into a bouquet of flowers by attaching a lollipop stick or wooden pop stick to the back of each cookie when coating in melted chocolate. Let stand until chocolate is firm. Decorate with assorted candies, sprinkles or colored sugars and decorating icings to resemble flowers. Tie 2 or 3 cookie flowers together with a ribbon. Wrap in cellophane for gift-giving.

easy petit fours

PREP: 5 min. | TOTAL: 5 min. | MAKES: 12 servings.

▶ what you need!

¼ cup PHILADELPHIA Strawberry Cream Cheese Spread

12 OREO White Fudge Covered Cookies

6 strawberries, halved

1 square BAKER'S Semi-Sweet Chocolate, melted

▶ make it!

SPREAD 1 tsp. cream cheese onto each cookie. Top each with strawberry half.

DRIZZLE each strawberry-topped cookie with melted chocolate.

chocolate-dipped coconut macaroons

PREP: 15 min. | TOTAL: 1 hour 5 min. | MAKES: 3 doz. or 36 servings, 1 cookie each.

▶ what you need!

- 1 pkg. (14 oz.) BAKER'S ANGEL FLAKE Coconut
- ⅔ cup sugar
- 6 Tbsp. flour
- ¼ tsp. salt
- 4 egg whites, lightly beaten
- 1 tsp. almond extract
- 1 pkg. (8 squares) BAKER'S Semi-Sweet Chocolate

▶ make it!

HEAT oven to 325°F.

COMBINE coconut, sugar, flour and salt. Add egg whites and extract; mix well. Drop by tablespoonfuls, 2 inches apart, onto greased and floured baking sheets.

BAKE 20 min. or until edges are golden brown. Cool 3 min. on baking sheets; remove to wire racks. Cool completely.

MELT chocolate as directed on package. Dip cookies halfway into chocolate. Let stand until chocolate is firm.

SUBSTITUTE:
Prepare using 1 tub (7 oz.) BAKER'S Dark Semi-Sweet Dipping Chocolate.

chocolate-marshmallow haystacks

PREP: 30 min. | **TOTAL:** 3 hours 30 min. | **MAKES:** about 4 doz. or 24 servings, 2 haystacks each.

▶ what you need!

3 cups BAKER'S ANGEL FLAKE Coconut

3 oz. PHILADELPHIA Cream Cheese, softened

2 Tbsp. milk

2 cups powdered sugar

2 squares BAKER'S Unsweetened Chocolate, melted

¼ tsp. vanilla

⅛ tsp. salt

3 cups JET-PUFFED Miniature Marshmallows

▶ make it!

PLACE coconut in shallow dish or pie plate; set aside. Beat cream cheese and milk in large bowl with electric mixer on medium speed until well blended. Gradually add sugar, beating until well blended after each addition. Add chocolate, vanilla and salt; mix well. Gently stir in marshmallows.

DROP rounded teaspoonfuls of the cream cheese mixture into coconut; toss gently until evenly coated. Place on baking sheet.

REFRIGERATE several hours or until firm.

SIZE-WISE:
You are much more likely to be successful in improving you and your family's eating habits if you don't deprive anybody of the foods they love. So, give them their favorites, like these chocolate-marshmallow treats, adhering to the serving size.

STORAGE KNOW-HOW:
Store in airtight container in refrigerator.

coconut-fudge bars

PREP: 15 min. | TOTAL: 2 hours 30 min. | MAKES: 32 servings, 1 bar each.

► what you need!

1 cup butter or margarine, divided

14 HONEY MAID Honey Grahams, finely
crushed (about 2½ cups crumbs)

1 cup sugar

1 can (5 oz.) evaporated milk (about ⅔ cup)

1 pkg. (10½ oz.) JET-PUFFED Miniature
Marshmallows

1½ pkg. (12 squares) BAKER'S Semi-Sweet
Chocolate, coarsely chopped

1 cup chopped PLANTERS Walnuts

1 cup BAKER'S ANGEL FLAKE Coconut

► make it!

LINE 13×9-inch pan with foil, with ends of foil extending over sides of pan. Grease foil. Melt ¾ cup of the butter; mix with graham crumbs. Press firmly onto bottom of prepared pan. Set aside.

PLACE remaining ¼ cup butter, the sugar, evaporated milk and marshmallows in large saucepan; bring to boil on medium heat, stirring constantly. Boil 5 min., stirring constantly. Add chocolate; cook until completely melted, stirring frequently. Pour immediately over crust; spread to evenly cover bottom of crust.

SPRINKLE with nuts and coconut; press lightly into chocolate layer with back of spoon. Refrigerate 2 hours or until firm. Lift dessert from pan, using foil handles. Cut into 32 bars. Store in airtight container in refrigerator.

STORAGE KNOW-HOW:
Unopened packages of BAKER'S ANGEL FLAKE Coconut can be kept on your kitchen shelf. After opening the package, store the coconut in a tightly closed package or in an airtight container. Refrigerate or freeze coconut for up to 6 months.

crunch "bars"

▶ what you need!

35 PREMIUM Saltine Crackers

½ cup butter or margarine

½ cup packed brown sugar

1 pkg. (8 squares) BAKER'S Semi-Sweet Chocolate, chopped

1 cup chopped PLANTERS Walnuts, toasted

▶ make it!

HEAT oven to 400°F.

PLACE crackers in single layer in foil-lined 15×10×1-inch pan.

COOK butter and sugar in saucepan on medium-high heat until butter is melted and mixture is well blended, stirring occasionally. Bring to boil; cook 3 min. without stirring. Spread onto crackers.

BAKE 5 to 7 min. or until topping is golden brown. Immediately sprinkle with chopped chocolate; let stand 5 min. or until softened. Spread over crackers; top with nuts. Cool. Break into pieces.

SHORTCUT:
Use a food processor to quickly chop the walnuts.

snow-covered almond crescents

PREP: 20 min. | TOTAL: 1 hour 12 min. | MAKES: 5 doz. or 30 servings, 2 cookies each.

▶ what you need!

1 pkg. (8 oz.) PHILADELPHIA Cream Cheese, softened

¾ cup butter, softened

1 cup granulated sugar

2 tsp. vanilla

½ tsp. almond extract

2¼ cups flour

½ tsp. baking soda

1 cup finely chopped PLANTERS Slivered Almonds

¾ cup powdered sugar

▶ make it!

BEAT first 5 ingredients in large bowl with mixer until well blended. Add flour and baking soda; mix well. Stir in nuts. Refrigerate 30 min.

HEAT oven to 350°F. Roll dough into 60 (1-inch) balls; shape each into crescent shape. Place, 2 inches apart, on baking sheets. Flatten slightly.

BAKE 10 to 12 min. or until lightly browned. Cool 3 min. on baking sheets; transfer to wire racks. Cool completely; sprinkle with powdered sugar.

PECAN CRESCENTS:
Substitute finely chopped PLANTERS Pecans for the almonds.

easy pudding cookies

PREP: 15 min. | TOTAL: 27 min. | MAKES: about 3½ doz. or 42 servings, 1 cookie each.

▶ what you need!

- 1 cup butter or margarine, softened
- 1 cup packed brown sugar
- 1 pkg. (3.9 oz.) JELL-O Chocolate Instant Pudding
- 2 eggs
- 1 tsp. baking soda
- 2 cups flour
- 1 pkg. (6 squares) BAKER'S White Chocolate, chopped

▶ make it!

HEAT oven to 350°F.

BEAT butter and sugar in large bowl with mixer until light and fluffy. Add dry pudding mix; beat until well blended. Add eggs and baking soda; mix well. Gradually add flour, beating after each addition until well blended. Stir in chocolate.

DROP tablespoonfuls of dough, 2 inches apart, onto baking sheets.

BAKE 10 to 12 min. or until edges are lightly browned. Cool 1 min. on baking sheets; remove to wire racks. Cool completely.

VARIATION:
Prepare using your favorite brand of JELL-O Instant Pudding.

gingerbread people

PREP: 20 min. | TOTAL: 1 hour 32 min. | MAKES: 20 servings.

▶ what you need!

¾ cup butter, softened

¾ cup packed brown sugar

1 pkg. (3.4 oz.) JELL-O Butterscotch Instant Pudding

1 egg

2 cups flour

1 tsp. baking soda

1 Tbsp. ground ginger

1½ tsp. ground cinnamon

▶ make it!

HEAT oven to 350°F.

BEAT butter, sugar, dry pudding mix and egg in large bowl with mixer until well blended. Mix remaining ingredients. Gradually add to pudding mixture, beating well after each addition. Refrigerate 1 hour or until firm.

ROLL out dough on lightly floured surface to ¼-inch thickness. Cut into gingerbread shapes with 4-inch cookie cutter. Place, 2 inches apart, on greased baking sheets.

BAKE 10 to 12 min. or until edges are lightly browned. Let stand on baking sheets 3 min. Remove to wire racks; cool completely. Decorate as desired.

MAKE IT EASY:
To easily decorate these cookies, fill resealable plastic bag with prepared frosting. Seal bag and cut small corner off one of the bottom corners of bag. Roll down top of bag to squeeze frosting over cookies to decorate as desired.

golden caramel cheesecake bars

PREP: 15 min. | TOTAL: 5 hours 20 min. | MAKES: 20 servings, 1 bar each.

▶ what you need!

24 Golden OREO Cookies, divided

2 Tbsp. butter or margarine, melted

25 KRAFT Caramels (½ of 14-oz. bag)

1 Tbsp. water

2 pkg. (8 oz. each) PHILADELPHIA
   Cream Cheese, softened

1 jar (7 oz.) JET-PUFFED Marshmallow
   Creme

1 egg

▶ make it!

HEAT oven to 350°F.

PLACE 14 of the cookies in food processor container; cover. Process until finely crushed. Mix with butter; press firmly onto bottom of 9-inch square baking pan. Bake 10 min. or until golden brown. Cool 10 min.

PLACE caramels and water in microwaveable bowl. Microwave on HIGH 1 min. or until caramels are completely melted, stirring every 30 sec. Set aside. Coarsely chop remaining 10 cookies. Beat cream cheese and marshmallow creme in large bowl with electric mixer on medium speed until well blended. Add egg; mix well. Stir in chopped cookies; pour over crust. Drop spoonfuls of the caramel mixture over batter; swirl gently with knife for marble effect.

BAKE 20 to 25 min. or until center is set. Cool completely. Refrigerate 4 hours or overnight. Cut into 20 bars. Store in tightly covered container in refrigerator.

SIZE-WISE:
Enjoy a serving, 1 square, of this cool dessert on occasion.

lemon-coconut squares

PREP: 10 min. | **TOTAL:** 3 hours 40 min. | **MAKES:** 20 servings, 1 square each.

▶ what you need!

- 35 NILLA Wafers, finely crushed (about 1⅓ cups)
- 1 cup sugar, divided
- ¼ cup butter or margarine, melted
- 1 tsp. grated lemon zest
- 2 eggs
- ¼ cup lemon juice
- 2 Tbsp. flour
- ½ tsp. CALUMET Baking Powder
- ¼ tsp. salt
- ⅓ cup BAKER'S ANGEL FLAKE Coconut

▶ make it!

HEAT oven to 350°F.

MIX wafer crumbs, ¼ cup of the sugar, the butter and lemon zest until well blended. Press firmly into 8-inch square baking pan. Bake 8 min.

BEAT eggs and remaining ¾ cup sugar in small bowl with wire whisk until thickened and well blended. Add lemon juice, flour, baking powder and salt; mix well. Pour over crust; sprinkle with coconut.

BAKE 25 to 30 min. or until center is set and top is lightly browned. Cool completely. Cover and refrigerate several hours or until chilled before cutting to serve. Store in tightly covered container in refrigerator.

lemony white chocolate chunk biscotti

PREP: 20 min. | TOTAL: 1 hour 10 min. | MAKES: 3½ doz. or 21 servings, 2 biscotti each.

▶ what you need!

2 cups flour

1 tsp. CALUMET Baking Powder

½ tsp. salt

¼ cup butter or margarine, softened

1 cup sugar

2 Tbsp. lemon zest

2 eggs

1 tsp. lemon extract

4 squares BAKER'S White Chocolate, chopped

⅓ cup PLANTERS Sliced Almonds, toasted

▶ make it!

HEAT oven to 350°F.

SIFT together flour, baking powder and salt; set aside. Beat butter, sugar and lemon zest in separate large bowl with mixer until well blended. Add eggs, 1 at a time, beating well after each. Blend in extract. Gradually beat in flour mixture. Stir in chocolate and nuts.

DIVIDE dough in half; shape each half into 12×1-inch log on floured surface. Place on greased baking sheet.

BAKE 35 min. or until golden brown. Cool on baking sheet 10 min. Transfer to cutting board. Cut each log diagonally into 21 slices, using serrated knife. Return, cut-sides down, to baking sheet. Bake 5 min. or until crisp. Remove to wire racks; cool completely.

HOW TO TOAST NUTS:
Heat oven to 350°F. Spread nuts in single layer on baking sheet. Bake 5 to 7 min. or until lightly toasted.

NILLA peppermint cremes

PREP: 30 min. | TOTAL: 3 hours 30 min. | MAKES: 10 servings, 2 cookie sandwiches each.

▶ what you need!

- 4 squares BAKER'S White Chocolate
- 2 Tbsp. whipping cream
- 1½ tsp. butter or margarine
- 6 drops peppermint extract
- 40 NILLA Wafers
- 4 starlight mints, crushed

▶ make it!

MICROWAVE chocolate, cream and butter in microwaveable bowl on HIGH 1 to 1½ min. or until butter is melted, stirring after 1 min. Stir until chocolate is completely melted. Blend in extract.

REFRIGERATE 3 hours or until firm.

SHAPE 1 tsp. of the chocolate mixture into ½-inch ball; place between 2 wafers to form sandwich. Press together gently. Roll edge in crushed mints. Repeat to make 20 cookie sandwiches.

HOW TO DOUBLE RECIPE:
This recipe can be easily doubled to make enough for a party. Just prepare as directed, doubling the chocolate, cream, butter, wafers and mints, and using ⅛ tsp. extract.

HOW TO STORE PEPPERMINT CREMES:
Store in tightly covered container in refrigerator up to 2 days.

peanut butter cookie bars

PREP: 10 min. | TOTAL: 40 min. | MAKES: 32 servings, 1 bar each.

▶ what you need!

½ cup butter

24 NUTTER BUTTER Cookies, divided

1½ cups BAKER'S ANGEL FLAKE Coconut

1 can (14 oz.) sweetened condensed milk

1 cup BAKER'S Semi-Sweet Chocolate Chunks

▶ make it!

HEAT oven to 350°F.

MELT butter in oven in foil-lined 13×9-inch baking pan.

CRUSH 12 cookies; sprinkle over butter. Top with coconut and sweetened condensed milk. Coarsely chop remaining cookies; sprinkle over milk. Top with chocolate.

BAKE 25 to 30 min. or until lightly browned. Cool completely before cutting into bars.

strawberry NILLA nibbles

PREP: 5 min. | TOTAL: 5 min. | MAKES: 1 serving.

▶ what you need!

4 Reduced Fat NILLA Wafers

2 Tbsp. thawed COOL WHIP LITE Whipped Topping

2 fresh strawberries, halved

▶ make it!

PLACE wafers on small dessert plate.

TOP with COOL WHIP and berries.

SERVE immediately.

SUBSTITUTE:
Prepare as directed, using COOL WHIP FREE Whipped Topping.

peanut butter cookie cheesecake bars

PREP: 15 min. | TOTAL: 3 hours 55 min. | MAKES: 32 servings, 1 bar each.

▶ what you need!

32 NUTTER BUTTER Cookies, divided

2 Tbsp. butter or margarine, melted

4 pkg. (8 oz. each) PHILADELPHIA Cream Cheese, softened

1 cup sugar

1 tsp. vanilla

4 eggs

▶ make it!

HEAT oven to 350°F.

CHOP 16 of the cookies; set aside. Place remaining 16 cookies in food processor container; cover. Process 30 to 45 sec. or until finely ground. Add butter; mix well. Press firmly onto bottom of 13×9-inch baking pan.

BEAT cream cheese, sugar and vanilla with electric mixer on medium speed until well blended. Add eggs, 1 at a time, mixing on low speed after each addition just until blended. Gently stir in 1½ cups of the chopped cookies. Pour over crust. Sprinkle with remaining chopped cookies.

BAKE 40 min. or until center is almost set. Cool. Refrigerate 3 hours or overnight. Cut into 32 bars. Store in tightly covered container in refrigerator.

SUBSTITUTE:
Prepare as directed, using PHILADELPHIA Neufchâtel Cheese.

HOW TO EASILY REMOVE BARS FROM PAN:
Line pan with foil before pressing crumb mixture onto bottom of pan, extending ends of foil beyond sides of pan. Use foil as handles to easily remove cooled dessert from pan.

PHILADELPHIA
snowmen cookies

PREP: 20 min. | TOTAL: 41 min. | MAKES: 22 servings, 2 cookies each.

▶ what you need!

1 pkg. (8 oz.) PHILADELPHIA Cream Cheese, softened

1 cup powdered sugar

¾ cup butter or margarine

½ tsp. vanilla

2 cups flour

½ tsp. baking soda

Suggested decorations: decorating gels, colored sprinkles, nonpareils and miniature peanut butter cups (optional)

▶ make it!

HEAT oven to 325°F.

BEAT cream cheese, sugar, butter and vanilla with electric mixer on medium speed until well blended. Add flour and baking soda; mix well.

SHAPE dough into equal number of ½-inch and 1-inch diameter balls. (You should have about 44 of each size ball.) Using 1 small and 1 large ball for each snowman, place balls, slightly overlapping on ungreased baking sheet. Flatten to ¾-inch thickness with bottom of glass dipped in additional flour. Repeat with remaining dough.

BAKE 19 to 21 min. or until lightly browned. Cool on wire rack. Decorate as desired.

SIZE-WISE:
A serving of these cookies along with a glass of low-fat milk is sure to be a hit as an after-school snack for your kids.

JAZZ IT UP:
Decorate with decorating gels, colored sprinkles and nonparells to resemble snowmen. Cut peanut butter cups in half. Place 1 candy half on top of each snowman for hat.

praline bars

PREP: 15 min. | TOTAL: 4 hours 8 min. | MAKES: 32 servings, 1 bar each.

▶ what you need!

- ¾ cup butter or margarine, softened
- 1 cup sugar, divided
- 1 tsp. vanilla, divided
- 1½ cups flour
- 2 pkg. (8 oz. each) PHILADELPHIA Cream Cheese, softened
- 2 eggs
- ½ cup toffee bits
- 3 Tbsp. caramel ice cream topping

▶ make it!

HEAT oven to 350°F.

BEAT butter, ½ cup of the sugar and ½ tsp. of the vanilla in large bowl with electric mixer on medium speed until light and fluffy. Gradually add flour, beating on low speed after each addition until well blended. Press firmly onto bottom of 13×9-inch baking pan. Bake 20 to 23 min. or until lightly browned.

BEAT cream cheese, remaining ½ cup sugar and remaining ½ tsp. vanilla in large bowl with electric mixer on medium speed until well blended. Add eggs; mix well. Stir in toffee bits. Pour over crust. Drop teaspoonfuls of the caramel topping evenly over cream cheese mixture. Cut through batter several times with knife for marble effect.

BAKE 30 min. or until center is almost set. Cool completely. Refrigerate several hours or until chilled. Cut into 32 bars to serve. Store leftover bars in tightly covered container in refrigerator.

SIZE-WISE:
Enjoy your favorite foods while keeping portion size in mind.

soft & chewy chocolate drops

PREP: 20 min. | TOTAL: 1 hour 20 min. | MAKES: about 5 doz. or 30 servings, 2 cookies each.

▶ what you need!

- 4 squares BAKER'S Unsweetened Chocolate
- ¾ cup butter (margarine: see below)
- 2 cups sugar
- 3 eggs
- 1 tsp. vanilla
- 2 cups flour
- 1 tub (8 oz.) COOL WHIP Whipped Topping (Do not thaw.)
- 6 squares BAKER'S Semi-Sweet Baking Chocolate

▶ make it!

HEAT oven to 350°F.

MICROWAVE unsweetened chocolate and butter in large microwaveable bowl on HIGH 2 min. or until butter is melted. Stir until chocolate is completely melted. Add sugar; mix well. Blend in eggs and vanilla. Add flour; mix well. Refrigerate 1 hour or until dough is easy to handle.

SHAPE dough into 1-inch balls; place, 2 inches apart, on greased baking sheets.

BAKE 8 min. or just until set. (Do not overbake.) Let stand on baking sheet 1 min.; transfer to wire racks. Cool completely.

PLACE COOL WHIP and semi-sweet chocolate in microwaveable bowl. Microwave on HIGH 1½ min. or until chocolate is completely melted and mixture is shiny and smooth, stirring after 1 min. Let stand 15 min. to thicken. Spread over cookies. Let stand until firm.

TIP:
For best results, use butter. If using margarine, add an additional ½ cup flour.

rugelach

PREP: 1 hour | TOTAL: 25 hours 25 min. | MAKES: about 5 doz. or 32 servings.

▶ what you need!

1 pkg. (8 oz.) PHILADELPHIA Cream Cheese, softened

1 cup butter or margarine, divided

2¼ cups flour

1 cup finely chopped PLANTERS Walnuts

½ cup plus 2 Tbsp. sugar, divided

1 Tbsp. ground cinnamon, divided

¼ cup raspberry preserves

▶ make it!

BEAT cream cheese and butter in large bowl with mixer until well blended. Gradually add flour, mixing well after each addition. (Dough will be very soft and sticky.) Divide dough into 4 portions; place each on sheet of plastic wrap. Use floured hands to pat each portion into 1-inch-thick round. Wrap individually in plastic wrap. Refrigerate overnight.

HEAT oven to 325°F. Cover baking sheets with foil or parchment paper. Mix nuts, ½ cup sugar and 2 tsp. cinnamon. Roll each portion of dough to 11-inch circle on lightly floured surface; spread each with 1 Tbsp. preserves.

SPRINKLE nut mixture over preserves. Cut each circle into 16 wedges. Roll up each wedge, starting from the wide side. Place, point-sides down, on prepared baking sheets; shape into crescents. Sprinkle with combined remaining cinnamon and sugar.

BAKE 25 min. or until lightly brown. Immediately remove from baking sheets to wire racks; cool completely.

SUBSTITUTE:
Substitute PLANTERS Pecans for the walnuts and/or apricot preserves for the raspberry preserves.

BAKER'S ONE BOWL
chocolate bliss cookies

PREP: 15 min. | TOTAL: 28 min. | MAKES: 2½ doz. cookies or 30 servings, 1 cookie each.

▶ what you need!

2 pkg. (8 squares each) BAKER'S Semi-Sweet Chocolate, divided

¾ cup firmly packed brown sugar

¼ cup butter, slightly softened

2 eggs

1 tsp. vanilla

½ cup flour

¼ tsp. CALUMET Baking Powder

2 cups chopped PLANTERS Walnuts

▶ make it!

HEAT oven to 350°F.

COARSELY chop 8 of the chocolate squares; set aside. Microwave remaining 8 chocolate squares in large microwaveable bowl on HIGH 2 min., stirring after 1 min. Stir until chocolate is completely melted. Add brown sugar, butter, eggs and vanilla; stir until well blended. Add flour and baking powder; mix well. Stir in chopped chocolate and nuts. (Note: If omitting nuts, increase flour to ¾ cup to prevent excessive spreading of cookies as they bake.)

DROP rounded tablespoonfuls of dough, 2 inches apart, onto ungreased baking sheets.

BAKE 12 to 13 min. or until cookies are puffed and shiny. Cool 1 min.; remove from baking sheets to wire racks. Cool completely.

NO-BAKE DELIGHTS

cappuccino dessert

PREP: 10 min. | TOTAL: 1 hour 10 min. | MAKES: 5 servings.

▶ what you need!

1 pkg. (1 oz.) JELL-O Vanilla Flavor Fat Free Sugar Free Instant Pudding

2 tsp. MAXWELL HOUSE Instant Coffee

2 cups cold fat-free milk

⅛ tsp. ground cinnamon

1 cup thawed COOL WHIP LITE Whipped Topping

▶ make it!

BEAT dry pudding mix , coffee granules and milk with whisk 2 min; pour into 5 dessert dishes.

REFRIGERATE 1 hour.

STIR cinnamon into COOL WHIP with whisk. Spoon over pudding.

awesome sundae pie

PREP: 20 min. | TOTAL: 3 hours 20 min. | MAKES: 8 servings.

▶ what you need!

6 squares BAKER'S Semi-Sweet Chocolate

1 Tbsp. butter or margarine

¾ cup finely chopped PLANTERS Pecans, toasted

¾ cup BAKER'S ANGEL FLAKE Coconut

1 qt. (4 cups) ice cream, any flavor, softened

1 cup thawed COOL WHIP Whipped Topping

3 maraschino cherries

▶ make it!

LINE 9-inch pie plate with foil; lightly grease foil. Microwave chocolate and butter in large microwaveable bowl on HIGH 1½ min. or until butter is melted, stirring after 1 min. Stir until chocolate is completely melted. Stir in nuts and coconut. Spread evenly onto bottom and up side of prepared pie plate.

REFRIGERATE 1 hour or until firm. Lift crust out of pie plate. Carefully peel off foil. Return crust to pie plate or place on serving plate. Fill with scoops of the ice cream; cover.

FREEZE 2 hours or until firm. Top with COOL WHIP and cherries just before serving. Store leftover pie in freezer.

TIP:
Before serving, remove pie from freezer. Let stand at room temperature 10 min. to allow pie to soften slightly for easier cutting.

caramel apple dessert

PREP: 15 min. | TOTAL: 5 hours 15 min. | MAKES: 16 servings.

▶ what you need!

60 NILLA Wafers, finely crushed (about 2 cups)

⅓ cup butter, melted

1 pkg. (8 oz.) PHILADELPHIA Cream Cheese, softened

¼ cup sugar

3¼ cups milk, divided

1 tub (8 oz.) COOL WHIP Whipped Topping, thawed, divided

2 pkg. (3.4 oz. each) JELL-O Vanilla Flavor Instant Pudding

½ cup caramel ice cream topping, divided

1 each red and green apple, chopped

¼ cup PLANTERS COCKTAIL Peanuts, chopped

▶ make it!

MIX wafer crumbs and butter; press onto bottom of 13×9-inch pan. Beat cream cheese, sugar and ¼ cup milk with mixer until well blended. Stir in 1 cup COOL WHIP; spread over crust.

BEAT dry pudding mixes and remaining milk with whisk 2 min. Stir in ¼ cup caramel topping. Spoon over cream cheese layer; top with remaining COOL WHIP.

REFRIGERATE 5 hours or until firm. Top with apples, nuts and remaining caramel topping just before serving.

KEEP APPLES FROM TURNING BROWN:
After cutting the apples, minimize browning by dipping them in 1 cup water mixed with 1 Tbsp. lemon juice before adding to dessert.

chocolate & peanut butter ribbon dessert

PREP: 15 min. | TOTAL: 4 hours 15 min. | MAKES: 12 servings.

▶ what you need!

12 NUTTER BUTTER Cookies, divided

2 Tbsp. butter, melted

1 pkg. (8 oz.) PHILADELPHIA Cream Cheese, softened

½ cup PLANTERS Creamy Peanut Butter

½ cup sugar

2 tsp. vanilla

1 tub (12 oz.) COOL WHIP Whipped Topping, thawed, divided

2 squares BAKER'S Semi-Sweet Chocolate, melted

▶ make it!

CRUSH 8 cookies; mix cookie crumbs and butter. Press onto bottom of foil-lined 9×5-inch loaf pan.

MIX next 4 ingredients with mixer until well blended. Whisk in 3 cups COOL WHIP. Spoon ½ cup into small bowl. Blend in melted chocolate. Spoon half the remaining cream cheese mixture over crust. Top evenly with chocolate mixture and remaining cream cheese mixture.

FREEZE 4 hours or until firm. Invert onto plate. Remove foil, then re-invert onto serving platter so that crumb layer is on bottom. Coarsely break the remaining cookies. Top dessert with remaining COOL WHIP and cookies.

HOW TO DOUBLE THE RECIPE:
Line 13×9-inch pan with foil, with ends of foil extending over sides of pan; set aside. Prepare recipe as directed, using the 1 tub (12 oz.) COOL WHIP but increasing the vanilla to 1 Tbsp. and doubling all remaining ingredients. Do not invert dessert to remove from pan but lift dessert from pan using foil handles. Cut into bars to serve. Makes 24 servings, 1 bar each.

MAKE AHEAD:
Dessert can be frozen overnight before unmolding and serving as directed.

CHIPS AHOY! ice cream cake

PREP: 30 min. | TOTAL: 4 hours 45 min. | MAKES: 12 servings.

▶ what you need!

1 pkg. (15.25 oz.) CHIPS AHOY! Cookies (39 cookies), divided

¼ cup butter or margarine, melted

¾ cup hot fudge ice cream topping, divided

3 cups vanilla ice cream, divided

3 cups chocolate ice cream, divided

¾ cup thawed COOL WHIP Whipped Topping

7 maraschino cherries

▶ make it!

SET aside 12 cookies. Crush remaining cookies; mix with butter. Press ⅔ onto bottom of 9-inch springform pan. Stand reserved cookies around edge. Microwave ½ cup fudge topping as directed on package; drizzle over crust. Freeze 15 min.

SOFTEN 1½ cups of <u>each</u> flavor ice cream; spread, 1 flavor at a time, over fudge layer in crust. Sprinkle with remaining crumb mixture. Scoop remaining ice cream into balls; place over crumb layer.

FREEZE 4 hours or until firm. When ready to serve, top dessert with COOL WHIP. Microwave remaining fudge topping as directed on package; drizzle over dessert. Garnish with cherries.

NOTE:
If you don't have a springform pan, you can prepare dessert in 9-inch pie plate instead.

tropical strawberry cream pie

PREP: 15 min. | TOTAL: 4 hours 20 min. | MAKES: 8 servings.

▶ what you need!

42 NILLA Wafers, divided

3 Tbsp. butter or margarine, melted

1 pkg. (8 oz.) PHILADELPHIA Cream Cheese, softened

¼ cup sugar

2 cups thawed COOL WHIP Whipped Topping, divided

1 can (8 oz.) crushed pineapple, drained

¾ cup boiling water

1 pkg. (3 oz.) JELL-O Strawberry Flavor Gelatin

1 cup ice cubes

2 cups sliced strawberries

▶ make it!

CRUSH 26 wafers; mix with butter until well blended. Press onto bottom of 9-inch pie plate. Stand remaining wafers around edge of pie plate.

BEAT cream cheese and sugar in large bowl with mixer until well blended. Gently stir in 1 cup COOL WHIP and pineapple; spread over crust.

ADD boiling water to dry gelatin mix in medium bowl; stir 2 min. until completely dissolved. Stir in ice until melted. Add strawberries; stir. Refrigerate 5 min. or until slightly thickened; spoon over cream cheese layer. Refrigerate 4 hours or until set. Top with remaining COOL WHIP, if desired.

CHIPS AHOY! wiches

PREP: 20 min. | TOTAL: 2 hours 20 min. | MAKES: 1 doz. or 12 servings.

▶ what you need!

3 cups vanilla ice cream, slightly softened

24 CHIP AHOY! Cookies

¾ cup sprinkles

▶ make it!

SPREAD ¼ cup ice cream onto flat side of each of 12 cookies. Cover with remaining cookies to make 12 sandwiches.

ROLL edges in sprinkles.

FREEZE 1 to 2 hours or until firm.

VARIATION:
Prepare using your favorite flavor of ice cream, sherbet or frozen yogurt. In addition, roll edges in chopped PLANTERS Nuts, colored sprinkles, chocolate chips or toasted BAKER'S ANGEL FLAKE Coconut instead of the sprinkles.

"cookie dough" ice cream

PREP: 5 min. | TOTAL: 5 min. | MAKES: 4 servings.

▶ what you need!

2 cups vanilla ice cream, softened

8 CHIPS AHOY! Cookies, crumbled

▶ make it!

MIX ingredients until well blended.

SERVE immediately.

SPECIAL EXTRA:
Garnish each serving with an additional CHIPS AHOY! Cookie, if desired.

NUTTER BUTTER frozen peanut butter pie

PREP: 15 min. | TOTAL: 4 hours 45 min. | MAKES: 12 servings.

► what you need!

24 NUTTER BUTTER Cookies, finely crushed

 5 Tbsp. butter, melted

 1 pkg. (8 oz.) PHILADELPHIA Cream Cheese, softened

 1 cup PLANTERS Creamy Peanut Butter

¾ cup sugar

 1 Tbsp. vanilla

 1 tub (8 oz.) COOL WHIP Whipped Topping, thawed, divided

► make it!

MIX cookie crumbs and butter; press onto bottom and up side of 9-inch pie plate.

BEAT next 4 ingredients in medium bowl with mixer until blended. Stir in 1½ cups COOL WHIP; spoon into crust.

FREEZE 4 hours or until firm. Remove from freezer 30 min. before serving. Let stand at room temperature to soften slightly. Top with remaining COOL WHIP.

SUBSTITUTE:
Substitute 1 HONEY MAID Graham Pie Crust (6 oz.) for the homemade crumb crust.

HOW TO EASILY CRUSH COOKIES:
Crush cookies in resealable plastic bag with rolling pin or in food processor.

OREO & fudge ice cream cake

PREP: 10 min. | TOTAL: 4 hours 10 min. | MAKES: 12 servings.

▶ what you need!

½ cup hot fudge ice cream topping, warmed

1 tub (8 oz.) COOL WHIP Whipped Topping, thawed, divided

1 pkg. (3.9 oz.) JELL-O Chocolate Instant Pudding

16 OREO Cookies, chopped (about 2 cups), divided

12 vanilla ice cream sandwiches

▶ make it!

POUR fudge topping into medium bowl. Whisk in 1 cup COOL WHIP. Add dry pudding mix; stir 2 min. Stir in 1 cup chopped cookies.

ARRANGE 4 ice cream sandwiches, side-by-side, on 24-inch-long piece of foil; top with half the COOL WHIP mixture. Repeat layers. Top with remaining sandwiches. Frost top and sides with remaining COOL WHIP; press remaining chopped cookies into COOL WHIP on top and sides of cake. Bring up foil sides; double fold top and ends to loosely seal packet.

FREEZE 4 hours.

NOTE:
The consistency of fudge topping can vary depending on what brand you purchase. If your fudge topping mixture is too thick to spread easily, stir in up to ¼ cup milk.

chocolate-layered no-bake cheesecake bars

PREP: 15 min. | TOTAL: 3 hours 15 min. | MAKES: 16 servings, 1 bar each.

▶ what you need!

1½ cups HONEY MAID Graham Cracker Crumbs

¼ cup butter, melted

2 Tbsp. sugar

1 pkg. (8 squares) BAKER'S Semi-Sweet Chocolate, divided

4 pkg. (8 oz. each) PHILADELPHIA Cream Cheese, softened

½ cup sugar

1 tsp. vanilla

1 tub (8 oz.) COOL WHIP Whipped Topping, thawed

▶ make it!

LINE 13×9-inch pan with foil, with ends of foil extending over sides of pan. Mix graham crumbs, butter and 2 Tbsp. sugar. Press firmly onto bottom of prepared pan. Refrigerate while preparing filling.

MICROWAVE 6 of the chocolate squares in microwaveable bowl on HIGH 1 min.; stir until chocolate is completely melted. Cool slightly. Beat cream cheese, ½ cup sugar and the vanilla in large bowl with electric mixer on medium speed until well blended. Gently stir in COOL WHIP. Pour half of the batter into medium bowl; stir in melted chocolate. Pour over crust; cover with remaining plain batter.

MELT remaining 2 chocolate squares as directed on package; drizzle over batter. Refrigerate 3 hours or until firm. Using foil handles, remove cheesecake from pan; cut into bars. Store in tightly covered container in refrigerator.

HOW TO NEATLY CUT DESSERT BARS:
When cutting creamy-textured bars, such as cheesecake bars, carefully wipe off the knife blade between cuts with a clean damp towel. This prevents the creamy filling from building up on the blade, ensuring clean cuts that leave the edges intact.

frosty orange creme layered dessert

PREP: 15 min. | TOTAL: 3 hours 15 min. | MAKES: 12 servings.

▶ what you need!

- 2 cups orange sherbet, softened
- 1 pkg. (8 oz.) PHILADELPHIA Cream Cheese, softened
- 1 can (14 oz.) sweetened condensed milk
- ½ cup orange juice
- 1 tub (8 oz.) COOL WHIP Whipped Topping, thawed

▶ make it!

LINE 9×5-inch loaf pan with foil. Spread sherbet onto bottom of prepared pan to form even layer. Freeze 10 min.

MEANWHILE, beat cream cheese in large bowl with mixer until creamy. Gradually add sweetened condensed milk and juice, beating until blended. Stir in COOL WHIP; spread over sherbet in pan.

FREEZE 3 hours. To unmold, invert pan onto plate; remove foil.

SPECIAL EXTRA:
Top with 1 cup fresh berries just before serving.

HOW TO EASILY CUT DESSERT:
Remove from freezer about 10 min. before serving to soften slightly before slicing.

frozen grasshopper squares

PREP: 15 min. | TOTAL: 3 hours 15 min. | MAKES: 16 servings.

▶ what you need!

28 OREO Cookies, divided

6 cups chocolate chip-mint ice cream, softened

1 tub (8 oz.) COOL WHIP Whipped Topping, thawed

1 square BAKER'S Semi-Sweet Chocolate, grated

▶ make it!

LINE 13×9-inch pan with foil, with ends of foil extending over sides. Crush 20 cookies; sprinkle crumbs onto bottom of prepared pan.

SPREAD ice cream evenly over crumbs in pan; top with COOL WHIP and grated chocolate.

FREEZE 3 hours. Remove from freezer 15 min. before serving. Let stand at room temperature to soften slightly. Lift dessert from pan with foil handles; cut into 16 squares. Cut remaining cookies in half; place 1 on each square.

HOW TO MAKE MESS-FREE COOKIE CRUMBS:
Crushing cookies into crumbs can be a messy task. To keep the crumbs contained, place the whole cookies in a resealable plastic bag. Squeeze the air from the bag, then seal the bag. Run a rolling pin back and forth over the cookies until finely crushed.

frozen lemonade squares

PREP: 20 min. | TOTAL: 4 hours 20 min. | MAKES: 9 servings.

▶ what you need!

9 HONEY MAID Low Fat Honey Grahams, finely crushed (about 1¼ cups)

⅓ cup margarine or butter, melted

4 cups frozen vanilla yogurt, softened

6 oz. (½ of 12-oz. can) frozen lemonade concentrate, thawed

½ cup thawed COOL WHIP LITE Whipped Topping

▶ make it!

MIX graham crumbs and margarine; press onto bottom of 9-inch square pan.

BEAT yogurt and concentrate with mixer until well blended; spread over crust.

FREEZE 4 hours or until firm. Serve topped with COOL WHIP.

SPECIAL EXTRA:
Garnish with fresh mint sprigs and lemon slices or lemon zest.

JELL-O magic mousse

PREP: 10 min. | TOTAL: 8 hours 10 min. | MAKES: 10 servings, about ½ cup each.

▶ what you need!

3 cups boiling water

1 pkg. (6 oz.) JELL-O Gelatin, any red flavor

1 tub (16 oz.) COOL WHIP Whipped Topping, thawed, divided

▶ make it!

STIR boiling water to dry gelatin mix in medium bowl; stir 2 min. until completely dissolved. Reserve 1 cup COOL WHIP; refrigerate. Whisk remaining COOL WHIP into gelatin until well blended. (Mixture will be thin.)

POUR into 1½-qt glass bowl or 10 glasses.

REFRIGERATE at least 8 hours or until firm. Top with the reserved COOL WHIP just before serving.

SUBSTITUTE:
Prepare as directed, using any flavor JELL-O Gelatin.

banana pudding squares

▶ what you need!

35 Reduced Fat NILLA Wafers, finely crushed (about 1¼ cups)

¼ cup margarine, melted

1 pkg. (8 oz.) PHILADELPHIA Neufchâtel Cheese, softened

½ cup powdered sugar

1 tub (8 oz.) COOL WHIP Sugar Free Whipped Topping, thawed, divided

3 bananas, sliced

2 pkg. (1 oz. each) JELL-O Vanilla Flavor Fat Free Sugar Free Instant Pudding

3 cups cold fat-free milk

½ square BAKER'S Semi-Sweet Chocolate, grated

▶ make it!

MIX wafer crumbs and margarine; press onto bottom of 13×9-inch dish. Refrigerate.

BEAT Neufchâtel and sugar in medium bowl with whisk until blended. Stir in 1½ cups COOL WHIP; spread over crust. Top with bananas.

BEAT dry pudding mixes and milk with whisk 2 min.; spread over bananas. Top with remaining COOL WHIP and chocolate. Refrigerate 3 hours.

MAKEOVER—HOW WE DID IT:
We've made over this favorite dessert to save you 80 calories and 13 grams of fat per serving compared to the traditional recipe. We used Reduced Fat NILLA Wafers and margarine instead of flour, butter and peanuts for the crust. In addition, we cut the amount of sugar and chocolate in half and used better-for-you products in the creamy layers. These simple changes result in a great-tasting dessert that can save you both fat and calories!

no-oven peanut butter squares

PREP: 10 min. | TOTAL: 1 hour 10 min. | MAKES: 24 servings, 2 squares each.

▶ what you need!

½ cup butter or margarine

2 cups powdered sugar

1½ cups NABISCO Graham Cracker Crumbs

1 cup PLANTERS Creamy Peanut Butter

1½ pkg. (8 squares each) BAKER'S Semi-Sweet Chocolate (12 squares), melted

▶ make it!

LINE 13×9-inch baking pan with foil, with ends of foil extending over sides of pan. Set aside.

MELT butter in large microwaveable bowl on HIGH 45 sec. Add next 3 ingredients; mix well. Spread into prepared pan; cover with chocolate.

CUT partially through dessert to mark 48 squares. Refrigerate 1 hour or until firm. Use foil handles to remove from pan; cut into squares.

HOW TO MAKE THICKER SQUARES:
Reduce chocolate to 1 pkg. (8 squares). Prepare recipe as directed, using 9-inch square pan. Cut into 24 squares to serve. Makes 24 servings, 1 square each.

peanut butter cup pie

PREP: 15 min. | TOTAL: 4 hours 30 min. | MAKES: 10 servings.

▶ what you need!

- 1 pkg. (8 oz.) PHILADELPHIA Cream Cheese, softened
- ½ cup plus 1 Tbsp. PLANTERS Creamy Peanut Butter, divided
- 1 cup cold milk
- 1 pkg. (3.4 oz.) JELL-O Vanilla Flavor Instant Pudding
- 2½ cups thawed COOL WHIP Whipped Topping, divided
- 1 OREO Pie Crust (6 oz.)
- 3 squares BAKER'S Semi-Sweet Chocolate

▶ make it!

BEAT cream cheese and ½ cup peanut butter until well blended. Add milk and dry pudding mix; beat 2 min. Whisk in 1 cup COOL WHIP; spoon into crust. Refrigerate until ready to use.

MEANWHILE, microwave remaining COOL WHIP and chocolate in microwaveable bowl on HIGH 1½ to 2 min. or until chocolate is completely melted and mixture is well blended, stirring after each min. Cool completely.

SPREAD chocolate mixture over pudding layer in crust. Microwave remaining peanut butter in small microwaveable bowl 30 sec.; stir. Drizzle over pie. Refrigerate 4 hours or until firm.

SUBSTITUTE:
Prepare using JELL-O Chocolate Instant Pudding.

peanut butter cup squares

PREP: 15 min. | TOTAL: 4 hours 30 min. | MAKES: 16 servings.

▶ what you need!

25 NUTTER BUTTER Cookies, divided

¼ cup butter or margarine, melted

1 pkg. (8 oz.) PHILADELPHIA Cream Cheese, softened

½ cup PLANTERS Creamy Peanut Butter

1 cup cold milk

1 pkg. (3.4 oz.) JELL-O Vanilla Flavor Instant Pudding

2½ cups thawed COOL WHIP Whipped Topping, divided

3 squares BAKER'S Semi-Sweet Chocolate

▶ make it!

LINE 9-inch square pan with foil, with ends of foil extending over sides. Finely crush 24 cookies. Mix with butter; press onto bottom of prepared pan.

BEAT cream cheese and peanut butter in medium bowl with whisk until well blended. Add milk and dry pudding mix; beat 2 min. Stir in 1 cup COOL WHIP; spoon over crust. Refrigerate until ready to use.

MICROWAVE remaining COOL WHIP and chocolate in microwaveable bowl on HIGH 1½ to 2 min. or until chocolate is completely melted and mixture is well blended, stirring after each min. Cool completely.

SPREAD chocolate mixture over pudding layer in pan. Chop remaining cookie; sprinkle over chocolate mixture. Refrigerate 4 hours or until firm. Use foil handles to lift dessert from pan before cutting to serve.

NILLA yogurt freeze

PREP: 5 min. | TOTAL: 1 hour 5 min. | MAKES: 1 serving.

▶ what you need!

2 Reduced Fat NILLA Wafers

2 Tbsp. thawed COOL WHIP LITE Whipped Topping

2 Tbsp. strawberry low-fat yogurt

▶ make it!

PLACE 1 wafer in paper-lined medium muffin cup; cover with combined COOL WHIP and yogurt.

TOP with remaining wafer.

FREEZE 1 hour or until firm.

SUBSTITUTE:
Prepare using your favorite flavor of yogurt.

CHEESECAKES

PHILADELPHIA
no-bake mini cheesecakes

PREP: 10 min. | TOTAL: 10 min. | MAKES: 12 servings.

▶ what you need!

1 pkg. (8 oz.) PHILADELPHIA Cream Cheese, softened

½ cup sugar

1 tub (8 oz.) COOL WHIP Whipped Topping, thawed

12 OREO Cookies

Multi-colored sprinkles

▶ make it!

BEAT cream cheese and sugar until well blended. Gently stir in COOL WHIP.

PLACE cookies on bottom of 12 paper-lined muffin cups.

SPOON cream cheese mixture into muffin cups. Top with multi-colored sprinkles. Refrigerate until ready to serve.

SUBSTITUTE:
Substitute miniature chocolate chips for sprinkles.

boston cream cheesecake

PREP: 25 min. | TOTAL: 5 hours 20 min. | MAKES: 12 servings.

▶ what you need!

1 pkg. (1-layer size) yellow cake mix

2 pkg. (8 oz. each) PHILADELPHIA Cream Cheese, softened

½ cup granulated sugar

2 tsp. vanilla, divided

2 eggs

⅓ cup BREAKSTONE'S or KNUDSEN Sour Cream

2 squares BAKER'S Unsweetened Chocolate

3 Tbsp. butter or margarine

2 Tbsp. boiling water

1 cup powdered sugar

▶ make it!

HEAT oven to 350°F.

GREASE bottom of 9-inch springform pan. Prepare cake mix as directed on package; pour batter evenly into prepared springform pan. Bake 20 min. Beat cream cheese, granulated sugar and 1 tsp. of the vanilla with electric mixer on medium speed until well blended. Add eggs, 1 at a time, mixing on low speed after each addition just until blended. Blend in sour cream; pour over cake layer.

BAKE an additional 35 min. or until center is almost set. Run knife or metal spatula around rim of pan to loosen cake; cool before removing rim of pan.

MELT chocolate and butter in medium saucepan over low heat, stirring until smooth. Remove from heat. Add water, powdered sugar and remaining 1 tsp. vanilla; mix well. Spread over cooled cheesecake. Refrigerate 4 hours or overnight.

cappuccino cheesecake

PREP: 25 min. | TOTAL: 6 hours 35 min. | MAKES: 16 servings.

▶ what you need!

1½ cups finely chopped PLANTERS Walnuts

3 Tbsp. butter or margarine, melted

2 Tbsp. sugar

4 pkg. (8 oz. each) PHILADELPHIA Cream Cheese, softened

1 cup sugar

3 Tbsp. flour

4 eggs

1 cup BREAKSTONE'S or KNUDSEN Sour Cream

1 Tbsp. MAXWELL HOUSE Instant Coffee

¼ tsp. ground cinnamon

¼ cup boiling water

1½ cups thawed COOL WHIP Whipped Topping

▶ make it!

HEAT oven to 325°F.

MIX nuts, butter and 2 Tbsp. sugar; press onto bottom of 9-inch springform pan. Bake 10 min. Remove from oven; cool. Increase oven temperature to 450°F.

BEAT cream cheese, 1 cup sugar and flour with mixer until well blended. Add eggs, 1 at a time, mixing on low speed after each just until blended. Blend in sour cream.

DISSOLVE instant coffee with cinnamon in water; cool. Gradually add to cream cheese mixture, mixing until well blended. Pour over crust.

BAKE 10 min. Reduce oven temperature to 250°F. Bake an additional 1 hour or until center is almost set. Run knife around rim of pan to loosen cake; cool before removing rim. Refrigerate 4 hours. Top with dollops of COOL WHIP. Garnish with a sprinkle of additional cinnamon, if desired.

NOTE:
Reduce oven temperature to 300°F if using a dark nonstick springform pan.

white chocolate-cranberry cheesecake

PREP: 15 min. | TOTAL: 5 hours 5 min. | MAKES: 12 servings.

▶ what you need!

15 OREO Cookies, finely crushed (about 1¼ cups)

¼ cup butter, melted

3 pkg. (8 oz. each) PHILADELPHIA Cream Cheese, softened

¾ cup sugar

3 eggs

4 squares BAKER'S White Chocolate, melted

½ cup dried cranberries

1 tsp. grated orange zest

▶ make it!

HEAT oven to 350°F.

MIX cookie crumbs and butter. Press firmly onto bottom of 9-inch springform pan.

BEAT cream cheese and sugar in large bowl with electric mixer on medium speed until well blended. Add eggs, 1 at a time, mixing just until blended after each addition. Stir in white chocolate, cranberries and orange zest; pour over crust.

BAKE 45 to 50 min. or until center is almost set if using a silver springform pan. (Or, bake at 325°F for 45 to 50 min. if using a dark nonstick springform pan.) Cool completely. Refrigerate 3 hours or overnight.

SPECIAL EXTRA:
Garnish with thawed COOL WHIP Whipped Topping, orange slices and additional dried cranberries just before serving.

chocolate chunk cheesecake

PREP: 10 min. | TOTAL: 4 hours 45 min. | MAKES: 16 servings.

▶ what you need!

18 OREO Cookies, crushed (about 1½ cups)

¼ cup butter, melted

3 pkg. (8 oz. each) PHILADELPHIA Cream Cheese, softened

¾ cup sugar

½ cup BREAKSTONE'S or KNUDSEN Sour Cream

3 eggs

12 squares (1½ pkg.) BAKER'S Semi-Sweet Chocolate, divided

½ cup whipping cream

▶ make it!

HEAT oven to 350°F.

MIX cookie crumbs and butter; press onto bottom of 9-inch springform pan.

BEAT cream cheese and sugar in large bowl with mixer until well blended. Add sour cream; mix well. Add eggs, 1 at a time, beating on low speed after each just until blended. Chop 8 chocolate squares; stir into batter. Pour over crust.

BAKE 45 to 50 min. or until center is almost set. Run knife around rim of pan to loosen cake. Cool completely.

BRING cream to simmer in small saucepan on low heat. Meanwhile, chop remaining chocolate squares. Remove pan from heat. Add chocolate; stir until completely melted. Cool slightly. Pour over cheesecake. Refrigerate 3 hours. Remove rim of pan before serving cheesecake.

SIZE-WISE:
Enjoy a serving of this decadent dessert on special occasions.

chocolate-hazelnut cheesecake

PREP: 30 min. | TOTAL: 5 hours 35 min. | MAKES: 16 servings.

▶ what you need!

18 OREO Cookies, crushed (about 1½ cups)

2 Tbsp. butter or margarine, melted

3 pkg. (8 oz. each) PHILADELPHIA Cream Cheese, softened

1 cup sugar

1 tsp. vanilla

1 pkg. (8 squares) BAKER'S Semi-Sweet Chocolate, melted, slightly cooled

¼ cup hazelnut-flavored liqueur

3 eggs

½ cup whole hazelnuts, toasted

▶ make it!

HEAT oven to 325°F if using a silver 9-inch springform pan (or to 300°F if using a dark nonstick 9-inch springform pan).

MIX crushed cookies and butter; press firmly onto bottom of pan. Bake 10 min.

BEAT cream cheese, sugar and vanilla in large bowl with electric mixer on medium speed until well blended. Add chocolate and liqueur; mix well. Add eggs, 1 at a time, mixing on low speed after each addition just until blended. Pour over crust.

BAKE 55 min. to 1 hour 5 min. or until center is almost set. Run knife or metal spatula around rim of pan to loosen cake; cool before removing rim of pan. Refrigerate 4 hours or overnight. Top with nuts just before serving.

PHILADELPHIA 3-STEP
coconut cheesecake

PREP: 10 min. | TOTAL: 4 hours 50 min. | MAKES: 10 servings.

▶ what you need!

2 pkg. (8 oz. each) PHILADELPHIA Cream Cheese, softened

½ cup cream of coconut

½ cup sugar

½ tsp. vanilla

2 eggs

1 HONEY MAID Graham Pie Crust (6 oz.)

2 cups thawed COOL WHIP Whipped Topping

½ cup BAKER'S ANGEL FLAKE Coconut, toasted

▶ make it!

HEAT oven to 350°F.

1. BEAT cream cheese, cream of coconut, sugar and vanilla with electric mixer on medium speed until well blended. Add eggs; mix just until blended.

2. POUR into crust.

3. BAKE 40 min. or until center is almost set. Cool. Refrigerate 3 hours or overnight. Top with COOL WHIP and toasted coconut just before serving. Store leftover cheesecake in refrigerator.

white chocolate-cherry pecan cheesecake

PREP: 30 min. | TOTAL: 6 hours 30 min. | MAKES: 16 servings.

▶ what you need!

1 cup PLANTERS Pecan Halves, toasted, divided

1½ cups HONEY MAID Graham Cracker Crumbs

¼ cup sugar

¼ cup margarine or butter, melted

3 pkg. (8 oz. each) PHILADELPHIA Cream Cheese, softened

1 can (14 oz.) sweetened condensed milk

1 pkg. (6 squares) BAKER'S White Chocolate, melted

2 tsp. vanilla, divided

4 eggs

1 can (21 oz.) cherry pie filling

1 cup thawed COOL WHIP Whipped Topping

▶ make it!

HEAT oven to 300°F if using a silver 9-inch springform pan (or to 275°F if using a dark nonstick 9-inch springform pan).

RESERVE 16 nut halves. Finely chop remaining nuts; mix with graham crumbs, sugar and margarine. Press firmly onto bottom of pan.

BEAT cream cheese in large bowl with electric mixer on medium speed until creamy. Gradually add sweetened condensed milk, beating until well blended. Add chocolate and 1 tsp. of the vanilla; mix well. Add eggs, 1 at a time, mixing on low speed just until blended. Pour over crust.

BAKE 1 hour or until center is almost set. Run knife around rim of pan to loosen cake; cool before removing rim. Refrigerate 4 hours or overnight.

MIX pie filling and remaining vanilla; spoon over cheesecake. Top with COOL WHIP and reserved nut halves.

double-decker OREO cheesecake

PREP: 25 min. | TOTAL: 5 hours 40 min. | MAKES: 16 servings.

▶ what you need!

1 pkg. (1 lb. 1 oz.) OREO Chocolate Creme Cookies (48 cookies), divided

¼ cup butter, melted

4 pkg. (8 oz. each) PHILADELPHIA Cream Cheese, softened

1 cup sugar

1 tsp. vanilla

1 cup BREAKSTONE'S or KNUDSEN Sour Cream

4 eggs

4 squares BAKER'S Semi-Sweet Chocolate, melted

▶ make it!

HEAT oven to 325°F.

PROCESS 30 cookies in food processor until finely ground. Add butter; mix well. Press onto bottom of 13×9-inch baking pan.

BEAT cream cheese, sugar and vanilla in large bowl with mixer until well blended. Add sour cream; mix well. Add eggs, 1 at a time, beating after each just until blended; pour half over crust. Stir melted chocolate into remaining batter; pour over batter in pan. Chop remaining cookies; sprinkle over batter.

BAKE 45 min. or until center is almost set. Cool completely. Refrigerate 4 hours.

SIZE-WISE:
Enjoy your favorite foods while keeping portion size in mind.

MAKE AHEAD:
Wrap cooled cheesecake tightly in foil. Freeze up to 2 months. Thaw in refrigerator overnight before serving.

HOW TO REMOVE FROM PAN EASILY:
Line pan with foil, with ends of foil extending over sides. Prepare as directed. Use foil handles to lift cheesecake from pan before cutting.

NILLA praline cheesecake

PREP: 20 min. | TOTAL: 6 hours 5 min. | MAKES: 16 servings.

▶ what you need!

66 NILLA Wafers, divided

1¼ cups sugar, divided

¼ cup margarine or butter, melted

3 pkg. (8 oz. each) PHILADELPHIA Cream Cheese, softened

½ cup BREAKSTONE'S or KNUDSEN Sour Cream

1 tsp. vanilla

3 eggs

25 KRAFT Caramels

3 Tbsp. milk

½ cup PLANTERS Pecan Pieces, toasted

▶ make it!

HEAT oven to 325°F.

FINELY crush 50 wafers; mix with ¼ cup sugar and margarine. Press onto bottom of 9-inch springform pan. Stand remaining wafers around edge, pressing gently into crust to secure.

BEAT cream cheese and remaining sugar in large bowl with mixer until well blended. Add sour cream and vanilla; mix well. Add eggs, 1 at a time, beating on low speed after each just until blended. Pour over crust.

BAKE 45 to 50 min. or until center is almost set. Run small knife around rim of pan to loosen cake; cool before removing rim. Refrigerate 4 hours. Microwave caramels and milk on HIGH 1 min. or until caramels are completely melted, stirring every 30 sec. Cool slightly. Pour over cheesecake; top with nuts.

SUBSTITUTE:
Line 13×9-inch pan with foil, with ends of foil extending over sides. Grease foil. Prepare recipe as directed, increasing whole NILLA Wafers around the side from 16 to 22. Bake 40 to 45 min. or until center is almost set. Use foil handles to lift dessert from pan before cutting into squares to serve.

NOTE:
If using a dark nonstick 9-inch springform pan, reduce oven temperature to 300°F.

HOW TO TOAST NUTS:
Toasting nuts adds crunch and intensifies their flavor. To toast nuts in the oven, spread nuts in single layer in shallow baking pan. Bake at 350°F for 10 to 15 min. or until golden brown, stirring occasionally.

mini OREO cheesecakes

PREP: 15 min. | TOTAL: 3 hours 35 min. | MAKES: 2 doz. or 24 servings.

▶ what you need!

44 OREO Cookies, divided

 3 pkg. (8 oz. each) PHILADELPHIA Cream Cheese, softened

¾ cup sugar

¾ cup BREAKSTONE'S or KNUDSEN Sour Cream

 1 tsp. vanilla

 3 eggs

 2 squares BAKER'S White Chocolate, melted

½ cup colored sprinkles

1½ cups thawed COOL WHIP Whipped Topping

▶ make it!

HEAT oven to 325°F.

PLACE 1 cookie in each of 24 foil- or paper-lined muffin pan cups. Chop 8 of the remaining cookies; set aside.

BEAT cream cheese and sugar with mixer until blended. Add sour cream and vanilla; mix well. Add eggs, 1 at a time, beating after each just until blended. Gently stir in chopped cookies. Spoon into baking cups.

BAKE 18 to 20 min. or until centers are set. Cool completely. Refrigerate 3 hours or until chilled. Meanwhile, cut remaining cookies in half. Dip cookie halves halfway in melted chocolate. Place on waxed paper-covered baking sheet; top with sprinkles. Let stand 15 min. or until chocolate is firm.

TOP each cheesecake with dollop of COOL WHIP and cookie half just before serving.

MAKE AHEAD:
Cheesecakes can be stored in refrigerator up to 3 days, or frozen up to 1 month, before topping with COOL WHIP and cookie half just before serving. If freezing cheesecakes, thaw overnight in refrigerator before garnishing.

OREO no-bake cheesecake

PREP: 15 min. | TOTAL: 4 hours 15 min. | MAKES: 16 servings, 1 piece each.

▶ what you need!

1 pkg. (16.6 oz.) OREO Cookies, divided

¼ cup butter, melted

4 pkg. (8 oz. each) PHILADELPHIA Cream Cheese, softened

½ cup sugar

1 tsp. vanilla

1 tub (8 oz.) COOL WHIP Whipped Topping, thawed

▶ make it!

LINE 13×9-inch pan with foil, with ends of foil extending over sides of pan. Coarsely chop 15 of the cookies; set aside. Finely crush remaining cookies; mix with butter. Press firmly onto bottom of prepared pan. Refrigerate while preparing filling.

BEAT cream cheese, sugar and vanilla in large bowl with electric mixer on medium speed until well blended. Gently stir in COOL WHIP and chopped cookies. Spoon over crust; cover.

REFRIGERATE 4 hours or until firm. Store leftover cheesecake in refrigerator.

VARIATION:
Prepare as directed, using 1 pkg. (1 lb. 2 oz.) Golden OREO Cookies or 1 pkg. (1 lb. 1 oz.) OREO Cool Mint Creme Cookies.

chocolate-berry no-bake cheesecake

PREP: 15 min. | TOTAL: 3 hours 15 min. | MAKES: 10 servings.

▶ what you need!

- 2 squares BAKER'S Semi-Sweet Chocolate
- 2 pkg. (8 oz. each) PHILADELPHIA Cream Cheese, softened
- ⅓ cup sugar
- 2 cups thawed COOL WHIP Chocolate Whipped Topping
- 1 OREO Pie Crust (6 oz.)
- 1½ cups quartered strawberries

▶ make it!

MICROWAVE chocolate in small microwaveable bowl on HIGH 1 min.; stir until chocolate is completely melted. Set aside.

BEAT cream cheese and sugar in large bowl with electric mixer on medium speed until well blended. Add chocolate, mix well. Gently stir in COOL WHIP. Spoon into crust.

REFRIGERATE 3 hours or until set. Top with strawberries just before serving. Store leftover cheesecake in refrigerator.

PHILADELPHIA blueberry no-bake cheesecake

PREP: 15 min. | TOTAL: 4 hours 15 min. | MAKES: 16 servings.

▶ what you need!

2 cups HONEY MAID Graham Cracker Crumbs

6 Tbsp. margarine, melted

1 cup sugar, divided

4 pkg. (8 oz. each) PHILADELPHIA Neufchâtel Cheese, softened

½ cup blueberry preserves

Grated zest from 1 lemon

1 pkg. (16 oz.) frozen blueberries, thawed, drained

1 tub (8 oz.) COOL WHIP LITE Whipped Topping, thawed

▶ make it!

MIX graham crumbs, margarine and ¼ cup of the sugar; press firmly onto bottom of 13×9-inch pan. Refrigerate while preparing filling.

BEAT Neufchâtel cheese and remaining ¾ cup sugar in large bowl with electric mixer on medium speed until well blended. Add preserves and lemon zest, mix until blended. Stir in blueberries. Gently stir in COOL WHIP. Spoon over crust; cover.

REFRIGERATE 4 hours or until firm. Garnish as desired. Store leftovers in refrigerator.

HOW TO MAKE IT WITH FRESH BLUEBERRIES:
Place 2 cups blueberries in small bowl with 2 Tbsp. sugar; mash with fork. Add to Neufchâtel cheese mixture; continue as directed.

PHILADELPHIA 3-STEP
luscious lemon cheesecake

PREP: 10 min. | TOTAL: 3 hours 50 min. | MAKES: 8 servings.

▶ what you need!

2 pkg. (8 oz. each) PHILADELPHIA Cream
  Cheese, softened

½ cup sugar

½ tsp. grated lemon zest

1 Tbsp. fresh lemon juice

½ tsp. vanilla

2 eggs

1 HONEY MAID Graham Pie Crust (6 oz.)

▶ make it!

HEAT oven to 350°F.

1. BEAT cream cheese, sugar, zest, juice and vanilla with electric mixer on medium speed until well blended. Add eggs; mix just until blended.

2. POUR into crust.

3. BAKE 40 min. or until center is almost set. Cool. Refrigerate 3 hours or overnight. Store leftover cheesecake in refrigerator.

VARIATION:
Prepare as directed, substituting lime juice for the lemon juice and grated lime zest for the lemon zest.

JAZZ IT UP:
Top with additional lemon zest before serving.

PHILADELPHIA blueberry crown cheesecake

PREP: 15 min. | TOTAL: 5 hours 15 min. | MAKES: 16 servings.

▶ what you need!

30 NILLA Wafers, crushed (about 1 cup)

1 cup plus 3 Tbsp. sugar, divided

3 Tbsp. butter or margarine, melted

5 pkg. (8 oz. each) PHILADELPHIA Cream Cheese, softened

3 Tbsp. flour

1 Tbsp. vanilla

Grated zest from 1 medium lemon

1 cup BREAKSTONE'S or KNUDSEN Sour Cream

4 eggs

2 cups fresh blueberries

▶ make it!

HEAT oven to 325°F.

MIX wafer crumbs, 3 Tbsp. of the sugar and butter until well blended. Press firmly onto bottom of 9-inch springform pan.

BEAT cream cheese, remaining 1 cup sugar, flour, vanilla and lemon zest with electric mixer on medium speed until well blended. Add sour cream; mix well. Add eggs, 1 at a time, beating on low speed after each addition just until blended. Pour over crust; top with blueberries.

BAKE 1 hour 10 min. to 1 hour 15 min. or until center is almost set. Run small knife or spatula around rim of pan to loosen cake; cool before removing rim of pan. Refrigerate at least 4 hours before serving. Store leftover cheesecake in refrigerator.

SIZE IT UP:
Savor a serving of this crowd-pleasing dessert on special occasions.

SPECIAL EXTRA:
Garnish with additional blueberries and fresh mint sprigs just before serving.

GREAT SUBSTITUTE:
Substitute 1 bag (16 oz.) thawed frozen blueberries or 1 can (15 oz.) blueberries, well drained, for the 2 cups fresh blueberries.

PHILADELPHIA chocolate-vanilla swirl cheesecake

PREP: 15 min. | TOTAL: 5 hours 25 min. | MAKES: 16 servings.

▶ what you need!

20 OREO Cookies, finely crushed

3 Tbsp. butter, melted

4 pkg. (8 oz. each) PHILADELPHIA Cream Cheese, softened

1 cup sugar

1 tsp. vanilla

1 cup BREAKSTONE'S or KNUDSEN Sour Cream

4 eggs

6 squares BAKER'S Semi-Sweet Chocolate, melted, cooled

▶ make it!

HEAT oven to 325°F.

MIX cookie crumbs and butter; press onto bottom of foil-lined 13×9-inch pan. Bake 10 min.

BEAT cream cheese, sugar and vanilla in large bowl with mixer until well blended. Add sour cream; mix well. Add eggs, 1 at a time, mixing after each just until blended.

RESERVE 1 cup batter. Stir chocolate into remaining batter; pour over crust. Top with spoonfuls of reserved plain batter.

SWIRL batters with knife. Bake 40 min. or until center is almost set. Cool. Refrigerate 4 hours.

SPECIAL EXTRA:
Garnish with chocolate curls just before serving. Use a vegetable peeler to shave the side of an additional square of BAKER'S Semi-Sweet Chocolate until desired amount of curls are obtained. Wrap remaining chocolate and store at room temperature for another use.

HOW TO BAKE IN A SPRINGFORM PAN:
Prepare as directed, using a 9-inch springform pan and reserving just ½ cup of the plain batter for swirling. Increase baking time to 55 min. to 1 hour or until center is almost set. Run small knife or spatula around rim of pan to loosen cake; cool before removing rim.

NOTE:
Use foil handles to remove chilled cheesecake from pan before cutting to serve.

PHILADELPHIA
classic cheesecake

PREP: 20 min. | TOTAL: 5 hours 45 min. | MAKES: 16 servings.

▸ what you need!

1½ cups HONEY MAID Graham Cracker Crumbs

3 Tbsp. sugar

⅓ cup butter or margarine, melted

4 pkg. (8 oz. each) PHILADELPHIA Cream Cheese, softened

1 cup sugar

1 tsp. vanilla

4 eggs

▸ make it!

HEAT oven to 325°F.

MIX graham crumbs, 3 Tbsp. sugar and butter; press onto bottom of 9-inch springform pan.

BEAT cream cheese, 1 cup sugar and vanilla with mixer until well blended. Add eggs, 1 at a time, mixing on low speed after each just until blended. Pour over crust.

BAKE 55 min. or until center is almost set. Loosen cake from rim of pan; cool before removing rim. Refrigerate 4 hours.

SIZE-WISE:
Sweets can add enjoyment to a balanced diet, but remember to keep tabs on portions.

SPECIAL EXTRA:
Top with fresh fruit just before serving.

PHILADELPHIA
new york cheesecake

PREP: 15 min. | TOTAL: 5 hours 25 min. | MAKES: 16 servings.

▶ what you need!

21 OREO Cookies, finely crushed (about 2 cups)

3 Tbsp. butter or margarine, melted

5 pkg. (8 oz. each) PHILADELPHIA Cream Cheese, softened

1 cup sugar

3 Tbsp. flour

1 Tbsp. vanilla

1 cup BREAKSTONE'S or KNUDSEN Sour Cream

4 eggs

1 can (21 oz.) cherry pie filling

▶ make it!

HEAT oven to 325°F.

LINE 13×9-inch pan with foil, with ends of foil extending over sides. Mix cookie crumbs and butter; press onto bottom of pan.

BEAT cream cheese, sugar, flour and vanilla with mixer until well blended. Add sour cream; mix well. Add eggs, 1 at a time, mixing on low speed after each just until blended. Pour over crust.

BAKE 40 min. or until center is almost set. Cool completely. Refrigerate 4 hours. Use foil handles to lift cheesecake from pan before cutting to serve. Top with pie filling.

PHILADELPHIA new york-style strawberry swirl cheesecake

PREP: 15 min. | TOTAL: 5 hours 25 min. | MAKES: 16 servings.

▶ what you need!

1 cup HONEY MAID Graham Cracker Crumbs

3 Tbsp. sugar

3 Tbsp. butter, melted

5 pkg. (8 oz. each) PHILADELPHIA Cream Cheese, softened

1 cup sugar

3 Tbsp. flour

1 Tbsp. vanilla

1 cup BREAKSTONE'S or KNUDSEN Sour Cream

4 eggs

⅓ cup seedless strawberry jam

▶ make it!

HEAT oven to 325°F.

LINE 13×9-inch pan with foil, with ends of foil extending over sides. Mix graham crumbs, 3 Tbsp. sugar and butter; press onto bottom of pan. Bake 10 min.

BEAT cream cheese, 1 cup sugar, flour and vanilla in large bowl with mixer until well blended. Add sour cream; mix well. Add eggs, 1 at a time, mixing on low speed after each just until blended. Pour over crust. Gently drop small spoonfuls of jam over batter; swirl with knife.

BAKE 40 min. or until center is almost set. Cool completely. Refrigerate 4 hours. Lift cheesecake from pan with foil handles before cutting to serve.

PHILADELPHIA peaches 'n cream no-bake cheesecake

PREP: 15 min. | TOTAL: 4 hours 15 min. | MAKES: 16 servings, 1 piece each.

▶ what you need!

- 2 cups HONEY MAID Graham Cracker Crumbs
- 6 Tbsp. margarine, melted
- 1 cup sugar, divided
- 4 pkg. (8 oz. each) PHILADELPHIA Neufchâtel Cheese, softened
- 1 pkg. (3 oz.) JELL-O Peach Flavor Gelatin
- 2 fresh peaches, chopped
- 1 tub (8 oz.) COOL WHIP LITE Whipped Topping, thawed

▶ make it!

MIX graham crumbs, margarine and ¼ cup sugar; press onto bottom of 13×9-inch pan. Refrigerate while preparing filling.

BEAT Neufchâtel cheese and remaining ¾ cup sugar in large bowl with mixer until well blended. Add dry gelatin mix; mix well. Stir in peaches and COOL WHIP. Spoon over crust; cover.

REFRIGERATE 4 hours or until firm. Store leftovers in refrigerator.

SIZE-WISE:
You'll know it's a special occasion when you get to enjoy a serving of this luscious cheesecake.

SUBSTITUTE:
Prepare as directed, using 1 drained 15-oz. can peaches.

PHILLY brownie cheesecake

PREP: 10 min. | TOTAL: 6 hours | MAKES: 16 servings.

▶ what you need!

- 1 pkg. (19 to 21 oz.) brownie mix (13×9-inch pan size)
- 4 pkg. (8 oz. each) PHILADELPHIA Cream Cheese, softened
- 1 cup sugar
- 1 tsp. vanilla
- ½ cup BREAKSTONE'S or KNUDSEN Sour Cream
- 3 eggs
- 2 squares BAKER'S Semi-Sweet Chocolate

▶ make it!

HEAT oven to 325°F.

PREPARE brownie batter as directed on package; pour into 13×9-inch pan sprayed with cooking spray. Bake 25 min. or until top is shiny and center is almost set.

MEANWHILE, beat cream cheese, sugar and vanilla in large bowl with mixer until well blended. Add sour cream; mix well. Add eggs, 1 at a time, mixing on low speed after each just until blended. Gently pour over brownie layer in pan. (Filling will come almost to top of pan.)

BAKE 40 min. or until center is almost set. Run knife or metal spatula around rim of pan to loosen sides; cool. Refrigerate 4 hours.

MELT chocolate squares as directed on package; drizzle over cheesecake. Refrigerate 15 min. or until chocolate is firm.

SIZE-WISE:
Balance your food choices throughout the day so you can enjoy a serving of this rich-and-indulgent cheesecake with your loved ones.

prize winning chocolate cheesecake

PREP: 20 min. | TOTAL: 4 hours 20 min. | MAKES: 10 servings.

▶ what you need!

1½ cups TEDDY GRAHAMS Chocolate Graham Snacks, crushed

¾ cup PLANTERS Sliced Almonds, finely chopped

¼ cup butter, melted

1 tsp. vanilla, divided

2 pkg. (8 oz. each) PHILADELPHIA Cream Cheese, softened

½ cup sugar

1 jar (13 oz.) chocolate-hazelnut spread

1 tub (8 oz.) COOL WHIP or COOL WHIP Extra Creamy Whipped Topping, thawed

▶ make it!

MIX graham crumbs, nuts, butter and ½ tsp. vanilla until well blended; press onto bottom and up side of 9-inch pie plate. Refrigerate until ready to use.

BEAT cream cheese and sugar in large bowl with mixer until well blended. Add hazelnut spread and remaining vanilla; mix well. Whisk in COOL WHIP. Spoon into crust.

REFRIGERATE 4 hours.

SIZE-WISE:
This sensational cheesecake is full of flavor. And since it makes 10 servings, it can feed a crowd at your next gathering or family party.

silky chocolate cheesecake

PREP: 15 min. | TOTAL: 5 hours 10 min. | MAKES: 12 servings.

▶ what you need!

21 OREO Cookies, crushed (about 2 cups)

2 Tbsp. sugar

⅓ cup butter or margarine, melted

2 pkg. (4 oz. each) BAKER'S GERMAN'S
Sweet Chocolate, divided

2 eggs

⅔ cup corn syrup

⅓ cup whipping cream

1½ tsp. vanilla

2 pkg. (8 oz. each) PHILADELPHIA Cream
Cheese, cubed, softened

▶ make it!

HEAT oven to 325°F if using a silver 9-inch springform pan (or to 300°F if using a dark nonstick 9-inch springform pan).

MIX cookie crumbs, sugar and butter until well blended. Press firmly onto bottom and 1½ inches up side of pan. Microwave 1½ pkg. (6 squares) of the chocolate in microwaveable bowl on HIGH 2 min., stirring after 1 min. Stir until chocolate is completely melted.

PLACE eggs, corn syrup, whipping cream and vanilla in blender container; cover. Blend until smooth. With blender running, gradually add cream cheese through small opening at top of blender, blending until smooth. Add melted chocolate; cover. Blend well. Pour into crust.

BAKE 50 to 55 min. or until center is almost set. Run knife or metal spatula around rim of pan to loosen cake; cool before removing from pan. Refrigerate 4 hours or overnight.

MELT remaining 2 squares of chocolate as directed on package. Drizzle over cheesecake just before serving. Store leftover cheesecake in refrigerator.

triple-citrus cheesecake

PREP: 30 min. | TOTAL: 6 hours 35 min. | MAKES: 16 servings.

▶ what you need!

1 cup HONEY MAID Graham Cracker Crumbs

⅓ cup firmly packed brown sugar

¼ cup butter or margarine, melted

4 pkg. (8 oz. each) PHILADELPHIA Cream Cheese, softened

1 cup granulated sugar

2 Tbsp. flour

1 tsp. vanilla

4 eggs

1 Tbsp. fresh lemon juice

1 Tbsp. fresh lime juice

1 Tbsp. fresh orange juice

1 Tbsp. grated lemon zest

1 Tbsp. grated lime zest

1 Tbsp. grated orange zest

▶ make it!

HEAT oven to 325°F if using a silver 9-inch springform pan (or to 300°F if using a dark nonstick 9-inch springform pan).

MIX graham crumbs, brown sugar and butter; press firmly onto bottom of pan. Bake 10 min.

BEAT cream cheese, granulated sugar, flour and vanilla with electric mixer on medium speed until well blended. Add eggs, 1 at a time, mixing on low speed after each addition just until blended. Stir in remaining ingredients; pour over crust.

BAKE 1 hour and 5 min. or until center is almost set. Run knife or metal spatula around rim of pan to loosen cake; cool before removing rim of pan. Refrigerate 4 hours or overnight. Store leftover cheesecake in refrigerator.

ultimate turtle cheesecake

PREP: 30 min. | TOTAL: 6 hours 10 min. | MAKES: 16 servings.

▶ what you need!

24 OREO Cookies, crushed (about 2 cups)

6 Tbsp. butter or margarine, melted

1 pkg. (14 oz.) KRAFT Caramels

½ cup milk

1 cup chopped PLANTERS Pecans

3 pkg. (8 oz. each) PHILADELPHIA Cream Cheese, softened

¾ cup sugar

1 Tbsp. vanilla

3 eggs

2 squares BAKER'S Semi-Sweet Chocolate

▶ make it!

HEAT oven to 325°F.

MIX cookie crumbs and butter; press onto bottom and 2 inches up side of 9-inch springform pan.

MICROWAVE caramels and milk in small microwaveable bowl on HIGH 3 min. or until caramels are completely melted, stirring after each min. Stir in nuts; pour half into crust. Refrigerate 10 min. Refrigerate remaining caramel mixture for later use.

BEAT cream cheese, sugar and vanilla with mixer until well blended. Add eggs, 1 at a time, mixing on low speed after each just until blended. Pour over caramel layer in crust.

BAKE 1 hour 5 min. to 1 hour 10 min. or until center is almost set. Run knife around rim of pan to loosen cake; cool before removing rim. Refrigerate 4 hours.

MICROWAVE reserved caramel mixture 1 min.; stir. Pour over cheesecake. Melt chocolate as directed on package; drizzle over cheesecake.

white chocolate cheesecake

PREP: 40 min. | TOTAL: 7 hours 5 min. | MAKES: 16 servings.

▶ what you need!

- ½ cup butter, softened
- ¾ cup sugar, divided
- 1½ tsp. vanilla, divided
- 1 cup flour
- 4 pkg. (8 oz. each) PHILADELPHIA Cream Cheese, softened
- 2 pkg. (6 squares each) BAKER'S White Chocolate, melted, slightly cooled
- 4 eggs
- 2 cups fresh raspberries

▶ make it!

HEAT oven to 325°F.

BEAT butter, ¼ cup sugar, and ½ tsp. vanilla in small bowl with mixer until light and fluffy. Gradually beat in flour until well blended; press onto bottom of 9-inch springform pan. Prick with fork. Bake 25 min. or until edge is lightly browned.

BEAT cream cheese, remaining sugar and vanilla in large bowl with mixer until well blended. Add chocolate; mix well. Add eggs, 1 at a time, beating on low speed after each addition just until blended. Pour over crust.

BAKE 55 min. to 1 hour or until center is almost set. Run knife around rim of pan to loosen cake; cool before removing rim. Refrigerate 4 hours. Top with raspberries just before serving.

WHITE CHOCOLATE-MACADAMIA CHEESECAKE:
Prepare as directed, stirring ¾ cup chopped PLANTERS Macadamias into the batter before pouring over crust and baking as directed.

fluffy cheesecake

PREP: 15 min. | TOTAL: 3 hours 15 min. | MAKES: 8 servings.

▶ what you need!

1 pkg. (8 oz.) PHILADELPHIA Cream Cheese, softened

⅓ cup sugar

1 tub (8 oz.) COOL WHIP Whipped Topping, thawed

1 HONEY MAID Graham Pie Crust (6 oz.)

1 apple, cored, thinly sliced (optional)

▶ make it!

BEAT cream cheese and sugar in large bowl with wire whisk or electric mixer until well blended. Gently stir in COOL WHIP.

SPOON into crust.

REFRIGERATE 3 hours or until set. Top with apple slices just before serving, if desired.

FLUFFY CHEESECAKE SQUARES:
Omit pie crust. Mix 1 cup HONEY MAID Graham Cracker Crumbs, 2 Tbsp. sugar and ⅓ cup melted butter or margarine. Press onto bottom of foil-lined 8-inch square baking pan. Continue as directed. Makes 9 servings.

CHOCOLATE DELICACIES

Chocolate
Delicacies

CHIPS AHOY! cheesecake sandwiches

PREP: 10 min. | TOTAL: 3 hours 10 min. | MAKES: 10 servings, 1 sandwich each.

▶ what you need!

4 oz. (½ of 8-oz. pkg.) PHILADELPHIA Cream Cheese, softened

2 Tbsp. sugar

1 cup thawed COOL WHIP Whipped Topping

20 CHIPS AHOY! Real Chocolate Chip Cookies

1 tub (7 oz.) BAKER'S Real Milk Dipping Chocolate, melted

▶ make it!

BEAT cream cheese and sugar in large bowl with electric mixer on medium speed until well blended. Stir in COOL WHIP.

COVER bottom (flat) side of each of 10 of the cookies with about 2 Tbsp. of the cream cheese mixture; top each with second cookie, bottom-side down, to form sandwich. Dip half of each sandwich in chocolate; gently shake off excess chocolate. Place in single layer in airtight container.

FREEZE 3 hours or until firm. Store leftover sandwiches in freezer.

white chocolate-berry pie

PREP: 20 min. | TOTAL: 1 hour 20 min. | MAKES: 8 servings.

▶ what you need!

- 1 ready-to-use refrigerated pie crust (½ of 14.1 oz. pkg.)
- 1 pkg. (6 squares) BAKER'S White Chocolate, divided
- 2 Tbsp. milk
- 4 oz. (½ of 8-oz. pkg.) PHILADELPHIA Cream Cheese, softened
- ⅓ cup powdered sugar
- 1 tsp. grated orange zest
- 2 cups thawed COOL WHIP Whipped Topping
- 2 cups raspberries

▶ make it!

PREPARE and bake pie crust in 9-inch pie plate as directed on package for unfilled 1-crust baked shell. Cool.

MICROWAVE 5 chocolate squares and milk in medium microwaveable bowl on HIGH 2 min. or until chocolate is almost melted, stirring after 1 min. Stir until chocolate is completely melted. Cool to room temperature.

BEAT cream cheese, sugar and zest with mixer until well blended. Add to chocolate mixture; beat with whisk until well blended. Stir in COOL WHIP; spoon into crust. Top with berries.

MELT remaining chocolate square as directed on package; drizzle over berries. Refrigerate 1 hour.

SUBSTITUTE:
Substitute sliced strawberries for the raspberries.

best-ever chocolate fudge layer cake

PREP: 10 min. | TOTAL: 1 hour 30 min. | MAKES: 18 servings.

▶ what you need!

- 1 pkg. (8 squares) BAKER'S Semi-Sweet Chocolate, divided
- 1 pkg. (2-layer size) chocolate cake mix
- 1 pkg. (3.9 oz.) JELL-O Chocolate Instant Pudding
- 4 eggs
- 1 cup BREAKSTONE'S or KNUDSEN Sour Cream
- ½ cup oil
- ½ cup water
- 1 tub (8 oz.) COOL WHIP Whipped Topping (Do not thaw.)
- 2 Tbsp. PLANTERS Sliced Almonds

▶ make it!

HEAT oven to 350°F.

CHOP 2 chocolate squares. Beat cake mix, dry pudding mix, eggs, sour cream, oil and water in large bowl with mixer on low speed just until moistened. Beat on medium speed 2 min. Stir in chopped chocolate. Pour into 2 greased 9-inch round pans.

BAKE 30 to 35 min. or until toothpick inserted in centers comes out clean. Cool in pans on wire racks 10 min. Loosen cakes from sides of pans. Invert onto racks; gently remove pans. Cool cakes completely.

PLACE COOL WHIP and remaining chocolate squares in microwaveable bowl. Microwave on HIGH 1½ min. or until chocolate is completely melted and mixture is well blended, stirring after 1 min. Let stand 15 min. to thicken. Stack cake layers on plate, filling and frosting with COOL WHIP mixture. Garnish with nuts. Keep refrigerated.

VARIATION:
Prepare as directed, using JELL-O Chocolate Fat Free Sugar Free Instant Pudding, BREAKSTONE'S Reduced Fat or KNUDSEN Light Sour Cream and COOL WHIP LITE Whipped Topping.

choco-cherry bars

▶ what you need!

- 4 squares BAKER'S Unsweetened Chocolate, divided
- 1 pkg. (8 oz.) PHILADELPHIA Cream Cheese, softened
- ¾ cup butter or margarine, softened
- 1 cup granulated sugar
- 2 eggs
- 1½ tsp. vanilla, divided
- 1¼ cups flour
- ½ tsp. baking soda
- ½ tsp. salt
- 1 cup chopped maraschino cherries, well drained
- ½ cup chopped PLANTERS Walnuts
- 1 cup sifted powdered sugar
- 2 to 3 Tbsp. milk, divided

▶ make it!

HEAT oven to 350°F.

MELT 2 chocolate squares; set aside. Beat cream cheese, butter and granulated sugar in large bowl with mixer until blended. Add eggs and 1 tsp. vanilla; mix well. Mix flour, baking soda and salt. Add to cream cheese mixture; mix well. Blend in melted chocolate. Stir in cherries and nuts.

SPREAD into greased and floured 15×10×1-inch pan.

BAKE 25 to 30 min. or until toothpick inserted in center comes out clean. Melt remaining chocolate squares in medium microwaveable bowl. Stir in powdered sugar, 2 Tbsp. milk and remaining vanilla. Add remaining 1 Tbsp. milk, if necessary for desired glaze consistency. Drizzle over dessert. Cool completely.

BAKER'S ONE BOWL
bittersweet torte

PREP: 20 min. | TOTAL: 1 hour | MAKES: 12 servings.

▶ what you need!

1 pkg. (6 squares) BAKER'S
   Bittersweet Chocolate, divided

¾ cup butter or margarine

1 cup sugar

3 eggs

1 tsp. vanilla

⅓ cup flour

¼ tsp. salt

½ cup chopped PLANTERS Pecans

▶ make it!

HEAT oven to 350°F.

GREASE and flour 9-inch round cake pan. Line bottom of pan with waxed paper; set aside.

MICROWAVE 4 of the chocolate squares and butter in large microwaveable bowl on HIGH 1½ to 2 min. or until chocolate is almost melted, stirring after 1 min. Stir until chocolate is completely melted. Add sugar; mix well. Blend in eggs and vanilla. Add flour and salt; mix well. Stir in nuts. Pour into prepared pan.

BAKE 40 min. or until toothpick inserted in center comes out with fudgy crumbs. (Do not overbake.) Cool in pan 5 min. Run small knife around side of pan to loosen edge. Invert torte onto serving platter; remove waxed paper. Melt remaining 2 chocolate squares. Drizzle over top of torte. Let stand until firm.

SUBSTITUTE:
Substitute BAKER'S Semi-Sweet Chocolate for the bittersweet chocolate.

BAKER'S ONE BOWL brownies

PREP: 15 min. | TOTAL: 50 min. | MAKES: 24 servings.

▶ what you need!

- 4 squares BAKER'S Unsweetened Chocolate
- ¾ cup butter or margarine
- 2 cups sugar
- 3 eggs
- 1 tsp. vanilla
- 1 cup flour
- 1 cup coarsely chopped PLANTER'S Pecans

▶ make it!

HEAT oven to 350°F.

LINE 13×9-inch baking pan with foil, with ends of foil extending over sides of pan. Grease foil.

MICROWAVE chocolate and butter in large microwavable bowl on HIGH 2 min. or until butter is melted. Stir until chocolate is completely melted. Stir in sugar. Blend in eggs and vanilla. Add flour and nuts; mix well. Spread into prepared pan.

BAKE 30 to 35 min. or until toothpick inserted into center comes out with fudgy crumbs. (Do not overbake.) Cool in pan on wire rack. Using foil handles, remove brownies from pan. Cut into 24 squares. Store in tightly covered container at room temperature.

chocolate bliss cheesecake

PREP: 20 min. | TOTAL: 6 hours | MAKES: 12 servings.

▶ what you need!

18 OREO Cookies, crushed (about 1½ cups)

2 Tbsp. butter or margarine, melted

3 pkg. (8 oz. each) PHILADELPHIA Cream Cheese, softened

¾ cup sugar

1 tsp. vanilla

1 pkg. (8 squares) BAKER'S Semi-Sweet Chocolate, melted, cooled slightly

3 eggs

▶ make it!

HEAT oven to 325°F.

MIX cookie crumbs and butter; press onto bottom of 9-inch springform pan.

BEAT cream cheese, sugar and vanilla with mixer until well blended. Add chocolate; mix well.

ADD eggs, 1 at a time, mixing on low speed after each just until blended. Pour over crust.

BAKE 55 min. to 1 hour or until center is almost set. Run knife around rim of pan to loosen cake; cool before removing rim. Refrigerate 4 hours. Garnish as desired.

NOTE:
If using a dark nonstick springform pan, reduce oven temperature to 300°F.

chocolate lover's cheesecake

PREP: 10 min. | TOTAL: 4 hours 50 min. | MAKES: 8 servings.

▶ what you need!

2 pkg. (8 oz. each) PHILADELPHIA Cream Cheese, softened

½ cup sugar

½ tsp. vanilla

4 squares BAKER'S Semi-Sweet Chocolate, melted, cooled

2 eggs

1 OREO Pie Crust (6 oz.)

▶ make it!

HEAT oven to 325°F.

BEAT cream cheese, sugar and vanilla in large bowl with mixer until well blended. Add chocolate; mix well. Add eggs; mix just until blended. Pour into crust.

BAKE 40 min. or until center is almost set; cool.

REFRIGERATE several hours.

MOCHA CHEESECAKE:
Prepare as directed, stirring 3 Tbsp. coffee-flavored liqueur or cooled brewed MAXWELL HOUSE Coffee into cheesecake batter before pouring into crust.

rich chocolatey mousse

PREP: 15 min. | TOTAL: 1 hour 15 min. | MAKES: 6 servings, about ½ cup each.

▶ what you need!

⅓ cup whipping cream

4 squares BAKER'S Bittersweet Chocolate

1 tsp. vanilla

1 tub (8 oz.) COOL WHIP Whipped Topping, thawed, divided

▶ make it!

MICROWAVE cream in large microwaveable bowl on HIGH 1½ min. or until cream comes to boil. Add chocolate; stir until completely melted. Blend in vanilla. Cool 5 min. or until mixture comes to room temperature, stirring occasionally.

ADD chocolate mixture to 2 cups of COOL WHIP; stir gently with wire whisk until well blended. Spoon evenly into 6 dessert dishes.

REFRIGERATE 1 hour or until set. Top with remaining COOL WHIP just before serving. Store leftover desserts in refrigerator.

CHOCOLATE-ORANGE MOUSSE:
Prepare as directed, stirring 1 tsp. grated orange zest into the mousse mixture before spooning into dessert dishes. Garnish with orange wedges, if desired.

chocolate pudding pie

PREP: 15 min. | **TOTAL:** 3 hours 15 min. | **MAKES:** 10 servings.

▶ what you need!

1 pkg. (3.9 oz.) JELL-O Chocolate Instant Pudding

1½ cups cold milk

1 OREO Pie Crust (6 oz.)

2 cups thawed COOL WHIP Whipped Topping, divided

▶ make it!

BEAT dry pudding mix and milk with whisk 2 min.; spoon half into crust.

STIR 1 cup COOL WHIP into remaining pudding; spoon over pudding layer in crust.

TOP with remaining COOL WHIP. Refrigerate 3 hours.

SPECIAL EXTRA:
Sprinkle 2 Tbsp. chopped toasted PLANTERS Pecans onto bottom of crust before adding filling as directed.

chocolate truffle cheesecake

PREP: 20 min. | TOTAL: 5 hours 30 min. | MAKES: 16 servings, 1 slice each.

► what you need!

18 OREO Cookies, finely crushed
(about 1¾ cups crumbs)

2 Tbsp. butter or margarine, melted

3 pkg. (8 oz. each) PHILADELPHIA
Cream Cheese, softened

1 can (14 oz.) sweetened condensed
milk

2 tsp. vanilla

1 pkg. (12 oz.) BAKER'S Semi-Sweet
Chocolate Chunks, melted,
slightly cooled

4 eggs

► make it!

HEAT oven to 300°F if using silver 9-inch springform pan (or to 275°F if using dark nonstick 9-inch springform pan).

MIX cookie crumbs and butter; press firmly onto bottom of pan. Set aside.

BEAT cream cheese, sweetened condensed milk and vanilla in large bowl with electric mixer on medium speed until well blended. Add chocolate; mix well. Add eggs, 1 at a time, mixing on low speed after each addition just until blended. Pour over crust.

BAKE 1 hour 5 min. to 1 hour 10 min. or until center is almost set. Run knife or metal spatula around rim of pan to loosen cake; cool before removing rim of pan. Refrigerate at least 4 hours or overnight. Store leftover cheesecake in refrigerator.

JAZZ IT UP:
Garnish with fresh raspberries just before serving.

MAKE IT EASY:
Use bottom of straight-sided glass to evenly press cookie crumb mixture onto bottom of springform pan.

VARIATION:
Add ¼ cup coffee-flavored liqueur along with the chocolate.

molten chocolate surprise

PREP: 15 min. | TOTAL: 23 min. | MAKES: 1 doz. or 12 servings.

▶ what you need!

- 4 squares BAKER'S Semi-Sweet Chocolate
- ½ cup butter or margarine
- 2 whole eggs
- 2 egg yolks
- 1 cup powdered sugar
- ⅓ cup flour
- 12 CHIPS AHOY! Cookies
- ½ cup thawed COOL WHIP Whipped Topping

▶ make it!

HEAT oven to 425°F.

MICROWAVE chocolate and butter in large microwaveable bowl on HIGH 2 min. or until butter is melted. Stir until chocolate is completely melted. Beat whole eggs, yolks, sugar and flour with whisk until well blended. Gradually beat into chocolate mixture.

LINE 12 muffin pan cups with paper liners; spray with cooking spray. Place 1 cookie, upside-down, on bottom of each cup; cover with batter.

BAKE 8 min. or until cakes are firm around edges but still soft in centers. Cool in pan 1 min. Carefully remove cakes from pan. Invert into dessert dishes; remove paper liners. Serve with COOL WHIP.

MAKE AHEAD:
Batter can be prepared ahead of time. Cover and refrigerate up to 24 hours. When ready to serve, pour batter evenly over cookies in prepared muffin cups and bake as directed.

PHILADELPHIA
triple-chocolate cheesecake

PREP: 20 min. | TOTAL: 5 hours 45 min. | MAKES: 16 servings.

▶ what you need!

24 OREO Cookies, finely crushed (about 2 cups)

2 Tbsp. butter or margarine, melted

1 pkg. (6 squares) BAKER'S White Chocolate, divided

4 pkg. (8 oz. each) PHILADELPHIA Cream Cheese, softened, divided

1 cup sugar, divided

½ tsp. vanilla

3 eggs

3 squares BAKER'S Semi-Sweet Chocolate, divided

1 tub (8 oz.) COOL WHIP Whipped Topping, thawed

▶ make it!

HEAT oven to 325°F.

MIX cookie crumbs and butter; press onto bottom of 9-inch springform pan. Melt 5 white chocolate squares as directed on package; cool slightly.

BEAT 3 packages cream cheese, ¾ cup sugar and vanilla with mixer until well blended. Add melted white chocolate; mix well. Add eggs, 1 at a time, mixing on low speed after each just until blended. Pour over crust.

BAKE 50 to 55 min. or until center is almost set. Run knife around rim of pan to loosen cake; cool completely. Meanwhile, melt 2 semi-sweet chocolate squares; cool.

BEAT remaining cream cheese and sugar in large bowl until well blended. Add melted semi-sweet chocolate; mix well. Whisk in COOL WHIP; spread over cheesecake. Refrigerate 4 hours. Garnish with chocolate curls from remaining white and semi-sweet chocolates.

VARIATION:
Substitute foil-lined 13×9-inch pan for the springform pan. Mix crust ingredients as directed. Press onto bottom of prepared pan; cover with prepared filling. Bake 45 min. or until center is almost set. Cool completely in pan. Spread with COOL WHIP mixture. Refrigerate 4 hours. Use ends of foil to remove cheesecake from pan before cutting to serve.

HOW TO SHAVE CHOCOLATE:
Warm 1 chocolate square by microwaving it on HIGH for a few sec. or just until you can smudge the chocolate with your thumb. Hold square steadily, then draw a vegetable peeler slowly over the chocolate to form shavings. Repeat with remaining chocolate square.

raspberry brownies

PREP: 20 min. | TOTAL: 2 hours 25 min. | MAKES: 32 servings, 1 brownie each.

▶ what you need!

4 squares BAKER'S Unsweetened Chocolate

¾ cup butter or margarine

2 cups sugar

3 eggs

1 tsp. vanilla

1 cup flour

¼ cup seedless raspberry jam

6 squares BAKER'S Semi-Sweet Baking Chocolate, chopped

¾ cup whipping cream

▶ make it!

HEAT oven to 350°F.

LINE 13×9-inch baking pan with foil, with ends of foil extending over sides of pan. Grease foil. Microwave unsweetened chocolate and butter in large microwaveable bowl on HIGH 2 min. or until butter is melted. Stir until chocolate is completely melted. Stir sugar into chocolate mixture until well blended. Add eggs and vanilla; mix well. Stir in flour until well blended. Spread into prepared pan.

BAKE 30 to 35 min. or until toothpick inserted in center comes out with fudgy crumbs. (Do not overbake.) Cool in pan.

SPREAD jam over brownies. Microwave semi-sweet chocolate and cream in microwaveable bowl on HIGH 2 min. or until simmering. Stir until chocolate is completely melted and mixture is well blended. Spread evenly over jam layer. Refrigerate 1 hour or until chocolate layer is set. Lift dessert from pan, using foil handles. Cut into 32 brownies to serve.

JAZZ IT UP:
Bake and glaze brownies as directed. Remove from pan; cut into diamond-shaped bars. Garnish each bar with a fresh raspberry.

raspberry ganache pie

PREP: 15 min. | TOTAL: 4 hours 15 min. | MAKES: 10 servings.

▶ what you need!

- 1 pkg. (8 squares) BAKER'S Semi-Sweet Chocolate, coarsely chopped
- 1 cup whipping cream
- 6 Tbsp. seedless raspberry jam, divided
- 1 OREO Pie Crust (6 oz)
- 2 cups fresh raspberries
- 1 Tbsp. water

▶ make it!

MICROWAVE chocolate and cream in microwaveable bowl on HIGH 2 min. or until chocolate is almost melted, stirring after each min. Beat with whisk until chocolate is completely melted and mixture is well blended. Stir in 2 Tbsp. jam.

POUR into crust. Refrigerate 4 hours.

ARRANGE berries on top of pie. Microwave remaining jam and water in small microwaveable bowl on HIGH 30 sec; stir until well blended. Brush onto berries. Keep refrigerated.

MAKE-AHEAD:
Pie can be prepared ahead of time. Freeze up to 2 days. Place in refrigerator to thaw for about 2 hours before serving.

ribbon bar cheesecake

PREP: 15 min. | TOTAL: 5 hours 15 min. | MAKES: 16 servings, 1 square each.

▶ what you need!

30 OREO Cookies, crushed

½ cup butter, melted

¼ cup chopped PLANTERS Pecans

¼ cup BAKER'S ANGEL FLAKE Coconut

4 pkg. (8 oz. each) PHILADELPHIA Cream Cheese, softened

1 cup sugar

4 eggs

½ cup whipping cream

6 squares BAKER'S Semi-Sweet Chocolate

▶ make it!

HEAT oven to 350°F.

MIX crushed cookies, butter, nuts and coconut; press firmly onto bottom of 13×9-inch baking pan. Refrigerate while preparing filling.

BEAT cream cheese and sugar in large bowl with electric mixer on medium speed until well blended. Add eggs, 1 at a time, mixing on low speed after each addition just until blended. Pour over crust.

BAKE 40 min. or until center is almost set. Cool. Refrigerate 3 hours or overnight. Place whipping cream and chocolate in saucepan. Cook on low heat until chocolate is completely melted and mixture is well blended, stirring occasionally. Pour over cheesecake. Refrigerate 15 min. or until chocolate is firm. Store leftover cheesecake in refrigerator.

JAZZ IT UP:
After chocolate topping is firm, place 1 additional chocolate square in microwaveable bowl. Microwave on MEDIUM (50%) 1 min., stirring after 30 sec. Stir until chocolate is completely melted. Pour into small resealable bag; seal bag. Snip off one small corner from bottom of bag; twist top of bag to squeeze chocolate from bag to pipe a special message, such as "Greetings," on top of cheesecake.

chocolate lover's pizza

PREP: 15 min. | **TOTAL:** 15 min. | **MAKES:** 20 servings, 1 wedge each.

▶ what you need!

- 1 pkg. (8 squares) BAKER'S Semi-Sweet Chocolate
- 10 squares BAKER'S White Chocolate, divided
- 2 cups JET-PUFFED Miniature Marshmallows
- 1 cup crisp rice cereal
- 1 cup PLANTERS COCKTAIL Peanuts
- ¼ cup red maraschino cherries, well drained, halved
- ¼ cup green maraschino cherries, well drained, halved
- ⅓ cup BAKER'S ANGEL FLAKE Coconut
- 1 tsp. vegetable oil

▶ make it!

MICROWAVE semi-sweet chocolate and 8 squares of the white chocolate in 2-qt. microwaveable bowl on HIGH 2 min; stir. Microwave an additional 1 to 2 min. or until chocolates are melted, stirring every 30 sec. Add marshmallows, cereal and nuts; mix well.

SPREAD evenly into lightly greased 12-inch pizza pan. Sprinkle with cherries and coconut.

MICROWAVE remaining 2 squares white chocolate with oil in 1-cup microwaveable bowl on HIGH 1 min; stir. Microwave an additional 30 sec. to 1 min. or until chocolate is completely melted, stirring every 15 sec. Drizzle over coconut. Cool completely or refrigerate until firm.

INDIVIDUAL CHOCOLATE LOVER'S PIZZAS:
Divide chocolate mixture into 24 greased muffin cups; refrigerate until firm. Let kids create their own pizzas by adding their toppings of choice.

ultimate chocolate caramel pecan pie

PREP: 30 min. | TOTAL: 3 hours 15 min. | MAKES: 10 servings.

▶ what you need!

3 cups chopped PLANTERS Pecans, divided

¼ cup granulated sugar

¼ cup butter or margarine, melted

1 pkg. (14 oz.) KRAFT Caramels

⅔ cup whipping cream, divided

1 pkg. (8 squares) BAKER'S Semi-Sweet Chocolate

¼ cup powdered sugar

½ tsp. vanilla

▶ make it!

HEAT oven to 350°F.

BLEND 2 cups nuts in blender until finely ground, using pulsing action. Mix with granulated sugar and butter; press onto bottom and up side of 9-inch pie plate. Bake 12 to 15 min. or until lightly browned. Cool completely. (If crust puffs up during baking, gently press down with back of spoon.)

MICROWAVE caramels and ⅓ cup whipping cream in microwaveable bowl on HIGH 2½ to 3 min. or until caramels are completely melted and mixture is well blended, stirring after each minute. Pour into crust. Chop remaining nuts; sprinkle over caramel layer.

COOK chocolate, remaining whipping cream, powdered sugar and vanilla in saucepan on low heat just until chocolate is completely melted, stirring constantly. Pour over pie; gently spread to evenly cover top. Refrigerate 2 hours.

rocky road no-bake cheesecake

PREP: 15 min. | **TOTAL:** 4 hours 15 min. | **MAKES:** 10 servings, 1 slice each.

▶ what you need!

- 3 squares BAKER'S Semi-Sweet Chocolate, divided
- 2 pkg. (8 oz. each) PHILADELPHIA Cream Cheese, softened
- ⅓ cup sugar
- ¼ cup milk
- 2 cups thawed COOL WHIP Whipped Topping
- ¾ cup JET-PUFFED Miniature Marshmallows
- ⅓ cup chopped PLANTERS COCKTAIL Peanuts
- 1 OREO Pie Crust (6 oz.)

▶ make it!

MICROWAVE 1 of the chocolate squares in small microwaveable bowl on HIGH 1 min.; stir until chocolate is completely melted. Set aside.

BEAT cream cheese, sugar and milk in large bowl with electric mixer on medium speed until well blended. Add melted chocolate; mix well. Gently stir in COOL WHIP, marshmallows and nuts. Coarsely chop remaining 2 chocolate squares; stir into cream cheese mixture. Spoon into crust.

REFRIGERATE 4 hours or until set. Garnish as desired. Store leftover pie in refrigerator.

SIZE-WISE:
Since this indulgent cheesecake makes 10 servings, it's the perfect dessert to serve at your next party.

so-easy german chocolate cake

PREP: 10 min. | TOTAL: 1 hour 40 min. | MAKES: 16 servings.

▶ what you need!

- 1 pkg. (19.5 oz.) brownie mix
- ¼ cup butter, cut up
- 4 oz. (½ of 8-oz. pkg.) PHILADELPHIA Cream Cheese, cubed
- ½ cup firmly packed brown sugar
- 1 cup BAKER'S ANGEL FLAKE Coconut
- 1 cup PLANTERS Pecan Pieces

▶ make it!

HEAT oven to 350°F.

PREPARE brownie mix as directed on package for cake-like brownies. Pour batter into greased 13×9-inch baking pan.

PLACE butter and cream cheese in small saucepan; cook on medium heat until cream cheese is completely melted and mixture is well blended, stirring frequently. Stir in sugar. Add coconut and nuts; mix well. (Mixture will be thick.) Drop spoonfuls of the cream cheese mixture over brownie batter in pan.

BAKE 30 min. or until toothpick inserted in center comes out clean. Cool 1 hour. Store leftover cake in the refrigerator.

EASY CLEANUP:
Make cleanup easier by lining baking pan with foil before using. To easily remove the baked cake from pan, extend foil beyond sides of pan. Then use the foil as handles to remove the cake from the pan.

triple-layer mud pie

PREP: 15 min. | TOTAL: 3 hours 15 min. | MAKES: 10 servings.

▶ what you need!

3 squares BAKER'S Semi-Sweet Chocolate, melted

¼ cup canned sweetened condensed milk

1 OREO Pie Crust (6 oz.)

½ cup chopped PLANTERS Pecans, toasted

2 pkg. (3.9 oz. each) JELL-O Chocolate Instant Pudding

2 cups cold milk

1 tub (8 oz.) COOL WHIP Whipped Topping, thawed, divided

▶ make it!

MIX chocolate and sweetened condensed milk. Pour into crust; sprinkle with nuts.

BEAT dry pudding mixes and milk with whisk 2 min.; spoon 1½ cups over nuts. Stir half the COOL WHIP into remaining pudding; spread over pudding layer in crust. Top with remaining COOL WHIP.

REFRIGERATE 3 hours.

HOW TO TOAST NUTS:
Heat oven to 350°F. Spread nuts in single layer in shallow pan. Bake 5 to 7 min. or until lightly toasted, stirring occasionally.

white chocolate fudge

PREP: 20 min. | TOTAL: 2 hours 20 min. | MAKES: 4 doz. pieces or 24 servings, 2 pieces each.

▶ what you need!

2 pkg. (6 squares each) BAKER'S White Chocolate

¾ cup sweetened condensed milk

1 cup coarsely chopped PLANTERS Almonds, toasted

½ cup dried cranberries

1 Tbsp. grated orange zest

▶ make it!

LINE 8-inch square pan with foil, with ends of foil extending over sides of pan; set aside. Microwave chocolate and sweetened condensed milk in large microwaveable bowl on HIGH 2 to 3 min. or until chocolate is almost melted; stir until chocolate is completely melted. Add nuts, cranberries and orange zest; stir until well blended.

SPREAD chocolate mixture into prepared pan. Refrigerate 2 hours or until firm.

LIFT fudge from pan, using foil handles. Cut into 48 pieces. Store in tightly covered container in refrigerator up to 3 weeks. (Do not freeze.)

WHAT TO DO WITH LEFTOVER SWEETENED CONDENSED MILK:
Store leftover sweetened condensed milk in tightly covered container in refrigerator up to 1 week. Serve over cut-up fruit or hot cooked oatmeal. Or for extra flavor, stir into your cup of hot brewed coffee or tea instead of regular milk.

cookies & cream freeze

▶ what you need!

4 squares BAKER'S Semi-Sweet Chocolate

14 OREO Cookies, divided

1 pkg. (8 oz.) PHILADELPHIA Cream Cheese, softened

¼ cup sugar

½ tsp. vanilla

1 tub (8 oz.) COOL WHIP Whipped Topping, thawed

▶ make it!

MELT chocolate as directed on package; set aside until ready to use. Line 8½×4½-inch loaf pan with foil, with ends of foil extending over sides of pan. Arrange 8 of the cookies evenly on bottom of pan. Crumble remaining 6 cookies; set aside.

BEAT cream cheese, sugar and vanilla in medium bowl with electric mixer until well blended. Stir in COOL WHIP. Remove about 1½ cups of the cream cheese mixture; place in medium bowl. Stir in melted chocolate.

SPREAD remaining cream cheese mixture over cookies in pan; sprinkle with crumbled cookies. Gently press cookies into cream cheese mixture with back of spoon; top with chocolate mixture. Cover. Freeze 3 hours or until firm. Remove from freezer about 15 min. before serving; invert onto serving plate. Peel off foil; let stand at room temperature to soften slightly before cutting to serve.

SPECIAL EXTRA:
Drizzle serving plates with additional melted BAKER'S Semi-Sweet Chocolate for a spectacular, yet simple, dessert presentation.

german chocolate cheesecake

PREP: 30 min. | TOTAL: 4 hours 20 min. | MAKES: 14 servings.

▶ what you need!

1 cup finely crushed FAMOUS Chocolate Wafers

1 cup sugar, divided

3 Tbsp. butter or margarine, melted

3 pkg. (8 oz. each) PHILADELPHIA Cream Cheese, softened

¼ cup flour

1 pkg. (4 oz.) BAKER'S GERMAN'S Sweet Chocolate, melted

2½ tsp. vanilla, divided

4 eggs, divided

⅓ cup canned evaporated milk

¼ cup butter or margarine

½ cup BAKER'S ANGEL FLAKE Coconut

½ cup PLANTERS Chopped Pecans

▶ make it!

HEAT oven to 350°F.

MIX chocolate wafer crumbs, 2 Tbsp. of the sugar and 3 Tbsp. butter; press firmly onto bottom of 9-inch springform pan. Bake 10 min.

BEAT cream cheese, ½ cup of the sugar and the flour in large bowl with electric mixer on medium speed until well blended. Add chocolate and 2 tsp. of the vanilla; mix well. Add 3 of the eggs, 1 at a time, mixing on low speed after each addition just until blended. Pour over crust.

BAKE 45 to 50 min. or until center is almost set. Run knife or metal spatula around rim of pan to loosen cake; cool before removing rim of pan. Refrigerate 4 hours or overnight.

PLACE evaporated milk, remaining sugar, the ¼ cup butter, remaining egg and remaining ½ tsp. vanilla in small saucepan; cook on medium-low heat until thickened, stirring constantly. Stir in coconut and nuts. Cool. Spread over cheesecake just before serving. Store leftover cheesecake in refrigerator.

chocolate-peanut butter candy dessert

PREP: 15 min. | TOTAL: 3 hours 15 min. | MAKES: 12 servings.

▶ what you need!

12 OREO Cookies, crushed

2 Tbsp. butter, melted

2 cups cold milk

½ cup PLANTERS Creamy Peanut Butter

2 pkg. (3.9 oz. each) JELL-O Chocolate Instant Pudding

2 cups thawed COOL WHIP Whipped Topping, divided

2 Tbsp. hot fudge ice cream topping

¼ cup candy-coated peanut butter pieces

▶ make it!

MIX crushed cookies and butter; press onto bottom of 8-inch square pan.

ADD milk gradually to peanut butter in large bowl, stirring with whisk until well blended. Add dry pudding mixes; beat 2 min. (Mixture will be thick.) Stir in 1 cup COOL WHIP. Spread onto crust; cover with remaining COOL WHIP.

REFRIGERATE 3 hours or until firm. When ready to serve, microwave fudge topping as directed on label; drizzle over dessert. Top with peanut butter pieces.

MAKE AHEAD:
Make this dessert the day before the party and keep in the refrigerator until ready to serve.

KID FAVORITES

apple-cinnamon bun dip

PREP: 5 min. | **TOTAL:** 20 min. | **MAKES:** 1¼ cups dip or 10 servings, 2 Tbsp. dip and 8 wafers each.

▶ what you need!

    1 container (6 oz.) vanilla low-fat yogurt

    ½ cup applesauce

    ½ tsp. lemon zest

    ½ tsp. ground cinnamon

    2 tsp. caramel ice cream topping

    4 NILLA Wafers, coarsely crushed

       Additional NILLA Wafers for dipping

▶ make it!

MIX first 4 ingredients until blended. Drizzle with caramel topping; top with wafer crumbs.

REFRIGERATE 15 min. or until chilled.

SERVE as dip with NILLA Wafers.

SPECIAL EXTRA:
For a unique dip container, cut off top and hollow out large red apple. Stand upright on serving platter; fill with dip. Surround with wafers.

aquarium cups

PREP: 15 min. | TOTAL: 1 hour 15 min. | MAKES: 4 servings, about ½ cup each.

▶ what you need!

¾ cup boiling water

1 pkg. (3 oz.) JELL-O Berry Blue Flavor Gelatin

Ice cubes

½ cup cold water

½ cup chopped strawberries

4 bite-size fish-shaped chewy fruit snacks

▶ make it!

ADD boiling water to gelatin in medium bowl; stir 2 min. until completely dissolved. Add enough ice cubes to cold water to measure 1¼ cups. Add to gelatin; stir until slightly thickened. Remove any unmelted ice. If gelatin is still thin, refrigerate until slightly thickened.

PLACE berries in 4 clear plastic cups; cover with gelatin. Press fruit snacks into gelatin until completely submerged.

REFRIGERATE 1 hour or until firm.

SUBSTITUTE:
Substitute your favorite fruit for the strawberries.

triple-layer peanut butter brownies

PREP: 40 min. | TOTAL: 2 hours 10 min. | MAKES: 32 servings.

▶ what you need!

- 1 pkg. (19 to 21 oz.) brownie mix (13×9-inch pan size)
- 1 pkg. (3.4 oz.) JELL-O Vanilla Flavor Instant Pudding
- 1 cup cold milk
- 1 cup PLANTERS Creamy Peanut Butter
- ½ cup powdered sugar
- 1½ cups COOL WHIP Whipped Topping (Do not thaw.)
- 3 squares BAKER'S Semi-Sweet Chocolate
- ½ cup PLANTERS Dry Roasted Peanuts, coarsely chopped

▶ make it!

PREPARE and bake brownies in 13×9-inch pan as directed on package; cool. Meanwhile, beat dry pudding mix and milk with whisk 2 min. Add peanut butter and powdered sugar; mix well. Refrigerate until brownies are completely cooled.

SPREAD pudding mixture over brownies.

MICROWAVE COOL WHIP and chocolate on HIGH 1 min., stirring every 30 sec. Spread over pudding; top with nuts. Refrigerate 1 hour.

SUBSTITUTE:
Prepare using JELL-O White Chocolate Flavor Instant Pudding.

CHIPS AHOY!
ice cream cheesecake

PREP: 15 min. | TOTAL: 4 hours 15 min. | MAKES: 16 servings.

▶ what you need!

1 pkg. (15.2 oz.) CHIPS AHOY! Cookies, divided

2 Tbsp. butter, melted

2 pkg. (8 oz. each) PHILADELPHIA Cream Cheese, softened

½ cup sugar

2 tsp. vanilla

1½ qt. (6 cups) vanilla ice cream, slightly softened

▶ make it!

CRUSH 20 cookies to form fine crumbs; mix with butter until well blended. Press onto bottom of 9-inch springform pan. Chop 16 of the remaining cookies.

BEAT cream cheese, sugar and vanilla in large bowl with mixer until well blended. Add ice cream; mix well. Stir in chopped cookies; pour over crust.

FREEZE 4 hours or until firm. Remove from freezer 10 min. before serving; let stand at room temperature to soften slightly. Top with remaining cookies.

SPECIAL EXTRA:
Drizzle chilled cheesecake with chocolate or caramel sauce, then top each serving with a dollop of thawed COOL WHIP Whipped Topping.

VARIATION:
Prepare in a 13×9-inch pan instead of the springform pan.

chocolate-peanut butter cupcakes

PREP: 10 min. | TOTAL: 1 hour 20 min. | MAKES: 2 doz. or 24 servings, 1 cupcake each.

▶ what you need!

1 pkg. (2-layer size) devil's food cake mix

1 cup cold milk

1 pkg. (3.4 oz.) JELL-O Vanilla Flavor Instant Pudding

½ cup PLANTERS Creamy Peanut Butter

1½ cups thawed COOL WHIP Whipped Topping

4 squares BAKER'S Semi-Sweet Chocolate

¼ cup PLANTERS Dry Roasted Peanuts, chopped

▶ make it!

HEAT oven to 350°F.

PREPARE cake mix and bake in 24 paper-lined muffin cups, as directed on package. Cool only 30 min. (Cupcakes need to still be warm to fill.)

POUR milk into medium bowl. Add dry pudding mix. Beat with wire whisk 2 min. or until well blended. Add peanut butter; beat well. Spoon into small freezer-weight resealable plastic bag or pastry bag; seal bag. (If using plastic bag, snip off one of the corners from bottom of bag.) Insert tip of bag into center of each cupcake; pipe in about 1 Tbsp. of the filling.

MICROWAVE COOL WHIP and chocolate in small microwaveable bowl on HIGH 1½ min. or until chocolate is completely melted and mixture is well blended, stirring after 1 min. Dip the top of each cupcake into glaze. Sprinkle evenly with nuts. Store cupcakes in refrigerator.

HOW TO:
To frost with flair, dip top of cupcake into glaze, twist slightly and lift up.

easy banana pudding parfaits

PREP: 15 min. | TOTAL: 30 min. | MAKES: 2 servings.

▶ what you need!

12 NILLA Wafers, divided

¼ cup thawed COOL WHIP Whipped Topping, divided

1 small banana, cut into 10 slices, divided

2 JELL-O Vanilla Pudding Snacks

▶ make it!

CRUSH 10 wafers to form coarse crumbs; place ¼ of the crumbs in each of 2 parfait glasses. Top each with 1 Tbsp. COOL WHIP, 2 banana slices and half of 1 pudding snack. Repeat layers of crumbs, bananas and pudding.

REFRIGERATE 15 min. Meanwhile, wrap reserved banana slices tightly in plastic wrap; refrigerate until ready to use.

TOP parfaits with remaining COOL WHIP, wafers and banana slices just before serving.

HOW TO PREVENT THE BANANA SLICES FROM TURNING BROWN:
Toss banana slices with small amount of lemon juice.

easy celebration pretzel sticks

PREP: 15 min. | TOTAL: 15 min. | MAKES: 28 servings.

▶ what you need!

28 pretzel rods

1 tub (7 oz.) BAKER'S Real Dark Semi-Sweet Dipping Chocolate, melted

Multi-colored sprinkles

▶ make it!

DIP pretzels halfway into chocolate; scrape off excess.

COAT lightly with sprinkles; place on waxed paper-covered tray.

REFRIGERATE until chocolate is firm.

JAZZ IT UP:
Also try sprinkling dipped pretzels with BAKER'S ANGEL FLAKE Coconut or drizzling with melted BAKER'S White Chocolate.

luscious "cream puffs"

PREP: 15 min. | TOTAL: 45 min. | MAKES: 9 servings.

▶ what you need!

1 sheet frozen puff pastry (½ of 17.3-oz. pkg.), thawed

1 pkg. (3.4 oz.) JELL-O Vanilla Flavor Instant Pudding

1 cup cold milk

½ cup thawed COOL WHIP Whipped Topping

1 square BAKER'S Semi-Sweet Chocolate

▶ make it!

HEAT oven to 400°F.

UNFOLD pastry on lightly floured surface; roll to 10-inch square. Cut into 9 circles with 3-inch cookie cutter. Place, 2 inches apart, on baking sheet. Bake 10 min. Remove to wire racks; cool completely.

MEANWHILE, beat dry pudding mix and milk in medium bowl with whisk 2 min. Stir in COOL WHIP. Refrigerate 15 min.

MELT chocolate as directed on package. Split pastry rounds; fill with pudding mixture. Drizzle with chocolate.

OREO cookies & creme pudding pops

PREP: 10 min. | TOTAL: 5 hours 10 min. | MAKES: 10 servings.

▶ what you need!

1 pkg. (3.4 oz.) JELL-O Vanilla Flavor Instant Pudding

2 cups cold milk

12 OREO Cookies, divided

½ cup thawed COOL WHIP Whipped Topping

▶ make it!

BEAT dry pudding mix and milk in medium bowl with whisk 2 min.

CHOP 6 cookies; crush remaining cookies. Spoon half the crushed cookies onto bottoms of 10 (3-oz.) paper or plastic cups.

ADD chopped cookies and COOL WHIP to pudding; stir just until blended.

SPOON pudding mixture into cups; top with remaining crushed cookies. Insert wooden pop stick or plastic spoon into each for handle. Freeze 5 hours or until firm.

HOW TO REMOVE FROZEN POPS FROM CUPS:
Hold frozen cups with hands on sides of cups to warm pops slightly before removing from cups. To remove pops, press firmly onto bottom of cup to release pop. Do not twist or pull pop stick.

OREO frogs

PREP: 20 min. | TOTAL: 15 min. | MAKES: 6 servings.

▶ what you need!

- 2 squares BAKER'S Semi-Sweet Chocolate
- 2 Tbsp. butter or margarine
- 12 OREO Cookies
- ¼ cup JET-PUFFED Marshmallow Creme
- 24 miniature pretzel twists
- 24 candy-coated chocolate pieces

▶ make it!

MICROWAVE chocolate and butter in microwaveable bowl on HIGH 1 min. or until chocolate is completely melted and mixture is well blended, stirring every 30 sec.

SPREAD bottom of each cookie with 1 tsp. marshmallow creme, then dip bottom in melted chocolate. Immediately press 2 pretzel twists into chocolate for each frog's legs, with wide part of each pretzel facing outward. Place, pretzel-sides down, on waxed paper-covered baking sheet.

USE remaining melted chocolate to attach candies to tops of cookies for frog's eyes. Let stand until chocolate is firm.

OREO milk shake

PREP: 10 min. | TOTAL: 10 min. | MAKES: 4 servings, about 1 cup each.

► what you need!

4 tsp. chocolate syrup

8 OREO Cookies, divided

1½ cups milk

2 cups BREYERS®* All Natural Vanilla Ice Cream, softened

► make it!

SPOON 1 tsp. syrup into each of 4 glasses. Roll each glass to coat bottom and inside of glass. Finely chop 4 cookies; set aside.

QUARTER remaining cookies; place in blender. Add milk and ice cream; blend until smooth.

POUR into prepared glasses; top with chopped cookies. Serve immediately.

SUBSTITUTE:
For a lower calorie and fat option, use Reduced Fat OREO and BREYERS® SMOOTH & DREAMY™ Fat-Free Vanilla Ice Cream.

*BREYERS® is a registered trademark of Unilever, N. V., used under license.

triple strawberry no-drip pops

PREP: 10 min. | TOTAL: 2 hours 10 min. | MAKES: 8 servings.

▶ what you need!

2 cups boiling water

1 pkg. (3 oz.) JELL-O Strawberry Flavor Gelatin

18 fresh strawberries, stemmed

⅔ cup (filled to 2-qt. line) KOOL-AID Strawberry Flavor Sugar-Sweetened Soft Drink Mix, or any red flavor

▶ make it!

ADD boiling water to dry gelatin mix; stir 2 min. until completely dissolved.

CUT strawberries in half. Mash berries and drink mix in large bowl with fork. Stir in gelatin.

POUR into 8 (5-oz.) paper cups.

COVER cups with foil, insert wooden pop stick into center of each for handle. Freeze 2 hours or until firm.

VARIATION TWIST ON YOUR POP FLAVOR!:
Mix and match this refreshing summer pop with your favorite flavor combination of JELL-O, KOOL-AID and fruit.

MAKE AHEAD:
Make ahead to have on hand for an "anytime" snack.

rich 'n thick hot chocolate

PREP: 5 min. | TOTAL: 20 min. | MAKES: 4 servings, about 1 cup each.

▶ what you need!

1 cup water

2 squares BAKER'S Unsweetened Chocolate

½ cup sugar

3 cups milk

1 tsp. vanilla

JET-PUFFED Miniature Marshmallows (optional)

▶ make it!

PLACE water and chocolate in heavy medium saucepan; cook on low heat until chocolate is completely melted and mixture is well blended, stirring constantly with wire whisk. Add sugar; mix well.

BRING to boil on medium-high heat. Boil 3 min., stirring constantly. Gradually add milk, stirring with wire whisk until well blended. Stir in vanilla. Reduce heat to medium.

COOK until mixture is heated through, stirring occasionally. Serve with marshmallows, if desired.

rocket pops

PREP: 30 min. | TOTAL: 7 hours 30 min. | MAKES: 16 servings, 1 pop each.

▶ what you need!

1 pkg. (4-serving size) JELL-O Cherry Flavor Gelatin

1 cup sugar, divided

2 cups boiling water, divided

   Ice cubes

2 cups cold water, divided

1 pkg. (4-serving size) JELL-O Berry Blue Flavor Gelatin

1 tub (8 oz.) COOL WHIP Whipped Topping, thawed

▶ make it!

COMBINE dry cherry gelatin mix and ½ cup of the sugar in medium bowl. Add 1 cup of the boiling water; stir at least 2 min. until gelatin is completely dissolved. Add enough ice cubes to 1 cup of the cold water to measure 2 cups. Add to gelatin; stir until ice is completely melted. Pour evenly into 16 (5-oz.) paper or plastic cups, adding about ¼ cup of the gelatin to each cup. Freeze 1 hour.

MEANWHILE, combine dry blue gelatin mix and remaining ½ cup sugar in medium bowl. Add remaining 1 cup boiling water; stir at least 2 min. until gelatin is completely dissolved. Add enough ice cubes to remaining 1 cup cold water to measure 2 cups. Add to gelatin; stir until ice is completely melted. Refrigerate 1 hour.

SPOON about 3 Tbsp. COOL WHIP over red gelatin in each cup; top evenly with blue gelatin, adding about ¼ cup of the gelatin to each cup. Freeze 1 hour or until almost firm. Insert wooden pop stick or plastic spoon into center of each cup for handle. Freeze an additional 4 hours or overnight. To remove pops from cups, place bottoms of cups under warm running water for 15 sec. Press firmly on bottoms of cups to release pops. (Do not twist or pull pop sticks.) Store leftover pops in freezer.

NOTE:
Wooden pop sticks can be found at craft stores.

chewy chips s'more

PREP: 5 min. | TOTAL: 5 min. | MAKES: 1 serving.

▶ what you need!

2 Chewy CHIPS AHOY! Real Chocolate Chip Cookies

1 JET-PUFFED Marshmallow

▶ make it!

PLACE 1 cookie, upside-down, on microwaveable plate; top with marshmallow.

MICROWAVE on HIGH 8 to 10 sec. or until marshmallow puffs.

TOP with second cookie; press down lightly to secure.

SUBSTITUTE:
Prepare using CHIPS AHOY! Cookies.

dirt cups

PREP: 15 min. | TOTAL: 1 hour 15 min. | MAKES: 10 servings.

▶ what you need!

1 pkg. (3.9 oz.) JELL-O Chocolate Instant Pudding

2 cups cold milk

1 tub (8 oz.) COOL WHIP Whipped Topping, thawed

15 OREO Cookies, finely crushed (about 1¼ cups), divided

10 worm-shaped chewy fruit snacks

▶ make it!

BEAT dry pudding mix and milk in large bowl with whisk 2 min. Let stand 5 min. Stir in COOL WHIP and ½ cup cookie crumbs.

SPOON into 10 (6- to 7-oz.) plastic or paper cups; top with remaining cookie crumbs.

REFRIGERATE 1 hour. Top with fruit snacks just before serving.

SAND CUPS:
Prepare using JELL-O Vanilla Flavor Instant Pudding and 35 NILLA Wafers.

s'mores dessert squares

PREP: 30 min. | TOTAL: 3 hours 36 min. | MAKES: 24 servings.

▶ what you need!

64 NILLA Wafers, divided

5 Tbsp. butter or margarine, melted

3 Tbsp. sugar

1 pkg. (3.9 oz.) JELL-O Chocolate Instant Pudding

3¼ cups cold milk, divided

2 pkg. (3.4 oz. each) JELL-O White Chocolate Flavor Instant Pudding

1½ cups thawed COOL WHIP Whipped Topping

1½ cups JET-PUFFED Miniature Marshmallows

½ square BAKER'S Semi-Sweet Chocolate, grated

▶ make it!

HEAT oven to 350°F.

CRUSH 40 wafers finely; place in medium bowl. Add butter and sugar; mix well. Press onto bottom of 13×9-inch pan. Bake 8 min. or until lightly browned. Cool.

BEAT 1 package chocolate pudding mix and 1¼ cups milk with whisk 2 min.; spread over crust. Cover with remaining wafers. Beat white chocolate pudding mixes and remaining milk in medium bowl with whisk 2 min. Stir in COOL WHIP. Spread over wafer layer in pan. Refrigerate 3 hours or until firm.

HEAT broiler just before serving dessert. Top dessert with marshmallows; broil, 6 inches from heat, 1 min. or until marshmallows are puffed and lightly browned. Sprinkle with grated chocolate.

TAKE ALONG:
Assemble dessert in 13×9-inch disposable foil pan. Wrap tightly in plastic wrap and refrigerate as directed. Store in an insulated cooler packed with plenty of ice or frozen gel packs to take along to your party destination. Uncover and top with marshmallows just before serving, then broil as directed.

snowman cups

PREP: 15 min. | TOTAL: 15 min. | MAKES: 10 servings. ½ cup each.

▶ what you need!

2 pkg. (3.9 oz. each) JELL-O Chocolate Instant Pudding

1 qt. (4 cups) cold milk

20 OREO Cookies, crushed (about 2 cups), divided

2 cups thawed COOL WHIP Whipped Topping

Assorted decorating gels

▶ make it!

BEAT dry pudding mixes and milk with whisk 2 min. Let stand 5 min. Stir in 1 cup cookie crumbs.

SPOON remaining cookie crumbs into 10 (6- to 7-oz.) plastic cups; cover with pudding mixture.

DROP spoonfuls of COOL WHIP onto desserts to resemble snowmen. Decorate with gels for the eyes, noses and scarves.

MAKE IT EASY:
Instead of dropping spoonfuls of the COOL WHIP onto desserts, fill resealable plastic bag with COOL WHIP; seal bag. Using scissors, diagonally snip off one corner from bottom of bag. Squeeze COOL WHIP from bag to create snowmen. Decorate as directed.

strawberry snow cones

PREP: 10 min. | TOTAL: 10 min. | MAKES: 8 servings.

▶ what you need!

1 cup boiling water

1 pkg. (6 oz.) JELL-O Gelatin, any red flavor

1 cup puréed strawberries

½ cup light corn syrup

½ cup ice cubes

8 cups crushed ice

▶ make it!

ADD boiling water to dry gelatin mix in large bowl; stir 2 min. until completely dissolved. Add strawberries, corn syrup and ice cubes; stir until ice is completely melted.

SPOON crushed ice into 8 (8-oz.) paper or plastic cups.

SPOON gelatin mixture over ice. Serve immediately.

FUN IDEA:
Let the kids make their own holders for the prepared snow cones. Use markers to decorate sheets of construction paper. Roll up each to form cone shape; secure with staples. Insert filled paper cups into holders just before serving.

STORAGE KNOW-HOW:
If you have more snow cones than kids, wrap filled cups well with plastic wrap; store in freezer up to 3 weeks. Remove from freezer about 5 min. before serving.

sun-in-a-cloud

PREP: 10 min. | **TOTAL:** 10 min. | **MAKES:** 1½ cups dip or 12 servings, 2 Tbsp. dip and 8 graham pieces each.

▶ what you need!

1 cup thawed COOL WHIP LITE Whipped Topping

1 JELL-O Vanilla Pudding Snack

½ tsp. colored sprinkles

24 HONEY MAID Cinnamon Grahams, broken into quarters

▶ make it!

USE large spoon to spread COOL WHIP onto small plate, indenting center slightly.

FILL center with pudding; top with sprinkles.

INSERT 8 graham pieces into COOL WHIP. Serve with remaining grahams.

FAMILY FUN:
This is a great recipe to prepare with the kids!

CRAZY
FOR FRUIT

cool raspberry fruit dip

PREP: 5 min. | TOTAL: 5 min. | MAKES: 1¼ cups or 10 servings, 2 Tbsp. each.

▶ what you need!

1   container (6 oz.) raspberry nonfat yogurt

¾   cup thawed COOL WHIP Sugar Free Whipped Topping

▶ make it!

MIX ingredients until well blended.

SERVE immediately as a dip for cut-up fresh fruit. Or, cover and refrigerate until ready to serve.

SUBSTITUTE:
Prepare as directed, using COOL WHIP LITE Whipped Topping.

NUTRITION BONUS:
Add extra flavor to your favorite fruit with this tasty low-fat dip.

banana cream pie
with caramel drizzle

PREP: 15 min. | TOTAL: 4 hours 15 min. | MAKES: 10 servings.

▶ what you need!

1½ bananas, divided

1 HONEY MAID Graham Pie Crust (6 oz.)

2 pkg. (3.4 oz. each) JELL-O Vanilla Flavor Instant Pudding

2 cups cold milk

2 cups thawed COOL WHIP Whipped Topping, divided

¼ cup caramel ice cream topping

▶ make it!

SLICE 1 of the bananas; spread onto bottom of crust.

BEAT dry pudding mixes and milk in medium bowl with whisk 2 min. Stir in 1 cup COOL WHIP. Pour into crust.

REFRIGERATE 4 hours or until firm. Drizzle with caramel topping just before serving. Top with remaining COOL WHIP and ½ banana. Store leftovers in refrigerator.

VARIATION:
Prepare as directed, using JELL-O Banana Cream Flavor Instant Pudding.

SUBSTITUTE:
Prepare as directed, using COOL WHIP LITE Whipped Topping.

beautifully easy fruit tart

PREP: 15 min. | TOTAL: 45 min. | MAKES: 9 servings.

▶ what you need!

- 1 sheet frozen puff pastry (½ of 17.3-oz. pkg.), thawed
- 1 pkg. (3.4 oz.) JELL-O Vanilla Flavor Instant Pudding
- 1 cup cold milk
- 1 cup thawed COOL WHIP Whipped Topping
- 1 square BAKER'S White Chocolate
- 1 cup quartered fresh strawberries
- 1 can (11 oz.) mandarin oranges, drained
- 1 kiwi, peeled, sliced and halved
- 3 Tbsp. apricot preserves
- 2 tsp. water

▶ make it!

HEAT oven to 400°F.

UNROLL pastry on baking sheet. Fold over edges of pastry to form ½-inch rim; press together firmly to seal. Prick pastry sheet with fork. Bake 10 to 15 min. or until puffed and golden brown. Cool completely. Place on tray.

BEAT dry pudding mix and milk in large bowl with whisk 2 min. Stir in COOL WHIP; spread onto pastry.

MELT chocolate as directed on package. Arrange fruit over pudding mixture. Mix preserves and water; brush onto fruit. Drizzle with chocolate. Let stand until chocolate is firm.

HOW TO DRIZZLE CHOCOLATE:
Dip a large spoon into the bowl of melted chocolate. Quickly move the spoon back and forth over the tart, letting the chocolate fall in thin ribbons from the end of the spoon. Repeat until all of the chocolate is used.

SUBSTITUTE:
Substitute orange marmalade or pineapple preserves for the apricot preserves.

floating fruit parfaits

PREP: 15 min. | TOTAL: 1 hour 15 min. | MAKES: 6 servings.

▶ what you need!

½ cup sliced fresh strawberries

¾ cup boiling water

1 pkg. (0.3 oz.) JELL-O Strawberry Flavor Sugar Free Gelatin

½ cup cold water

¾ cup ice cubes

1 cup plus 6 Tbsp. thawed COOL WHIP LITE Whipped Topping, divided

▶ make it!

SPOON berries into 6 parfait or dessert glasses. Add boiling water to dry gelatin mix in medium bowl; stir 2 min. until completely dissolved. Add cold water and ice cubes; stir until ice is melted. Pour ¾ cup gelatin over berries. Refrigerate 20 min. or until gelatin is set but not firm.

ADD 1 cup COOL WHIP to remaining gelatin; whisk until well blended. Spoon over gelatin in glasses.

REFRIGERATE 1 hour or until firm. Serve topped with remaining COOL WHIP.

VARIATION:
Prepare as directed, using JELL-O Orange Flavor Sugar Free Gelatin and substituting cantaloupe balls for the strawberries.

SPECIAL EXTRA:
Add ½ cup seedless grapes with the strawberries.

STORING FRESH FRUIT:
Most fruits keep best when stored in the refrigerator. Berries, cherries and plums should not be washed before refrigeration, since excess moisture will cause these fruits to spoil more quickly.

NUTRITION BONUS:
Satisfy your sweet tooth with this elegant low-fat dessert. As a bonus, the strawberries provide a good source of vitamin C.

cherry-vanilla ice cream pie

PREP: 20 min. | TOTAL: 4 hours 20 min. | MAKES: 10 servings.

► what you need!

18 OREO Cookies, finely crushed (about 1½ cups)

3 Tbsp. butter or margarine, melted

3 cups vanilla ice cream, softened

1 can (21 oz.) cherry pie filling, divided

1 Tbsp. chocolate syrup

► make it!

COMBINE cookie crumbs and butter; press onto bottom and up side of 9-inch pie plate sprayed with cooking spray. Refrigerate until ready to use.

MIX ice cream and 1½ cups pie filling; spoon into crust. Freeze 4 hours or until firm.

DRIZZLE chocolate syrup over pie. Serve topped with remaining cherry pie filling.

SUBSTITUTE:
Prepare using a chocolate syrup that hardens to form a "shell" when drizzled over the pie.

COOL WHIP fruit dip

PREP: 10 min. | TOTAL: 3 hours 10 min. | MAKES: 24 servings, 2 Tbsp. each.

▶ what you need!

1 cup plain nonfat yogurt

¼ cup sugar

1 Tbsp. grated orange zest

¼ cup orange juice

2 cups thawed COOL WHIP Whipped Topping

▶ make it!

WHISK first 4 ingredients in medium bowl.

STIR in COOL WHIP.

REFRIGERATE 3 hours.

SERVING SUGGESTION:
Serve with strawberries and other cut-up fresh fruit for dipping.

HOW TO WASH FRESH BERRIES:
For best results, wash fresh berries just before use. Place in a colander and gently rinse with a cold water spray. Then, place on sheets of paper towels to dry.

creamy layered peach squares

PREP: 30 min. | TOTAL: 4 hours 30 min. | MAKES: 20 servings.

▶ what you need!

2 cups HONEY MAID Graham Cracker Crumbs

½ cup sugar, divided

½ cup butter or margarine, melted

1½ pkg. (8 oz. each) PHILADELPHIA Cream Cheese, softened

1 tub (8 oz.) COOL WHIP Whipped Topping, thawed, divided

3 large fresh peaches (about 1¼ lb.), peeled, sliced

1½ cups boiling water

1 pkg. (6 oz.) JELL-O Raspberry Flavor Gelatin

2 cups ice cubes

▶ make it!

MIX graham crumbs, ¼ cup sugar and butter in 13×9-inch pan; press onto bottom of pan.

BEAT cream cheese and remaining sugar in medium bowl until well blended. Whisk in 1½ cups COOL WHIP; spread over crust. Top with peaches. Refrigerate until ready to use.

ADD boiling water to dry gelatin mix in large bowl; stir 2 min. until completely dissolved. Stir in ice cubes until melted. Refrigerate 5 min. or until thickened. Whisk in remaining COOL WHIP; spread over peach layer. Refrigerate 4 hours or until firm.

SPECIAL EXTRA:
Garnish with fresh raspberries and peach slices.

vanilla cherry cheesecake

PREP: 15 min. | TOTAL: 3 hours 55 min. | MAKES: 10 servings.

▶ what you need!

2 pkg. (8 oz. each) PHILADELPHIA Cream Cheese, softened

⅓ cup GENERAL FOODS INTERNATIONAL Vanilla Crème

¼ cup sugar

¼ cup milk

2 eggs

1 HONEY MAID Pie Crust (6 oz.)

1 cup cherry pie filling

▶ make it!

HEAT oven to 325°F.

BEAT cream cheese, vanilla beverage mix and sugar in large bowl with electric mixer on medium speed until well blended. Gradually add milk, beating until well blended. Add eggs, 1 at a time, beating just until blended after each addition. Pour into crust.

BAKE 40 min. or until center is almost set. Cool.

REFRIGERATE 3 hours or overnight. Top with cherry pie filling just before serving. Store leftover cheesecake in refrigerator.

fruit pizza

PREP: 25 min. | TOTAL: 2 hours 59 min. | MAKES: 12 servings, 1 wedge each.

▶ what you need!

1 pkg. (20 oz.) refrigerated sliceable sugar cookies, sliced

1 pkg. (8 oz.) PHILADELPHIA Cream Cheese, softened

¼ cup sugar

½ tsp. vanilla

Assorted fruit, such as sliced kiwi, strawberries, blueberries and drained, canned mandarin orange segments

¼ cup apricot preserves, pressed through sieve to remove lumps

1 Tbsp. water

▶ make it!

HEAT oven to 375°F.

LINE 12-inch pizza pan with foil; spray with cooking spray. Arrange cookie dough slices in single layer in prepared pan; press together to form crust. Bake 14 min.; cool. Invert onto serving plate; carefully remove foil. Invert onto large serving plate or tray so crust is right-side-up.

BEAT cream cheese, sugar and vanilla with electric mixer on medium speed until well blended. Spread over crust.

ARRANGE fruit over cream cheese layer. Mix preserves and water; brush over fruit. Refrigerate 2 hours. Cut into 12 wedges to serve. Store leftover dessert in refrigerator.

PHILADELPHIA 3-STEP
low-fat berry cheesecake

PREP: 10 min. | TOTAL: 4 hours 55 min. | MAKES: 10 servings.

► what you need!

3 pkg. (8 oz. each) PHILADELPHIA Fat
  Free Cream Cheese, softened

¾ cup sugar

1 tsp. grated lemon zest

1 Tbsp. fresh lemon juice

½ tsp. vanilla

3 eggs

¼ cup crushed HONEY MAID Low Fat
  Honey Grahams

½ cup sliced strawberries

½ cup blueberries

½ cup raspberries

2 Tbsp. strawberry jelly, melted

► make it!

HEAT oven to 300°F.

1. BEAT cream cheese, sugar, lemon zest, lemon juice and vanilla with electric mixer on medium speed until well blended. Add eggs, 1 at a time, mixing on low speed after each addition just until blended. Spray 9-inch pie plate with cooking spray; sprinkle bottom with crumbs.

2. POUR cream cheese mixture into prepared pie plate.

3. BAKE 45 min. or until center is almost set. Cool. Refrigerate 3 hours or overnight. Top with fruit; drizzle with jelly.

OREO-apple snack stacks

PREP: 15 min. | TOTAL: 15 min. | MAKES: 8 servings.

▶ what you need!

- 1 pkg. (8 oz.) PHILADELPHIA Cream Cheese, softened
- 2 Tbsp. honey
- ½ tsp. zest and 2 Tbsp. juice from 1 orange, divided
- 6 OREO Cookies, chopped
- 4 small apples (1 lb.)
- 4 pretzel sticks
- 8 worm-shaped chewy fruit snacks

▶ make it!

MIX cream cheese, honey and zest in medium bowl until well blended. Stir in chopped cookies. Core apples. Cut each crosswise into 4 rings; brush cut sides with orange juice. Discard any remaining juice.

PAT apple slices dry with paper towels; spread with cream cheese mixture. Restack slices for each apple. Insert pretzel into top of each for the stem.

GARNISH with fruit snacks. Cut horizontally in half to serve.

MAKE AHEAD:
Snacks can be made ahead of time. Prepare as directed; wrap with plastic wrap. Refrigerate until ready to serve.

layered strawberry cheesecake bowl

PREP: 20 min. | TOTAL: 4 hours 20 min. | MAKES: 14 servings, ⅔ cup each.

▶ what you need!

3 cups sliced fresh strawberries

3 Tbsp. sugar

2 pkg. (8 oz. each) PHILADELPHIA Neufchâtel Cheese, softened

1½ cups cold milk

1 pkg. (3.4 oz.) JELL-O Vanilla Flavor Instant Pudding

2 cups thawed COOL WHIP LITE Whipped Topping, divided

2 cups frozen pound cake cubes (1 inch)

1 square BAKER'S Semi-Sweet Chocolate

▶ make it!

COMBINE berries and sugar; refrigerate until ready to use. Beat Neufchâtel with mixer until creamy. Gradually beat in milk. Add dry pudding mix; mix well.

BLEND in 1½ cups COOL WHIP. Spoon half into 2½-qt. bowl.

TOP with layers of cake, berries and remaining Neufchâtel mixture. Refrigerate 4 hours.

MELT chocolate; drizzle over trifle. Top with remaining COOL WHIP.

SPECIAL EXTRA:
Garnish with a chocolate-dipped strawberry just before serving.

NOTE:
You will need about half of a 10.75-oz. pkg. pound cake to get the 2 cups cake cubes needed to prepare this recipe.

PHILADELPHIA 3-STEP
pina colada cheesecake

PREP: 10 min. | TOTAL: 3 hours 50 min. | MAKES: 8 servings.

▶ what you need!

2 pkg. (8 oz. each) PHILADELPHIA Cream Cheese, softened

½ cup sugar

½ tsp. vanilla

2 eggs

⅓ cup thawed frozen pina colada tropical fruit mixer concentrate

1 HONEY MAID Graham Pie Crust (6 oz.)

4 canned pineapple rings, drained and sliced

¼ cup BAKER'S ANGEL FLAKE Coconut

▶ make it!

HEAT oven to 350°F.

1. **BEAT** cream cheese, sugar and vanilla with electric mixer on medium speed until well blended. Add eggs; mix just until blended. Stir in fruit mixer concentrate.

2. **POUR** into crust.

3. **BAKE** 40 min. or until center is almost set. Cool. Refrigerate at least 3 hours before serving. Top with pineapple and coconut. Store leftover cheesecake in refrigerator.

STRAWBERRY DAIQUIRI CHEESECAKE:
Prepare as directed, using frozen strawberry daiquiri concentrate. Garnish with fresh strawberries just before serving.

LIME MARGARITA CHEESECAKE:
Prepare as directed, using frozen margarita concentrate. Garnish with lime slices just before serving.

PHILADELPHIA strawberry fields no-bake cheesecake

PREP: 15 min. | TOTAL: 4 hours 15 min. | MAKES: 16 servings.

▶ what you need!

2 cups HONEY MAID Graham Cracker Crumbs

6 Tbsp. margarine, melted

1 cup sugar, divided

4 pkg. (8 oz. each) PHILADELPHIA Neufchâtel Cheese, softened

½ cup strawberry preserves

1 pkg. (16 oz.) frozen strawberries, thawed, drained

1 tub (8 oz.) COOL WHIP LITE Whipped Topping, thawed

▶ make it!

MIX graham crumbs, margarine and ¼ cup of the sugar; press firmly onto bottom of 13×9-inch pan. Refrigerate while preparing filling.

BEAT Neufchâtel cheese and remaining ¾ cup sugar in large bowl with electric mixer on medium speed until well blended. Add preserves; mix until blended. Stir in strawberries. Gently stir in COOL WHIP. Spoon over crust; cover.

REFRIGERATE 4 hours or until firm. Store leftovers in refrigerator.

HOW TO MAKE IT WITH FRESH STRAWBERRIES:
Place 2 cups fresh strawberries in small bowl with additional 2 Tbsp. sugar; mash with fork. Add to Neufchâtel cheese mixture; continue as directed.

scrumptious apple-pecan cheesecake

PREP: 25 min. | TOTAL: 6 hours 10 min. | MAKES: 12 servings.

▸ what you need!

1 cup HONEY MAID Graham Cracker Crumbs

¾ cup finely chopped PLANTERS Pecans, divided

3 Tbsp. sugar

1 tsp. ground cinnamon, divided

¼ cup butter or margarine, melted

2 pkg. (8 oz. each) PHILADELPHIA Cream Cheese, softened

½ cup sugar

½ tsp. vanilla

2 eggs

⅓ cup sugar

4 cups thin peeled apple slices

▸ make it!

HEAT oven to 325°F.

MIX graham crumbs, ½ cup nuts, 3 Tbsp. sugar, ½ tsp. cinnamon and butter; press onto bottom of 9-inch springform pan. Bake 10 min.

BEAT cream cheese, ½ cup sugar and vanilla with mixer until well blended. Add eggs, 1 at a time, beating on low speed after each just until blended. Pour over crust. Mix ⅓ cup sugar and remaining cinnamon in large bowl. Add apples; toss to coat. Spoon over cream cheese layer; sprinkle with remaining nuts.

BAKE 1 hour 10 min. to 1 hour 15 min. or until center is almost set. Run knife around rim of pan to loosen cake; cool before removing rim. Refrigerate 4 hours.

SIZE-WISE:
Enjoy a serving of this rich-and-indulgent treat on special occasions.

COOKING KNOW-HOW:
For best results, use firm apples, such as Granny Smith or McIntosh.

strawberry pretzel squares

PREP: 20 min. | TOTAL: 5 hours | MAKES: 20 servings.

▶ what you need!

2 cups finely crushed pretzels

½ cup sugar, divided

⅔ cup butter or margarine, melted

1½ pkg. (8 oz. each) PHILADELPHIA Cream
    Cheese, softened

2 Tbsp. milk

1 cup thawed COOL WHIP Whipped Topping

2 cups boiling water

1 pkg. (6 oz.) JELL-O Strawberry Flavor Gelatin

1½ cups cold water

4 cups fresh strawberries, sliced

▶ make it!

HEAT oven to 350°F.

MIX pretzel crumbs, ¼ cup of the sugar and the butter; press onto bottom of 13×9-inch baking pan. Bake 10 min. Cool.

BEAT cream cheese, remaining sugar and milk until well blended. Stir in COOL WHIP; spread over crust. Refrigerate.

ADD boiling water to dry gelatin mix in large bowl; stir 2 min. until completely dissolved. Stir in cold water. Refrigerate 1½ hours or until thickened.

STIR berries into gelatin; spoon over cream cheese layer. Refrigerate 3 hours or until firm.

MAKE IT EASY:
Substitute 1 pkg. (20 oz.) frozen whole strawberries, sliced, for the fresh strawberries. Stir into gelatin along with the cold water. Refrigerate 10 to 15 min. or until thickened, then spoon over cream cheese layer. Continue as directed.

SUBSTITUTE:
Prepare using 2 pkg. (3 oz. each) JELL-O Strawberry Flavor Gelatin.

triple-berry cheesecake tart

PREP: 15 min. | TOTAL: 3 hours 30 min. | MAKES: 10 servings.

▶ what you need!

1¼ cups finely crushed NILLA Wafers (about 45 wafers)

¼ cup butter, melted

1 pkg. (8 oz.) PHILADELPHIA Cream Cheese, softened

¼ cup sugar

1 cup thawed COOL WHIP Whipped Topping

2 cups mixed berries (raspberries, sliced strawberries, blueberries)

¾ cup boiling water

1 pkg. (3 oz.) JELL-O Lemon Flavor Gelatin

1 cup ice cubes

▶ make it!

MIX wafer crumbs and butter; press firmly onto bottom and up side of 9-inch tart pan. Place in freezer while preparing filling.

BEAT cream cheese and sugar in large bowl with electric mixer on medium speed until well blended. Gently stir in COOL WHIP. Spoon into crust. Top with berries. Cover and refrigerate while preparing gelatin.

STIR boiling water into dry gelatin mix in medium bowl 2 min. until completely dissolved. Add ice cubes; stir until ice is completely melted. Refrigerate 15 min., or until slightly thickened (consistency of unbeaten egg whites). Spoon gelatin over fruit in pan. Refrigerate 3 hours or until set. Store leftover tart in refrigerator.

SIZE-WISE:
This colorful berry dessert makes a great treat to share with friends and family.

tropical cheesecake

PREP: 25 min. | TOTAL: 4 hours 25 min. | MAKES: 8 servings.

▶ what you need!

1 pkg. (8 oz.) PHILADELPHIA Cream Cheese, softened

⅓ cup sugar

1 tub (8 oz.) COOL WHIP Whipped Topping, thawed

2 kiwis, peeled, quartered, sliced and divided

1 medium mango, peeled, chopped and divided

1 cup BAKER'S ANGEL FLAKE Coconut, toasted, divided

1 HONEY MAID Graham Pie Crust (6 oz.)

▶ make it!

BEAT cream cheese and sugar in large bowl with wire whisk or electric mixer until well blended.

ADD COOL WHIP; stir gently until well blended. Reserve ¼ cup <u>each</u> kiwi, mango and coconut for garnish. Stir remaining kiwi, mango and coconut into cream cheese mixture. Spoon into crust.

REFRIGERATE 3 hours or until set. Top with reserved mango, kiwi and coconut. Store leftover cheesecake in refrigerator.

HOW TO TOAST COCONUT:
Place coconut in small nonstick skillet. Cook on medium heat until lightly toasted, stirring frequently.

ginger snap-apple mallow crisp

▶ what you need!

6 Granny Smith apples (3 lb.), peeled, thinly sliced

1 cup JET-PUFFED Miniature Marshmallows

18 NABISCO Ginger Snaps, finely crushed (about 1 cup)

½ cup chopped PLANTERS Pecans

¼ cup butter or margarine, softened

1 cup thawed COOL WHIP Whipped Topping

▶ make it!

HEAT oven to 350°F.

PLACE apples in 8-inch square baking dish sprayed with cooking spray; top with marshmallows.

MIX ginger snap crumbs, nuts and butter until well blended; sprinkle over marshmallow layer.

BAKE 20 to 25 min. or until apples are tender. Serve topped with COOL WHIP.

NOTE:
Check dessert after the first 10 min. of the baking time. If it's becoming too brown, cover it loosely with foil for the rest of the baking time.

cranberry-pineapple minis

PREP: 15 min. | TOTAL: 2 hours 45 min. | MAKES: 24 servings.

▶ what you need!

   1 can (20 oz.) crushed pineapple in juice, undrained

   2 pkg. (3 oz. each) JELL-O Raspberry Flavor Gelatin

   1 can (16 oz.) whole berry cranberry sauce

   ⅔ cup chopped PLANTERS Walnuts

   1 apple, chopped

▶ make it!

DRAIN pineapple, reserving juice. Add enough water to reserved juice to measure 2½ cups; pour into saucepan. Bring to boil. Add to dry gelatin mixes in large bowl; stir 2 min. until completely dissolved.

STIR in pineapple, cranberry sauce, nuts and apple. Spoon into 24 paper-lined muffin cups.

REFRIGERATE 2½ hours or until firm. Remove desserts from liners before serving.

SUBSTITUTE:
Prepare using JELL-O Cherry Flavor Gelatin or JELL-O Raspberry Flavor Sugar Free Gelatin.

GIFT-GIVING

CHIPS AHOY! bark

PREP: 20 min. | TOTAL: 1 hour 20 min. | MAKES: 14 servings.

▶ what you need!

1 pkg. (8 squares) BAKER'S Semi-Sweet Chocolate, chopped

1 pkg. (6 squares) BAKER'S White Chocolate, chopped

10 CHIPS AHOY! Cookies, coarsely broken, divided

¼ cup dried cranberries, divided

▶ make it!

MICROWAVE semi-sweet and white chocolates in separate medium microwaveable bowls as directed on package. Stir ⅓ cup cookies and 1 Tbsp. cranberries into chocolate in each bowl.

DROP spoonfuls of the 2 chocolate mixtures alternately onto waxed paper-covered baking sheet; swirl gently with knife. Sprinkle with remaining cookies and cranberries.

REFRIGERATE 1 hour or until firm. Break into pieces.

SPECIAL EXTRA:
Toast ¼ cup PLANTERS Slivered Almonds. Add 1 Tbsp. nuts to melted chocolate in each bowl before dropping onto baking sheet and swirling as directed. Sprinkle with remaining nuts, cookies and cranberries.

chocolate, cranberry & oat bars

PREP: 15 min. | TOTAL: 45 min. | MAKES: 32 servings.

▶ what you need!

1 cup dried cranberries

¼ cup orange juice

1½ cups flour

1½ cups quick-cooking oats

1 tsp. CALUMET Baking Powder

¼ tsp. salt

¾ cup margarine, softened

1½ cups firmly packed brown sugar

2 eggs

4 squares BAKER'S Semi-Sweet Chocolate, coarsely chopped

½ cup PLANTERS Pecan Pieces

▶ make it!

HEAT oven to 350°F.

MICROWAVE cranberries and orange juice in microwaveable bowl on HIGH 30 sec. Mix next 4 ingredients; set aside. Beat margarine and brown sugar in large bowl with mixer until light and fluffy. Add eggs, 1 at a time, beating after each until well blended. Gradually beat in flour mixture. Stir in cranberry mixture, chocolate and nuts.

SPREAD onto bottom of 13×9-inch pan sprayed with cooking spray.

BAKE 25 to 30 min. or until lightly browned. Cool completely before cutting into bars.

SUBSTITUTE:
Substitute raisins for the cranberries.

BAKER'S ONE BOWL white chocolate blonde brownies

PREP: 15 min. | TOTAL: 50 min. | MAKES: 16 servings.

▶ what you need!

1 pkg. (6 squares) BAKER'S White Chocolate

¼ cup butter or margarine

¾ cup sugar

2 eggs

1 cup flour

½ tsp. CALUMET Baking Powder

½ tsp. salt

1 cup chopped PLANTERS Pecans, toasted

▶ make it!

HEAT oven to 350°F.

LINE 8-inch square pan with foil, with ends of foil extending over sides. Spray with cooking spray. Microwave chocolate and butter in large microwaveable bowl on HIGH 1½ min. or until butter is melted. Stir until chocolate is completely melted. Add sugar; mix well. Blend in eggs. Add flour, baking powder and salt; mix well. Stir in nuts.

SPREAD into prepared pan.

BAKE 30 to 35 min. or until toothpick inserted in center comes out with fudgy crumbs. (Do not overbake.) Cool in pan. Use foil handles to lift brownies from pan before cutting to serve.

sweet peanut brittle

PREP: 5 min. | TOTAL: 50 min. | MAKES: about 1½ lb. or 16 servings.

▶ what you need!

1 cup sugar

½ cup light corn syrup

1 Tbsp. butter

2 cups PLANTERS COCKTAIL Peanuts

1 tsp. baking soda

1 tsp. vanilla

4 squares BAKER'S Semi-Sweet Chocolate

¼ cup PLANTERS Creamy Peanut Butter

▶ make it!

SPRAY large baking sheet with cooking spray. Microwave sugar and corn syrup in large glass microwaveable bowl on HIGH 5 min. Stir in butter and nuts. Microwave 3 to 4 min. or until pale golden brown. Stir in baking soda and vanilla. (Mixture will foam.) Spread onto prepared baking sheet. Cool completely. Break into pieces.

MICROWAVE chocolate in 1-cup glass measuring cup on HIGH 1 to 2 min. or until chocolate is melted when stirred. Add peanut butter; stir until melted. Dip half of each candy piece in chocolate mixture; scrape bottom against edge of cup to remove excess chocolate. Place on sheet of foil or waxed paper. Refrigerate 20 min. or until chocolate is firm.

HOT AND SWEET PEANUT BRITTLE:
Stir 1 tsp. hot pepper sauce into candy along with the vanilla.

FUN IDEA:
Use crushed peanut brittle as a topping for ice cream.

CHIPS AHOY! turtles

PREP: 20 min. | TOTAL: 1 hour 5 min. | MAKES: 1 doz. or 12 servings.

▶ what you need!

3 squares BAKER'S Semi-Sweet Chocolate, divided

1 Tbsp. butter or margarine

12 CHIPS AHOY! Cookies

6 KRAFT Caramels

2 tsp. milk

12 PLANTERS Pecan Halves

▶ make it!

MICROWAVE 2 chocolate squares and butter in microwaveable bowl on HIGH 1 min. or until chocolate is melted and mixture is well blended, stirring every 30 sec. Spread onto tops of cookies. Let stand 15 min. or until chocolate is firm.

MICROWAVE caramels and milk in small microwaveable bowl on HIGH 1 min.; stir until smooth. Melt remaining chocolate square as directed on package.

SPOON caramel onto centers of cookies; top with nuts. Drizzle with melted chocolate. Let stand 30 min.

GIFT-GIVING:
To give as a gift, pack several cookie turtles in decorative container or tin lined with colorful plastic wrap or tissue paper.

chocolate cookie bark

PREP: 20 min. | TOTAL: 1 hour 20 min. | MAKES: 14 servings, 1 piece each.

▶ what you need!

1 pkg. (8 squares) BAKER'S Semi-Sweet Chocolate

1 pkg. (6 squares) BAKER'S White Chocolate

2 Tbsp. PLANTERS Creamy Peanut Butter

10 OREO Cookies

▶ make it!

PLACE semi-sweet chocolate and white chocolate in separate medium microwaveable bowls. Microwave until completely melted, following directions on package. Add peanut butter to white chocolate; stir until well blended. Crumble half the cookies over chocolate in each bowl; mix well.

DROP spoonfuls of the chocolate mixtures onto waxed paper-covered baking sheet, alternating the colors of the chocolates. Cut through chocolate mixtures several times with knife for marble effect.

REFRIGERATE at least 1 hour or until firm. Break into 14 pieces. Store in airtight container in refrigerator.

chocolate-dipped apples

PREP: 10 min. | TOTAL: 40 min. | MAKES: 6 apples or 12 servings, ½ apple each.

▶ what you need!

   6 wooden pop sticks

   6 small to medium apples, washed and well dried

   1 tub (7 oz.) BAKER'S Dipping Chocolate, any variety

  ¾ cup PLANTERS Chopped Pecans

▶ make it!

INSERT 1 wooden pop stick into stem end of each apple.

MICROWAVE chocolate as directed on package. Dip bottom half of each apple into chocolate, turning until evenly coated. Sprinkle nuts over chocolate. Place on waxed paper-covered tray.

REFRIGERATE 30 min. or until chocolate is firm. Cut each apple in half to serve. Cover and store any leftover uncut apples in refrigerator.

SUBSTITUTE:
Substitute BAKER'S ANGLE FLAKE Coconut, chopped PLANTERS COCKTAIL Peanuts or chopped OREO Cookies for the pecans.

chocolate-dipped strawberries

PREP: 10 min. | TOTAL: 40 min. | MAKES: 3 doz. or 18 servings, 2 strawberries each.

▶ what you need!

1 pkg. (7 oz.) BAKER'S Milk Chocolate Dipping Chocolate

36 medium strawberries

▶ make it!

MELT chocolate as directed on package.

DIP strawberries into chocolate; let excess chocolate drip off.

PLACE on waxed paper-covered baking sheet or tray. Let stand at room temperature or store in refrigerator for 30 min. or until chocolate is firm.

VARIATION:
Prepare as directed, using BAKER'S Dark Semi-Sweet Dipping Chocolate. Or, substitute 7 oz. melted BAKER'S GERMAN'S Sweet Chocolate for the dipping chocolate.

COOKING KNOW-HOW:
For best results, serve strawberries the same day they are dipped.

SUBSTITUTE:
Prepare as directed, using 18 large strawberries.

HOW TO SELECT AND STORE FRESH STRAWBERRIES:
When purchasing fresh strawberries, look for plump, brightly colored berries with a strong strawberry fragrance. If prepackaged in plastic cartons, be sure to check the bottom of the container for any mushy berries or signs of mold. Store strawberries in the refrigerator and wash just before using.

easy OREO truffles

PREP: 30 min. | TOTAL: 1 hour 30 min. | MAKES: 3½ doz. or 42 servings, 1 truffle each.

▶ what you need!

1 pkg. (15.3 oz.) OREO Cookies (about 4¼ cups), finely crushed, divided

1 pkg. (8 oz.) PHILADELPHIA Cream Cheese, softened

2 pkg. (8 squares each) BAKER'S Semi-Sweet Chocolate, melted

▶ make it!

MIX 3 cups of the cookie crumbs and the cream cheese until well blended. Shape into 42 (1-inch) balls.

DIP balls in melted chocolate; place on waxed paper-covered baking sheet. (Any leftover melted chocolate can be stored in tightly covered container at room temperature and saved for another use.) Sprinkle with remaining cookie crumbs.

REFRIGERATE 1 hour or until firm. Store any leftover truffles in tightly covered container in refrigerator.

JAZZ IT UP:
Sprinkle truffles with colored sugar or sprinkles in addition to or in place of the cookie crumbs.

chocolate-peanut butter mallow bars

PREP: 20 min. | TOTAL: 38 min. | MAKES: 32 servings.

▸ what you need!

1 pkg. (2-layer size) devil's food cake mix

½ cup butter, melted

⅔ cup milk, divided

¾ cup PLANTERS Creamy Peanut Butter

1 jar (7 oz.) JET-PUFFED Marshmallow Creme

½ cup PLANTERS Salted Peanuts

6 squares BAKER'S Semi-Sweet Chocolate, coarsely chopped

▸ make it!

HEAT oven to 350°F.

MIX dry cake mix, butter and ⅓ cup milk until blended; press ⅔ onto bottom of 13×9-inch pan. Bake 12 to 14 min. or until center is almost set; cool 3 min.

COMBINE peanut butter and remaining milk; spread onto crust. Top with small spoonfuls of the marshmallow creme and remaining cake mixture. Sprinkle with nuts and chocolate; press gently into cake mixture.

BAKE 18 min. or just until center is set. Cool completely before cutting into bars.

MAKE AHEAD:
Prepare as directed; cool completely. Do not cut into bars. Wrap dessert tightly; freeze up to 1 month. Thaw before cutting into bars.

graham break-aways

PREP: 10 min. | TOTAL: 25 min. | MAKES: 24 servings, 2 pieces each.

▶ what you need!

12 HONEY MAID Honey Grahams, broken in half (24 squares)

½ cup butter or margarine

¾ cup firmly packed brown sugar

1 cup BAKER's Semi-Sweet Chocolate Chunks

½ cup finely chopped PLANTERS Pecans

▶ make it!

HEAT oven to 350°F.

ARRANGE graham squares in single layer in 15×10×1-inch baking pan.

PLACE butter and sugar in medium saucepan. Bring to boil on medium heat; cook 2 min. Pour over grahams; immediately spread to completely cover all grahams.

BAKE 6 to 8 min. or until sugar mixture is lightly browned and bubbly. Sprinkle with chocolate chunks. Bake an additional 1 to 2 min. or until chocolate is melted. Remove from oven; immediately spread chocolate over grahams. Sprinkle with nuts; press lightly into chocolate with back of spoon. Cool completely. Break into 24 squares; break squares in half to form rectangles.

SUBSTITUTE:
Substitute PLANTERS Cocktail Peanuts for the pecans.

GIFT-GIVING:
Save cookie tins of all shapes and sizes throughout the year. Or buy inexpensive jars, baking pans, mugs or festive serving dishes for packaging your edible gifts. The packaging then becomes a gift too!

pecan tassies

PREP: 20 min. | TOTAL: 2 hours 15 min. | MAKES: 2 doz. or 24 servings.

▶ what you need!

4 oz. (½ of 8-oz. pkg.) PHILADELPHIA Cream Cheese, softened

½ cup butter or margarine, softened

1 cup flour

1 egg

¾ cup packed brown sugar

1 tsp. vanilla

¾ cup finely chopped PLANTERS Pecans

3 squares BAKER'S Semi-Sweet Chocolate, melted

▶ make it!

HEAT oven to 350°F.

BEAT cream cheese and butter in large bowl with mixer until well blended. Add flour; mix well. Refrigerate 1 hour or until chilled.

DIVIDE dough into 24 balls; place 1 in each of 24 miniature muffin pan cups; press onto bottoms and up sides of cups to form shells. Beat egg in medium bowl. Add sugar and vanilla; mix well. Stir in nuts; spoon into pastry shells, filling each ¾ full.

BAKE 25 min. or until lightly browned. Let stand 5 min. in pans; remove to wire racks. Cool completely. Drizzle with melted chocolate. Let stand until set.

VARIATION:
For a quick garnish, dust cooled tarts with powdered sugar instead of drizzling with the melted chocolate.

million dollar fudge

PREP: 5 min. | TOTAL: 25 min. | MAKES: 5 doz. pieces or 60 servings, 1 piece each.

▶ what you need!

½ cup butter or margarine

4½ cups sugar

1 can (13 oz.) evaporated milk

3 pkg. (12 oz. each) BAKER'S Semi-Sweet Chocolate Chunks

1 jar (7 oz.) JET-PUFFED Marshmallow Creme

3 cups PLANTERS Chopped Pecans

1 tsp. salt

1 tsp. vanilla

▶ make it!

PLACE butter, sugar and evaporated milk in heavy 4-qt. saucepan. Bring to full rolling boil on medium heat, stirring constantly. Boil 5 min., stirring constantly to prevent scorching.

REMOVE from heat. Gradually add chocolate chunks, stirring until chocolate is completely melted. Add remaining ingredients; beat until well blended.

POUR into greased 15×10×1-inch pan. Cool completely. Cut into 60 pieces.

TIP:
To make Rocky Road Fudge, prepare as directed, stirring 2 cups JET-PUFFED Miniature Marshmallows into the hot fudge mixture before pouring into pan.

OREO chocolate-raspberry truffle cups

PREP: 30 min. | TOTAL: 2 hours 30 min. | MAKES: 2 doz. or 24 servings.

▶ what you need!

- ¼ cup butter or margarine, divided
- 12 OREO Cookies (about 1 cup), finely crushed
- 2 Tbsp. raspberry jam
- 1 pkg. (6 squares) BAKER'S White Chocolate
- ½ cup whipping cream, divided
- 6 squares BAKER'S Semi-Sweet Chocolate
- 2 Tbsp. white or multi-colored sprinkles

▶ make it!

MELT 2 Tbsp. butter; mix with cookie crumbs. Press onto bottoms of 24 miniature paper-lined muffin cups. Add ¼ tsp. jam to each. Refrigerate until ready to use.

MICROWAVE white chocolate, ¼ cup cream and 1 Tbsp. of the remaining butter in microwaveable bowl on HIGH 1 min.; stir until chocolate is melted and mixture is well blended. Spoon over jam. Freeze 10 min.

MEANWHILE, melt semi-sweet chocolate with remaining cream and butter as directed for white chocolate. Spoon over white chocolate layer; top with sprinkles. Refrigerate 1 to 2 hours or until firm.

SUBSTITUTE:
For variety, substitute marshmallow creme, PLANTERS Creamy Peanut Butter, caramel sauce or a different flavor of jam for the raspberry jam in the recipe.

two-layer fudge

PREP: 20 min. | TOTAL: 2 hours 20 min. | MAKES: 24 servings.

▸ what you need!

- 1 pkg. (8 squares) BAKER'S Semi-Sweet Chocolate

- 1 can (14 oz.) sweetened condensed milk, divided

- ½ cup chopped PLANTERS Walnuts

- 1 tsp. vanilla

- 1 pkg. (6 squares) BAKER'S White Chocolate

▸ make it!

MICROWAVE semi-sweet chocolate and ¾ cup sweetened condensed milk in medium microwaveable bowl on HIGH 2 min. or until chocolate is almost melted, stirring after 1 min. Stir until chocolate is completely melted.

ADD nuts and vanilla; mix well. Spread onto bottom of foil-lined 8-inch square pan.

MICROWAVE white chocolate and remaining milk in medium microwaveable bowl on HIGH 1½ min. or until chocolate is almost melted, stirring after 1 min. Stir until chocolate is completely melted. Spread over semi-sweet chocolate layer. Refrigerate 2 hours.

DOUBLE-CHOCOLATE ORANGE-NUT FUDGE:
Prepare as directed, stirring 1 tsp. orange zest into white chocolate mixture before using as directed.

NILLA-cinnamon snack mix

PREP: 10 min. | TOTAL: 20 min. | MAKES: 6 cups or 24 servings, ¼ cup each.

▶ what you need!

3 cups NILLA Wafers

1 cup PLANTERS Pecan Halves

1 cup pretzel sticks

3 Tbsp. butter or margarine, melted

2 Tbsp. sugar

1 tsp. ground cinnamon

¼ tsp. kosher salt

½ cup yogurt-covered raisins

▶ make it!

HEAT oven to 375°F.

COMBINE first 3 ingredients in large bowl. Mix butter, sugar, cinnamon and salt. Drizzle over wafer mixture; toss to coat.

SPREAD onto bottom of foil-lined 15×10×1-inch pan.

BAKE 10 min. or until lightly toasted, stirring after 5 min. Cool. Stir in raisins.

HOW TO STORE:
Store in airtight container at room temperature.

nutty NILLA mallow bites

PREP: 15 min. | TOTAL: 15 min. | MAKES: 8 doz. or 24 servings, 4 squares each.

▶ what you need!

3 Tbsp. butter or margarine

1 pkg. (10½ oz.) JET-PUFFED Miniature Marshmallows (about 6 cups)

1 pkg. (12 oz.) NILLA Wafers, coarsely crushed (about 5 cups)

1 cup PLANTERS Cashews, chopped

½ cup dried cherries, chopped

▶ make it!

LINE 13×9-inch pan with foil, with ends of foil extending over sides; spray with cooking spray.

MICROWAVE butter in large microwaveable bowl on HIGH 45 sec. or until melted. Add marshmallows; toss to coat. Microwave 1½ min. or until marshmallows are completely melted and mixture is well blended, stirring every 45 sec.

ADD remaining ingredients; mix well. Press onto bottom of prepared pan; cool. Use foil handles to lift dessert from pan; cut into 1-inch squares.

GIFT-GIVING:
These bite-size treats make perfect gifts for family and friends. Place in paper candy cups or mini cupcake liners, then pack in a holiday gift box for a one-of-a-kind gift.

white chocolate fruit and nut clusters

PREP: 10 min. | TOTAL: 20 min. | MAKES: 12 servings, 4 clusters each.

▶ what you need!

1 pkg. (6 squares) BAKER'S White Chocolate

⅓ cup PLANTERS Sunflower Kernels

⅓ cup PLANTERS Slivered Almonds

⅓ cup dried cranberries

▶ make it!

MICROWAVE chocolate in large microwaveable bowl on HIGH 2 min. or until chocolate is almost melted; stir until chocolate is completely melted. Stir in remaining ingredients.

SPOON 1 tsp. of the chocolate mixture into each of 48 miniature muffin cup liners. Refrigerate at least 10 min. or until ready to serve.

SUBSTITUTE:
Prepare as directed, substituting 6 squares BAKER's Semi-Sweet Chocolate for the white chocolate.

banana-nut graham muffins

PREP: 15 min. | TOTAL: 33 min. | MAKES: 1 doz. or 12 servings.

▶ what you need!

16 HONEY MAID Honey Grahams, finely crushed (about 2⅔ cups)

¼ cup sugar

2 tsp. CALUMET Baking Powder

1 egg

1 cup fat-free milk

2 Tbsp. honey

2 fully ripe bananas, mashed

¼ cup chopped PLANTERS Walnuts

▶ make it!

HEAT oven to 400°F.

COMBINE graham crumbs, sugar and baking powder until well blended. Mix all remaining ingredients except nuts in large bowl. Add graham mixture; stir just until moistened.

SPOON into 12 paper-lined muffin cups; top with nuts.

BAKE 15 to 18 min. or until toothpick inserted in centers comes out clean. Cool in pan 5 min. Remove to wire rack; cool slightly.

SUBSTITUTE:
Substitute semi-sweet chocolate chips for the nuts.

white chocolate-mallow clusters

PREP: 15 min. | TOTAL: 1 hour 15 min. | MAKES: 8 servings, 2 clusters each.

▶ what you need!

2 pkg. (6 squares each) BAKER'S White Chocolate

1 cup JET-PUFFED Miniature Marshmallows

½ cup pretzel twists, coarsely broken

⅓ cup pastel-colored candy-coated chocolate pieces

▶ make it!

COVER baking sheet with waxed paper. Microwave chocolate in medium microwaveable bowl on MEDIUM (50%) 2 min., stirring after each minute. Cool.

ADD remaining ingredients; toss to coat. Drop tablespoonfuls of marshmallow mixture into 16 clusters on prepared baking sheet.

REFRIGERATE 1 hour or until firm.

SIZE-WISE:
One serving of this sweet treat goes a long way on flavor.

CUPCAKES, FROSTINGS & MINI CHEESECAKES

angel lush cupcakes

PREP: 15 min. | TOTAL: 1 hour 30 min. | MAKES: 30 servings.

▸ what you need!

- 1 pkg. (16 oz.) angel food cake mix
- 1 pkg. (3.4 oz.) JELL-O Vanilla Flavor Instant Pudding
- 2 cans (8 oz. each) DOLE Crushed Pineapple in Juice, undrained
- 1 cup thawed COOL WHIP Whipped Topping
- 2 cups assorted fresh berries (blueberries, raspberries and sliced strawberries)

▸ make it!

HEAT oven to 375°F.

PREPARE cake batter as directed on package; pour into 30 paper-lined muffin cups, filling each cup ⅔ full. Bake 12 to 15 min. or until tops are golden brown and cracks feel dry. (Note: If baking in batches, refrigerate remaining batter in bowl until ready to pour into lined muffin cups and bake.) Cool cupcakes in pans 10 min.; remove to wire racks. Cool completely.

MIX dry pudding mix and pineapple in medium bowl. Gently stir in COOL WHIP; spread onto cupcakes.

TOP with berries.

SUBSTITUTE:
Substitute 15 fresh strawberries, halved, for the 2 cups assorted fresh berries.

DOLE is a registered trademark of Dole Food Company, Inc.

mini OREO surprise cupcakes

PREP: 10 min. | TOTAL: 52 min. | MAKES: 24 servings.

▶ what you need!

    1 pkg. (2-layer size) chocolate cake mix

    1 pkg. (8 oz.) PHILADELPHIA Cream Cheese, softened

    1 egg

    2 Tbsp. sugar

    48 Mini OREO Bite Sized Cookies

    1½ cups thawed COOL WHIP Whipped Topping

▶ make it!

HEAT oven to 350°F.

PREPARE cake batter as directed on package; set aside. Beat cream cheese, egg and sugar until well blended.

SPOON cake batter into 24 paper-lined muffin cups. Top each with about 1½ tsp. of the cream cheese mixture and 1 cookie. Cover with remaining cake batter.

BAKE 19 to 22 min. or until wooden toothpick inserted in centers comes out clean. Cool 5 min.; remove from pans to wire racks. Cool completely.

FROST with COOL WHIP. Top with remaining cookies.

MAKE IT EASY:
For easy portioning of cream cheese mixture into cake batter, spoon cream cheese mixture into large resealable plastic bag. Seal bag securely. Snip small corner of bag with scissors. Squeeze about 1½ tsp. of the cream cheese mixture over batter in each muffin cup.

PHILADELPHIA 3-STEP
mini cheesecakes

PREP: 10 min. | TOTAL: 3 hours 30 min. | MAKES: 12 servings.

▶ what you need!

2	pkg. (8 oz. each) PHILADELPHIA Cream Cheese, softened
½	cup sugar
½	tsp. vanilla
2	eggs
12	OREO Cookies
1	kiwi, peeled, cut into 6 slices
36	blueberries (about ½ cup)
12	raspberries (about ⅓ cup)

▶ make it!

HEAT oven to 350°F.

1. BEAT cream cheese, sugar and vanilla in large bowl with electric mixer on medium speed until well blended. Add eggs, 1 at a time, beating on low speed after each addition just until blended.

2. PLACE 1 cookie in bottom of each of 12 medium paper-lined muffin cups. Fill evenly with batter.

3. BAKE 20 min. or until centers are almost set. Cool. Refrigerate 3 hours or overnight. Cut kiwi slices in half. Top each cheesecake with 1 kiwi half, 3 blueberries and 1 raspberry just before serving.

CHEESECAKE SQUARES:
Line 8-inch square baking pan with foil. Mix 1½ cups finely crushed OREO Cookies or HONEY MAID Honey Grahams with ¼ cup melted butter; press firmly onto bottom of pan. Prepare cheesecake batter as directed. Pour over crust. Bake and refrigerate as directed. Cut into 16 squares. Top evenly with the fruit mixture just before serving. Makes 16 servings, 1 square each.

carrot-ginger cupcakes with spiced cream cheese

PREP: 20 min. | TOTAL: 35 min. | MAKES: 24 servings, 1 cupcake each.

▶ what you need!

1 pkg. (16 oz.) pound cake mix

¾ cup shredded carrots

1 Tbsp. ground ginger

1 tsp. ground cinnamon, divided

½ cup PLANTERS Walnut Pieces, toasted

1 pkg. (8 oz.) PHILADELPHIA Cream Cheese, softened

2 cups thawed COOL WHIP Whipped Topping

▶ make it!

HEAT oven to 350°F.

PREPARE cake batter as directed on package; stir in carrots, ginger, ¾ tsp. of the cinnamon and nuts.

SPOON batter into 24 paper-lined medium muffin cups. Bake 15 min. or until toothpick comes out clean.

BEAT cream cheese in medium bowl with wire whisk until smooth. Gently stir in COOL WHIP. Spread over tops of cupcakes. Sprinkle with reserved ¼ tsp. cinnamon. Refrigerate until ready to serve.

SUBSTITUTE:
Substitute PLANTERS Pecans for the walnuts.

HOW TO STORE NUTS:
Nuts have a high oil content that can become rancid quickly and will ruin any dish that they are used in. Store shelled nuts in a tightly covered container in the refrigerator for up to 4 months. For longer storage, place shelled nuts in a freezer-weight resealable plastic bag and store in the freezer for up to 6 months. Do not chop nuts before storing; nuts stay fresh longer when stored in larger pieces.

bears at the beach

PREP: 30 min. | TOTAL: 1 hour 20 min. | MAKES: 24 servings.

▶ what you need!

1 pkg. (2-layer size) white cake mix

2¼ cups thawed COOL WHIP Whipped Topping, divided

6 drops blue food coloring

½ cup HONEY MAID Graham Cracker Crumbs

24 JET-PUFFED FUNMALLOWS Miniature Marshmallows

48 TEDDY GRAHAMS Graham Snacks

▶ make it!

PREPARE cake batter and bake as directed on package for 24 cupcakes. Cool in pans 15 min. Remove from pans to wire racks; cool completely.

REMOVE 1¼ cups COOL WHIP; set aside. Tint remaining COOL WHIP with food coloring. Spread top of each cupcake with some of each color COOL WHIP to resemble the ocean and its beach. Sprinkle 1 tsp. graham crumbs over white COOL WHIP on each cupcake for sand.

INSERT 1 small cocktail umbrella into marshmallows; insert into each cupcake for the umbrella. Decorate cupcakes with TEDDY GRAHAMS as shown in photo. Keep refrigerated.

SHORTCUT:
Spoon each color of COOL WHIP into separate resealable plastic bag; cut small corner off bottom of each bag. Use to squeeze COOL WHIP from bag to frost cupcakes.

SPECIAL EXTRA:
Flatten additional marshmallows with rolling pin to resemble beach towels. Or, cut wide, soft candy ribbon into pieces to resemble towels.

coconut-cream cheese frosting

PREP: 10 min. | TOTAL: 10 min. | MAKES: 2½ cups or 20 servings, 2 Tbsp. each.

▶ what you need!

4 oz. (½ of 8-oz. pkg.) PHILADELPHIA Cream Cheese, softened

¼ cup butter, softened

1 pkg. (16 oz.) powdered sugar

2 Tbsp. milk

½ tsp. vanilla

½ cup BAKER'S ANGEL FLAKE Coconut, toasted

▶ make it!

BEAT cream cheese and butter in large bowl with electric mixer on medium speed until light and fluffy.

ADD sugar alternately with the milk, beating until well blended after each addition. Add vanilla; mix well. Stir in coconut.

USE to frost your favorite cake or cupcake recipe.

HOW TO TOAST COCONUT:
Heat oven to 350°F. Spread coconut into shallow baking pan. Bake 8 to 10 min. or until lightly browned, stirring frequently.

NOTE:
Recipe makes enough to frost tops and sides of 2 (8- or 9-inch) cake layers, top and sides of 13×9-inch cake or tops of 3 (8- or 9-inch) cake layers.

"eyeball" cupcakes

PREP: 15 min. | TOTAL: 1 hour 10 min. | MAKES: 2 doz. or 24 servings, 1 cupcake each.

▶ what you need!

1 pkg. (2-layer size) chocolate cake mix

1 pkg. (3.9 oz.) JELL-O Chocolate Instant Pudding

1 pkg. (8 oz.) PHILADELPHIA Cream Cheese, softened

¼ cup butter, softened

1 tsp. vanilla

1 pkg. (16 oz.) powdered sugar

24 ring-shaped chewy fruit snacks

24 miniature candy-coated chocolate pieces

1 tube (19.28 g) red decorating gel

▶ make it!

PREPARE cake batter as directed on package. Add dry pudding mix; mix well. Spoon evenly into 24 paper-lined medium muffin cups. Bake as directed on package for cupcakes. Cool completely.

BEAT cream cheese, butter and vanilla in medium bowl with electric mixer on medium speed until well blended. Gradually add sugar, beating well after each addition. Spread evenly onto tops of cupcakes.

PLACE 1 fruit snack on top of each cupcake. Add 1 candy-coated chocolate piece to center of each fruit snack for the eyeball. Draw squiggly lines with decorating gel from the eyeballs to outsides of fruit snacks to resemble eyeball veins.

SUBSTITUTE:
Prepare as directed, using any flavor cake mix.

holiday poke cupcakes

PREP: 30 min. | TOTAL: 1 hour | MAKES: 24 servings.

▸ what you need!

1 pkg. (2-layer size) white cake mix

1 cup boiling water

1 pkg. (3 oz.) JELL-O Gelatin, any red flavor

1 tub (8 oz.) COOL WHIP Whipped Topping, thawed

Red or green food coloring

Suggested decorations: colored sugar, colored sprinkles, crushed candy canes and/or JET-PUFFED HOLIDAY MALLOWS Marshmallows

▸ make it!

PREPARE cake batter and bake as directed for cupcakes. Cool in pans 10 min. Pierce tops with fork.

ADD boiling water into dry gelatin mix; stir 2 min. until completely dissolved. Spoon over cupcakes. Refrigerate 30 min. Remove from pans.

TINT COOL WHIP with food coloring; spread onto cupcakes. Decorate as desired.

VARIATION:
Omit food coloring.

berry patriotic cupcakes

PREP: 10 min. | TOTAL: 10 min. | MAKES: 1 doz. or 12 servings, 1 cupcake each.

▶ what you need!

- 12 chocolate cupcakes, cooled
- 1½ cups thawed COOL WHIP Whipped Topping
- 12 small strawberries, stems removed, each cut into 5 slices
- ¼ cup blueberries

▶ make it!

SPREAD cupcakes evenly with COOL WHIP.

ARRANGE 5 of the strawberry slices on top of each cupcake to form a star.

FILL center of stars evenly with blueberries. Store in refrigerator.

SUBSTITUTE:
Substitute 60 fresh raspberries for strawberries, using 5 raspberries to decorate top of each cupcake.

SUBSTITUTE:
Prepare as directed, using your favorite flavor of cupcakes.

hot chocolate
brownie cupcakes

PREP: 20 min. | TOTAL: 1 hour 8 min. | MAKES: 24 servings.

▶ what you need!

30 CHIPS AHOY! Cookies, divided

1 pkg. (19 to 21 oz.) brownie mix (13×9-inch pan size)

4 oz. (½ of 8-oz. pkg.) PHILADELPHIA Cream Cheese, softened

1 jar (7 oz.) JET-PUFFED Marshmallow Creme

1 tsp. vanilla

1 tub (8 oz.) COOL WHIP Whipped Topping, thawed

1 tsp. unsweetened cocoa powder

1 cup JET-PUFFED Miniature Marshmallows

▶ make it!

HEAT oven to 350°F.

SPRAY 24 muffin pan cups with cooking spray. Press 1 cookie onto bottom of each cup. (No problem if cookies crack.) Cut remaining cookies into quarters; set aside.

PREPARE brownie batter as directed on package; spoon into cups. Bake 15 to 18 min. or until toothpick inserted in centers comes out with fudgy crumbs. (Do not overbake.) Cool completely.

BEAT cream cheese, marshmallow creme and vanilla in large bowl with mixer until well blended. Add COOL WHIP and cocoa powder; beat just until blended. Spread onto cupcakes; top with marshmallows. Keep refrigerated. Insert 1 cookie piece into side of each cupcake to resemble coffee mug just before serving.

SPECIAL EXTRA:
Dust with additional cocoa powder just before serving.

lemon-cream
cheese cupcakes

PREP: 10 min. | TOTAL: 1 hour 34 min. | MAKES: 24 servings, 1 cupcake each.

▶ what you need!

1 pkg. (2-layer size) white cake mix

1 pkg. (3.4 oz.) JELL-O Lemon Flavor Instant Pudding

1 cup water

4 egg whites

2 Tbsp. oil

1 pkg. (16 oz.) powdered sugar

1 pkg. (8 oz.) PHILADELPHIA Cream Cheese, softened

¼ cup butter, softened

2 Tbsp. lemon juice

▶ make it!

HEAT oven to 350°F.

BEAT cake mix, dry pudding mix, water, egg whites and oil in large bowl with electric mixer on low speed until moistened. (Batter will be thick.) Beat on medium speed 2 min. Spoon batter evenly into 24 paper-lined muffin cups.

BAKE 21 to 24 min. or until wooden toothpick inserted in centers comes out clean. Cool in pans 10 min.; remove to wire racks. Cool completely.

MEANWHILE, beat sugar, cream cheese, butter and juice with electric mixer on low speed until well blended. Frost cupcakes.

SUBSTITUTE:
Prepare as directed, using PHILADELPHIA Neufchâtel Cheese.

JAZZ IT UP:
Stir 1 tsp. grated lemon zest into frosting mixture.

martians-ate-my-OREO cupcakes

PREP: 30 min. | TOTAL: 1 hour 20 min. | MAKES: 24 servings.

▶ what you need!

- 1 pkg. (2-layer size) chocolate cake mix
- 1 pkg. (8 oz.) PHILADELPHIA Cream Cheese, softened
- 1 egg
- 2 Tbsp. sugar
- 54 Mini OREO Cookies, divided
- 2 or 3 drops green food coloring
- 2 cups thawed COOL WHIP Whipped Topping
- 4 OREO Cookies
- ¼ cup JET-PUFFED Miniature Marshmallows
- 4 JET-PUFFED Marshmallows, cut in half
- 2 pieces string licorice
- 1 Tbsp. assorted round candies

▶ make it!

HEAT oven to 350°F.

PREPARE cake batter as directed on package. Mix cream cheese, egg and sugar until well blended. Spoon half the cake batter into 24 paper-lined muffin cups. Top each with about 2 tsp. cream cheese mixture and 1 mini cookie; cover with remaining batter.

BAKE 19 to 22 min. or until toothpick inserted in centers comes out clean. Cool 5 min.; remove from pans to wire racks. Cool completely.

STIR green food coloring into COOL WHIP; spread onto cupcakes. Split remaining mini and regular-size cookies, leaving all the filling on half of each cookie. Use with remaining ingredients to decorate cupcakes to resemble martians as shown in photo.

monster "cake"

PREP: 15 min. | TOTAL: 1 hour 5 min. | MAKES: 24 servings.

▶ what you need!

1 pkg. (2-layer size) yellow cake mix

1 pkg. (3.4 oz.) JELL-O Vanilla Flavor Instant
  Pudding

1 pkg. (8 oz.) PHILADELPHIA Cream Cheese,
  softened

¼ cup butter, softened

1 tsp. vanilla

6 drops green food coloring

1 pkg. (16 oz.) powdered sugar

1 tube (0.75 oz.) black decorating gel

8 OREO Cookies, finely crushed

3 JET-PUFFED Miniature Marshmallows, cut in half

▶ make it!

PREPARE cake batter and bake as directed on package for 24 cupcakes, blending dry
pudding mix into batter before spooning into paper-lined cups. Cool completely.

BEAT cream cheese, butter, vanilla and food coloring in medium bowl with mixer until well
blended. Gradually add sugar, beating well after each addition.

ARRANGE cupcakes on platter or tray to resemble a monster's head; spread with frosting.
Use decorating gel to outline the eyes, mouth, scars and hairline on cupcakes. Fill in hair
with cookie crumbs. Place 1 marshmallow half in center of each eye; place remaining
marshmallow halves in mouth for teeth. Keep refrigerated.

SUBSTITUTE:
Prepare using your favorite flavor cake mix.

HOW TO CREATE YOUR OWN UNIQUE CAKE:
Let your imagination run wild and create your own unique cake. Just assemble the cupcakes into a
shape, such as a ghost, jack-o'-lantern or witch face, then frost and decorate. It's easy!

mini strawberry cheesecakes

PREP: 15 min. | TOTAL: 1 hour 15 min. | MAKES: 24 servings.

▶ what you need!

- 1 pkg. (8 oz.) PHILADELPHIA Neufchâtel Cheese, softened
- 1 pkg. (3.4 oz.) JELL-O Strawberry Crème Flavor Instant Pudding
- 1 cup cold fat-free milk
- 2 cups thawed COOL WHIP LITE Whipped Topping
- 24 NILLA Wafers
- 1 cup sliced fresh strawberries

▶ make it!

BEAT Neufchâtel with mixer until creamy. Blend in dry pudding mix. Gradually beat in milk. Stir in COOL WHIP.

PLACE 1 wafer on bottom of each of 24 paper baking cups; place in muffin pan. Cover with pudding mixture.

FREEZE 1 hour. Top with berries just before serving.

mini lemon cheesecakes

PREP: 30 min. | TOTAL: 2 hours 30 min. | MAKES: 12 servings, 1 cheesecake each.

▶ what you need!

40 NILLA Wafers, finely crushed (about 1⅔ cups crumbs)

¼ cup butter or margarine, softened

3 tsp. grated lemon zest, divided

1 pkg. (8 oz.) PHILADELPHIA Cream Cheese, softened

½ cup sugar

1 egg

1 Tbsp. lemon juice

▶ make it!

HEAT oven to 350°F.

MIX wafer crumbs, butter and 2 tsp. of the lemon zest until well blended. Spoon about 2 Tbsp. of the crumb mixture into each of 12 paper-lined or greased medium muffin cups. Press crumb mixture firmly onto bottom and up side of each cup to form crust.

BEAT cream cheese with electric mixer on medium speed until creamy. Gradually add sugar and remaining 1 tsp. lemon zest, beating after each addition until well blended. Add egg and lemon juice; beat just until blended. Spoon batter evenly into crusts.

BAKE 40 min. or until lightly browned. Turn oven off. Let cheesecakes stand in oven for 20 min., leaving door slightly ajar. Remove to wire rack to cool. Refrigerate at least 1 hour before serving.

REMOVE from paper liners before serving. Store leftover cheesecakes in refrigerator.

GREAT SUBSTITUTE:
Prepare as directed, using PHILADELPHIA Neufchâtel Cheese.

SPECIAL EXTRA:
Garnish with fresh strawberries and mint sprigs just before serving.

no-bake chocolate cream cupcakes

PREP: 10 min. | TOTAL: 1 hour 10 min. | MAKES: 2 servings, 1 cupcake each.

▶ what you need!

½ cup thawed COOL WHIP Whipped Topping, divided

2 oz. (¼ of 8-oz. pkg.) PHILADELPHIA Cream Cheese, softened

1 square BAKER'S Semi-Sweet Chocolate, melted, cooled

1 Tbsp. powdered sugar

8 NILLA Wafers

▶ make it!

MIX ¼ cup COOL WHIP, the cream cheese, melted chocolate and sugar until well blended.

PLACE 2 of the wafers in bottom of each of 2 paper-lined medium muffin cups. Cover with 1 Tbsp. COOL WHIP mixture. Repeat layers. Top evenly with remaining COOL WHIP. Cover.

REFRIGERATE at least 1 hour.

JAZZ IT UP:
Garnish with a sprinkling of unsweetened cocoa powder just before serving.

PHILADELPHIA
cream cheese frosting

PREP: 10 min. | TOTAL: 10 min. | MAKES: about 2½ cups or 20 servings, 2 Tbsp. each.

▶ what you need!

1 pkg. (8 oz.) PHILADELPHIA Cream Cheese, softened

¼ cup butter or margarine, softened

1 tsp. vanilla

1 pkg. (16 oz.) powdered sugar

▶ make it!

BEAT cream cheese, butter and vanilla in large bowl with electric mixer on medium speed until well blended.

ADD sugar gradually, beating after each addition until well blended.

CHOCOLATE PHILADELPHIA FROSTING:
Prepare as directed, blending in 3 squares BAKER'S Unsweetened Baking Chocolate, melted.

NOTE:
Recipe makes enough to fill and frost 2 (8- or 9-inch) cake layers or top and sides of 13×9-inch cake.

COOKING KNOW-HOW:
Sift the powdered sugar first before adding to the cream cheese mixture for a smoother frosting.

red velvet cupcakes

PREP: 15 min. | TOTAL: 1 hour 10 min. | MAKES: 24 servings.

▶ what you need!

- 1 pkg. (2-layer size) red velvet cake mix
- 1 pkg. (3.9 oz.) JELL-O Chocolate Instant Pudding
- 1 pkg. (8 oz.) PHILADELPHIA Cream Cheese, softened
- ½ cup butter or margarine, softened
- 1 pkg. (16 oz.) powdered sugar
- 1 cup thawed COOL WHIP Whipped Topping
- 1 square BAKER'S White Chocolate, shaved into curls

▶ make it!

PREPARE cake batter and bake as directed on package for 24 cupcakes, blending dry pudding mix into batter before spooning into prepared muffin cups. Cool.

MEANWHILE, beat cream cheese and butter in large bowl with mixer until well blended. Gradually beat in sugar. Whisk in COOL WHIP. Spoon 1½ cups into small freezer-weight resealable plastic bag; seal bag. Cut small corner off bottom of bag.

INSERT tip of bag into top of each cupcake to pipe about 1 Tbsp. frosting into center of cupcake. Frost cupcakes with remaining frosting. Top with chocolate curls. Keep refrigerated.

HOW TO MAKE CHOCOLATE CURLS:
Warm a square of BAKER'S Chocolate by microwaving it, unwrapped, on HIGH for a few sec. or just until you can smudge the chocolate with your thumb. Hold the square steadily and draw a peeler slowly over flat bottom of square, allowing a thin layer of chocolate to curl as it is peeled off the bottom of the square to make long, delicate curls. Use the same technique along the narrow side of the square to make short curls.

skull cakes

PREP: 15 min. | TOTAL: 40 min. | MAKES: 24 servings, 1 cupcake each.

▶ what you need!

1 pkg. (2-layer size) white cake mix

1 pkg. (3.4 oz.) JELL-O Vanilla Flavor Instant Pudding

1 pkg. (8 oz.) PHILADELPHIA Cream Cheese, softened

¼ cup butter, softened

1 tsp. vanilla

1 pkg. (16 oz.) powdered sugar

12 JET-PUFFED Marshmallows, cut in half

¾ cup semi-sweet chocolate chips

▶ make it!

PREPARE cake batter as directed on package; blend in dry pudding mix. Spoon into 24 paper-lined muffin cups. Bake as directed on package for cupcakes. Cool completely.

BEAT cream cheese, butter and vanilla with mixer until well blended. Add sugar gradually, beating well after each addition.

PULL each cupcake liner partially away from cake. Place a marshmallow half between paper and cupcake to create skull's jaw. Frost cupcakes with cream cheese mixture. Decorate with chocolate chips.

SUBSTITUTE:
Prepare as directed, using any flavor cake mix. Decorate with assorted fall candy instead of chocolate chips.

OREO cheesecake bites

PREP: 20 min. | TOTAL: 5 hours 5 min. | MAKES: 36 servings, 1 bar each.

▶ what you need!

36 OREO Cookies, divided

½ cup butter or margarine, divided

4 pkg. (8 oz. each) PHILADELPHIA Cream Cheese, softened

1 cup sugar

1 tsp. vanilla

1 cup BREAKSTONE'S or KNUDSEN Sour Cream

4 eggs

4 squares BAKER'S Semi-Sweet Chocolate

▶ make it!

HEAT oven to 325°F.

LINE 13×9-inch baking pan with foil. Finely crush 24 cookies. Melt ¼ cup butter; mix with crumbs. Press onto bottom of pan.

BEAT cream cheese, sugar and vanilla with mixer until blended. Add sour cream; mix well. Add eggs, 1 at a time, beating just until blended after each addition. Chop remaining cookies. Gently stir into batter; pour over crust.

BAKE 45 min. or until center is almost set. Cool. Meanwhile, place chocolate and remaining ¼ cup butter in microwaveable bowl. Microwave on HIGH 1 min. Stir until smooth. Cool slightly; pour over cheesecake. Spread to cover top of cheesecake. Refrigerate at least 4 hours. Remove cheesecake from pan before cutting to serve.

HOW TO MAKE MESS-FREE COOKIE CRUMBS:
Crushing cookies into crumbs can be a messy task. To keep the mess to a minimum, place the whole cookies in a resealable plastic bag. Flatten bag to remove excess air, then seal bag. Crush the cookies into crumbs by rolling a rolling pin across the bag until the crumbs are as fine as you need.

NOTE:
When lining pan with foil, extend ends of foil over sides of pan to use as handles when removing cheesecake from pan.

pumpkin cream cupcakes

PREP: 10 min. | TOTAL: 31 min. | MAKES: 24 servings, 1 cupcake each.

▶ what you need!

1 pkg. (2-layer size) spice cake mix

1 pkg. (3.4 oz.) JELL-O Vanilla Flavor Instant Pudding

1 cup canned pumpkin

1 pkg. (8 oz.) PHILADELPHIA Cream Cheese, softened

¼ cup sugar

1 egg

▶ make it!

HEAT oven to 350°F.

PREPARE cake batter as directed on package. Add dry pudding mix and pumpkin; mix well. Spoon into 24 paper-lined muffin cups.

BEAT cream cheese with mixer until creamy. Blend in sugar and egg; spoon over batter.

BAKE 18 to 21 min. or until toothpick inserted in centers comes out clean. Cool 5 min.; remove to wire racks. Cool completely.

SPECIAL EXTRA:
Stir ¼ tsp. ground nutmeg into 1½ cups thawed COOL WHIP Whipped Topping; spread over cooled cupcakes. Keep refrigerated.

HEALTHY
LIVING

lemonade cheesecake

PREP: 15 min. | TOTAL: 4 hours 15 min. | MAKES: 8 servings.

▶ what you need!

1 pkg. (8 oz.) PHILADELPHIA Fat Free Cream Cheese, softened

1 tsp. CRYSTAL LIGHT Lemonade Flavor Drink Mix

¼ cup cold fat-free milk

1 tub (8 oz.) COOL WHIP FREE Whipped Topping, thawed

1 ready-to-use reduced-fat graham cracker crumb crust (6 oz.)

▶ make it!

BEAT cream cheese and drink mix in large bowl with mixer until well blended. Gradually add milk, mixing until well blended.

STIR in COOL WHIP; spoon into crust.

REFRIGERATE 4 hours or until firm.

SPECIAL EXTRA:
Garnish with fruit just before serving.

NUTRIENTS PER SERVING: Calories: 180, Total Fat: 5g, Saturated Fat: 2.5g, Protein: 6g, Carbohydrate: 27g, Cholesterol: 5mg, Fiber: 0g, Sodium: 300mg.

cafe ladyfinger dessert

PREP: 20 min. | TOTAL: 1 hour 20 min. | MAKES: 12 servings.

▶ what you need!

2 pkg. (3 oz. each) ladyfingers, split, separated

1 cup freshly brewed strong MAXWELL HOUSE Coffee or YUBAN Coffee, any variety, at room temperature, divided

1 pkg. (8 oz.) PHILADELPHIA Fat Free Cream Cheese

2 cups cold fat-free milk

2 pkg. (1.5 oz. each) JELL-O Vanilla Flavor Fat Free Sugar Free Instant Pudding

1 tub (8 oz.) COOL WHIP FREE Whipped Topping, thawed, divided

▶ make it!

BRUSH cut side of ladyfingers with about ¼ cup of the coffee. Place ladyfingers on bottom and up side of 2-qt. serving bowl.

BEAT cream cheese and remaining coffee in large bowl with whisk until blended. Gradually beat in milk. Add dry pudding mixes. Beat 2 min. Gently stir in half of the COOL WHIP. Spoon into prepared bowl; cover.

REFRIGERATE 1 hour. Top with remaining COOL WHIP just before serving.

SHORTCUT:
Substitute 2 tsp. MAXWELL HOUSE Instant Coffee, dissolved in 1 cup hot water, for freshly brewed coffee.

NUTRIENTS PER SERVING: Calories: 140, Total Fat: 2.5g, Saturated Fat: 1.5g, Protein: 6g, Carbohydrate: 24g, Cholesterol: 55mg, Fiber: 0g, Sodium: 42mg.

cool yogurt smoothie

PREP: 5 min. | TOTAL: 5 min. | MAKES: 4 servings, 1 cup each.

▶ what you need!

1 container (6 oz.) strawberry low-fat yogurt

1¾ cups thawed COOL WHIP FREE Whipped Topping, divided

2 cups fresh strawberries

2 cups ice cubes

▶ make it!

PLACE yogurt, 1½ cups COOL WHIP, the strawberries and ice in blender; blend until smooth.

POUR into 4 glasses. Top each with 1 Tbsp. of the remaining COOL WHIP.

SERVE immediately.

STORAGE KNOW-HOW:
Smoothie can be covered and stored in refrigerator up to 24 hours, or frozen up to 1 week. Reblend before serving. If smoothie was frozen, thaw 20 min. to soften slightly before blending.

VARIATION:
Prepare as directed, using your favorite flavor yogurt, regular COOL WHIP Whipped Topping and/or frozen strawberries or any other cut-up seasonal fruit.

TO HALVE:
Prepare as directed, cutting all ingredients in half. Makes 2 servings, 1 cup each.

NUTRIENTS PER SERVING: Calories: 130, Total Fat: 2g, Saturated Fat: 2g, Protein: 2g, Carbohydrate: 25g, Cholesterol: 5mg, Fiber: 2g, Sodium: 50mg.

creamy layered squares

PREP: 15 min. | TOTAL: 4 hours | MAKES: 9 servings, 1 square each.

▶ what you need!

1½ cups boiling water

1 pkg. (0.6 oz.) JELL-O Strawberry Flavor Sugar Free Gelatin

Ice cubes

1 cup cold water

1½ cups thawed COOL WHIP Sugar Free Whipped Topping, divided

▶ make it!

ADD boiling water to dry gelatin mix in large bowl; stir 2 min. until completely dissolved. Add enough ice to cold water to measure 1½ cups. Add to gelatin; stir until ice is completely melted. Remove 1½ cups gelatin; set aside on counter. Refrigerate remaining gelatin 30 min. or until slightly thickened.

ADD ¾ cup of the COOL WHIP to chilled, thickened gelatin; stir with wire whisk until well blended. Pour into 8-inch square dish. Refrigerate 15 min. or until gelatin mixture is set but not firm. Carefully pour reserved gelatin over creamy layer in dish.

REFRIGERATE 3 hours or until firm. Cut into squares; top with remaining COOL WHIP.

GELATIN SUCCESS TIP:
To make JELL-O Gelatin that is clear and uniformly set, be sure the gelatin is completely dissolved in the boiling water before adding the cold liquid. Stirring with a rubber spatula will help ensure that all the crystals are dissolved.

SUBSTITUTE:
Prepare as directed, using any flavor JELL-O Sugar Free Gelatin.

NUTRIENTS PER SERVING: Calories: 35, Total Fat: 1.5g, Saturated Fat: 1.5g, Protein: 1g, Carbohydrate: 4g, Cholesterol: 0mg, Fiber: 0g, Sodium: 60mg.

fast & easy tiramisu

PREP: 15 min. | TOTAL: 4 hours 15 min. | MAKES: 12 servings.

► what you need!

2 Tbsp. MAXWELL HOUSE Instant Coffee

1 Tbsp. sugar

1 cup boiling water

2 pkg. (3 oz. each) ladyfingers, split, divided

2 pkg. (8 oz. each) PHILADELPHIA Fat Free Cream Cheese, softened

½ cup sugar

2 cups thawed COOL WHIP LITE Whipped Topping

1 tsp. unsweetened cocoa powder

► make it!

DISSOLVE combined coffee granules and 1 Tbsp. sugar in boiling water. Arrange 1 package ladyfingers on bottom of 13×9-inch baking dish. Brush with ½ cup coffee.

BEAT cream cheese in large bowl with mixer until creamy. Add ½ cup sugar; mix well. Whisk in COOL WHIP.

SPREAD half of the cream cheese mixture over ladyfingers in dish; top with remaining ladyfingers. Brush with remaining coffee mixture; cover with remaining cream cheese mixture. Sprinkle with cocoa powder. Refrigerate at least 4 hours.

SPECIAL EXTRA:
Add 2 Tbsp. almond-flavored liqueur or brandy to cream cheese along with the ½ cup sugar.

NUTRIENTS PER SERVING: Calories: 150, Total Fat: 3g, Saturated Fat: 2g, Protein: 7g, Carbohydrate: 24g, Cholesterol: 55mg, Fiber: 0g, Sodium: 250mg.

light COOL 'N EASY pie

PREP: 15 min. | TOTAL: 4 hours 45 min. | MAKES: 8 servings, 1 slice each.

▶ what you need!

⅔ cup boiling water

1 pkg. (0.3 oz.) JELL-O Cherry Flavor Sugar Free Gelatin

Ice cubes

½ cup cold water

1 tub (8 oz.) COOL WHIP FREE Whipped Topping, thawed, divided

1 ready-to-use reduced-fat graham cracker crumb crust (6 oz.)

▶ make it!

ADD boiling water to dry gelatin mix in large bowl; stir 2 min. until completely dissolved. Add enough ice to cold water to measure 1 cup. Add to gelatin; stir until slightly thickened. Remove any unmelted ice. Add 2 cups COOL WHIP; stir until well blended. Refrigerate 30 min. or until mixture is thick enough to mound.

SPOON into crust. Refrigerate 4 hours or until firm.

TOP with the remaining COOL WHIP just before serving.

SPECIAL EXTRA:
Garnish with assorted cut-up fresh fruit just before serving.

SUBSTITUTE:
Prepare as directed, using your favorite flavor of JELL-O Sugar Free Gelatin.

NUTRIENTS PER SERVING: Calories: 150, Total Fat: 5g, Saturated Fat: 2g, Protein: 3g, Carbohydrate: 25g, Cholesterol: 0mg, Fiber: 0g, Sodium: 160mg.

lime chiffon pie

PREP: 10 min. | TOTAL: 4 hours 30 min. | MAKES: 8 servings.

▶ what you need!

⅔ cup boiling water

1 pkg. (0.3 oz.) JELL-O Lime Flavor Sugar Free Gelatin

Ice cubes

½ cup cold water

2 cups thawed COOL WHIP FREE Whipped Topping

1½ tsp. grated lime zest

2 Tbsp. lime juice

1 ready-to-use reduced fat graham cracker crumb crust (6 oz.)

▶ make it!

ADD boiling water to dry gelatin mix in large bowl; stir 2 min. until completely dissolved. Add enough ice to cold water to make 1 cup. Add to gelatin; stir until ice is melted.

WHISK in COOL WHIP, zest and juice. Refrigerate 15 min. or until mixture is thick enough to mound. Spoon into crust.

REFRIGERATE 4 hours or until firm.

LEMON CHIFFON PIE:
Prepare as directed using JELL-O Lemon Flavor Sugar Free Gelatin, lemon zest and lemon juice.

SPECIAL EXTRA:
Garnish with thin lime wedges and/or additional lime zest.

NUTRIENTS PER SERVING: Calories: 140, Total Fat: 4.5g, Saturated Fat: 2g, Protein: 2g, Carbohydrate: 22g, Cholesterol: 0mg, Fiber: 0g, Sodium: 140mg.

low-fat chocolate-berry dessert

PREP: 15 min. | TOTAL: 2 hours 15 min. | MAKES: 12 servings, ⅔ cup each.

▸ what you need!

7 oz. (½ of 14-oz. loaf) fat-free marble loaf cake, cut into ¼-inch-thick slices

2 pkg. (1.4 oz. each) JELL-O Chocolate Fat Free Sugar Free Instant Pudding

2½ cups cold fat-free milk

2 cups thawed COOL WHIP FREE Whipped Topping, divided

2 cups fresh raspberries

¼ cup chocolate syrup

▸ make it!

COVER bottom of 9-inch square pan with cake slices, cutting and piecing slices to fit. Beat dry pudding mixes and milk with whisk 2 min. (Pudding will be thick.) Stir in 1 cup COOL WHIP; spread over cake slices.

REFRIGERATE 2 hours or until firm.

TOP with remaining COOL WHIP and berries just before serving. Drizzle with syrup.

SUBSTITUTE:
Substitute sliced fresh strawberries for the raspberries.

NUTRIENTS PER SERVING: Calories: 130, Total Fat: 1g, Saturated Fat: 1g, Protein: 3g, Carbohydrate: 28g, Cholesterol: 0mg, Fiber: 2g, Sodium: 310mg.

low-fat orange dream cheesecake

PREP: 15 min. | TOTAL: 4 hours 15 min. | MAKES: 8 servings.

► what you need!

1 HONEY MAID Honey Graham, crushed

⅔ cup boiling water

1 pkg. (3 oz.) JELL-O Orange Flavor Sugar Free Gelatin

1 cup BREAKSTONE'S or KNUDSEN 2% Milkfat Low Fat Cottage Cheese

1 tub (8 oz.) PHILADELPHIA Fat Free Cream Cheese

2 cups thawed COOL WHIP FREE Whipped Topping

► make it!

SPRINKLE graham crumbs onto bottom of 8- or 9-inch springform pan sprayed with cooking spray.

ADD boiling water to dry gelatin mix; stir 2 min. until completely dissolved. Cool 5 min.; pour into blender. Add cottage cheese and cream cheese; blend well. Pour into large bowl. Gently stir in COOL WHIP. Pour into prepared pan; smooth top.

REFRIGERATE 4 hours or until set. Remove rim of pan before serving. Refrigerate leftovers.

SUBSTITUTE:
Substitute 9-inch pie plate for the springform pan.

SPECIAL EXTRA:
Garnish with fresh mint sprigs and thin orange slices just before serving.

NUTRITION BONUS:
You're sure to love the creamy orange flavor of this low-fat cheesecake. As a bonus, the fat-free cream cheese is a good source of calcium.

NUTRIENTS PER SERVING: Calories: 100, Total Fat: 2g, Saturated Fat: 1.5g, Protein: 8g, Carbohydrate: 11g, Cholesterol: 10mg, Fiber: 0g, Sodium: 330mg.

mimosa mold

PREP: 15 min. | TOTAL: 6 hours 45 min. | MAKES: 12 servings, ½ cup each.

▶ what you need!

1½ cups boiling water

1 pkg. (0.6 oz.) JELL-O Orange Flavor Sugar
   Free Gelatin

2 cups cold club soda

1 can (11 oz.) mandarin oranges, drained

1 cup sliced fresh strawberries

▶ make it!

ADD boiling water to dry gelatin mix in large bowl; stir 2 min. until completely dissolved. Stir in club soda. Refrigerate 1½ hours or until thickened.

STIR in fruit. Pour into 6-cup mold sprayed with cooking spray.

REFRIGERATE 4 hours or until firm. Unmold.

HOW TO UNMOLD GELATIN:
Dip mold in warm water for 15 sec. Gently pull gelatin from around edge with moist fingers. Place moistened serving plate on top of mold. Invert plate and mold; holding mold and plate together, shaking slightly to loosen. Gently remove mold and center gelatin on plate.

SUBSTITUTE:
Substitute cold seltzer for the club soda.

SUBSTITUTE:
Prepare using JELL-O Lemon Flavor Gelatin.

NUTRITION BONUS:
Not only do the mandarin oranges and strawberries make this recipe refreshing, but they also team up to provide an excellent source of vitamin C.

NUTRIENTS PER SERVING: Calories: 15, Total Fat: 0g, Saturated Fat: 0g, Protein: 1g, Carbohydrate: 0g, Cholesterol: 0mg, Fiber: 1g, Sodium: 35mg.

angel lush with pineapple

▶ what you need!

- 1 can (20 oz.) DOLE Crushed Pineapple in Juice, undrained
- 1 pkg. (1.5 oz.) JELL-O Vanilla Flavor Instant Pudding
- 1 cup thawed COOL WHIP Whipped Topping
- 1 pkg. (10 oz.) round angel food cake, cut into 3 layers
- 1 cup fresh mixed berries

▶ make it!

MIX pineapple and dry pudding mix. Gently stir in COOL WHIP.

STACK cake layers on plate, spreading pudding mixture between layers and on top of cake.

REFRIGERATE 1 hour. Top with berries.

HOW TO CUT CAKE:
Use toothpicks to mark cake into 3 layers. Use a serrated knife to cut cake, in sawing motion, into layers.

LEMON-BERRY LUSH WITH PINEAPPLE:
Prepare using JELL-O Lemon Flavor Instant Pudding.

NUTRIENTS PER SERVING: Calories: 160, Total Fat: 1.5g, Saturated Fat: 1g, Protein: 2g, Carbohydrate: 37g, Cholesterol: 0mg, Fiber: 1g, Sodium: 360mg.

DOLE is a registered trademark of Dole Food Company, Inc.

low-fat raspberry summer sensation

PREP: 15 min. | TOTAL: 3 hours 25 min. | MAKES: 12 servings.

▶ what you need!

- 2 cups raspberry sorbet, softened
- 1 pkg. (1 oz.) JELL-O Vanilla Flavor Fat Free Sugar Free Instant Pudding
- 1 cup cold fat-free milk
- 1 tub (8 oz.) COOL WHIP Sugar Free Whipped Topping, thawed
- 1 cup raspberries

▶ make it!

SPOON sorbet into foil-lined 9×5-inch loaf pan; freeze 10 min.

BEAT dry pudding mix and milk in medium bowl with whisk 2 min. Stir in COOL WHIP. Spread over sorbet.

FREEZE 3 hours or until firm. Unmold onto plate; remove foil. Let dessert stand 10 min. to soften slightly before slicing to serve. Top with berries.

HELPFUL HINT:
Soften sorbet in microwave on MEDIUM (50%) 10 to 15 sec.

NUTRIENTS PER SERVING: Calories: 110, Total Fat: 2.5g, Saturated Fat: 2.5g, Protein: 1g, Carbohydrate: 21g, Cholesterol: 0mg, Fiber: 1g, Sodium: 115mg.

JELL-O strawberry mousse cups

PREP: 15 min. | TOTAL: 2 hours 15 min. | MAKES: 6 servings.

▸ what you need!

¾ cup boiling water

1 pkg. (0.3 oz.) JELL-O Strawberry Flavor Sugar Free Gelatin

1 cup ice cubes

2 cups thawed COOL WHIP FREE Whipped Topping, divided

2 cups strawberries, sliced, divided

▸ make it!

ADD boiling water to dry gelatin mix in large serving bowl; stir 2 min. until completely dissolved. Add ice; stir until completely melted. Gently stir in 1½ cups each COOL WHIP and berries until well blended.

SPOON into dessert dishes. Refrigerate 2 hours or until firm.

TOP with remaining COOL WHIP and berries just before serving.

VARIATION:
Prepare gelatin mixture as directed, but do not stir in strawberries. Spoon 1½ cups of the strawberries evenly into 6 dessert dishes; top with gelatin mixture. Refrigerate 2 hours or until firm. Top with remaining COOL WHIP and berries just before serving.

NUTRITION BONUS:
The strawberries in these low-fat desserts are an excellent source of vitamin C.

NUTRIENTS PER SERVING: Calories: 70, Total Fat: 1.5g, Saturated Fat: 1g, Protein: 1g, Carbohydrate: 13g, Cholesterol: 0mg, Fiber: 1g, Sodium: 50 mg.

low-fat strawberry shortcut

PREP: 15 min. | TOTAL: 15 min. | MAKES: 12 servings.

▶ what you need!

1½ qt. (6 cups) strawberries, sliced

¼ cup sugar

1 pkg. (13.6 oz.) prepared fat-free pound cake, cut into 12 slices

1 tub (8 oz.) COOL WHIP FREE Whipped Topping, thawed

▶ make it!

TOSS strawberries with sugar; let stand 10 min. or until sugar is dissolved, stirring occasionally.

CUT each slice of pound cake horizontally in half. Place 1 cake slice on each of 12 dessert plates.

TOP each with about ¼ cup of the strawberries and 2 Tbsp. COOL WHIP. Repeat layers. Serve immediately.

SPECIAL EXTRA:
Garnish with fresh mint sprigs.

NUTRITION BONUS:
This luscious dessert is low in fat, cholesterol free and an excellent source of vitamin C from the strawberries.

NUTRIENTS PER SERVING: Calories: 170, Total Fat: 1.5g, Saturated Fat: 1g, Protein: 2g, Carbohydrate: 36g, Cholesterol: 0mg, Fiber: 2g, Sodium: 120mg.

Index

MY RECIPES